Y0-DBZ-045

SHEEP AMONG Wolves

WITHDRAWN

WITHDRAWN

SHEEP AMONG *Wolves*

Texas Churches and the Law

DAVID D. BALKUM

PLEASANT LIBRARY
BUILDING PACIFIC UNIV.-M. B. STRAWBERRY
FRESNO CA 93710

© 2003 by David D. Balkum. All rights reserved

Packaged by Pleasant Word, PO Box 428, Enumclaw, WA 98022. The views expressed or implied in this work do not necessarily reflect those of Pleasant Word. The author(s) is ultimately responsible for the design, content and editorial accuracy of this work.

No part of this publication may be reproduced, stored in a retrieval system or transmitted in any way by any means—electronic, mechanical, photocopy, recording or otherwise—without the prior permission of the copyright holder, except as provided by USA copyright law.

Unless otherwise noted, all Scriptures are taken from the Holy Bible, New International Version, Copyright © 1973, 1978, 1984 by the International Bible Society. Used by permission of Zondervan Publishing House. The "NIV" and "New International Version" trademarks are registered in the United States Patent and Trademark Office by International Bible Society.

Scripture references marked KJV are taken from the King James Version of the Bible.

Scripture references marked NASB are taken from the New American Standard Bible, © 1960, 1963, 1968, 1971, 1972, 1973, 1975, 1977 by The Lockman Foundation. Used by permission.

ISBN 1-4141-0092-2
Library of Congress Catalog Card Number: 2003115235

Table of Contents

Acknowledgements

I wish to express my thanks to my family. My wife, Kimberly, and my daughters, Laurianne and Lesleigh, tolerated, as families must, my days of manic writing on the book, followed by my refusal to touch it for months afterward. They suffered the indignity of having personal stories revealed out of a shared hope that something good would emerge. They endured it patiently, encouraged me, and never indicated a moment's doubt about the wisdom of a sole practitioner with limited resources pouring such time and energy into a book that few people may read. My parents, Doug and Darlene, provided an earlier atmosphere in which faith and education were absolute priorities. Those ingredients are a recipe for a book and these people are my family in the best and fullest sense of the word.

Many ministers also encouraged me, lending their perspectives about ministry issues which face them. Among them are William Arnold, Robert Creech, Norman Fry, Ernest Izard, and Phill Martin. Attorneys who reviewed portions of the book and whose expertise and suggestions lent important contributions include Scott Agthe, Scott Brazil, Blake Coffee, Dan Conley, Leslie Guhl, and Patrick Quigley. David Holcomb's early encouragement also was vital to my crossing the finish line, albeit very belatedly, and Nancy Ferrell's and John Bethany's unique insights on conflict and the church challenged and greatly improved my original thoughts. Despite their collective influence, though, there will be mistakes in the book. When you find them, remember that they are mine and that those who encouraged and assisted me in this project bear no responsibility for its faults.

Finally, I must thank my clients, who have allowed me to gain the experience necessary to write a book like this. Each file, whether belonging to an individual, a business, or a church, has allowed me an opportunity to develop new insights and to expand my own professional horizons. May the lessons represented by those files bear fruit by protecting and edifying your church and its mission, ministries, and members.

Preface

My goal in writing this book is to provide a fairly comprehensive set of survey materials for anyone who deals with or is interested in legal issues confronting Texas churches. In aiming for that goal, I try to strike a balance between simply raising current issues and going unabridged. If I find the law to be confusing, complicated, or ambiguous or if disagreement exists about a topic, then I devote more space to it than otherwise might seem justified.

I avoid analysis of almost all federal issues. Such issues, *e.g.* taxation of ministers and First Amendment issues, are of vital interest to our churches and should receive our best critical thought. However, those resources already exist in abundance and, not practicing in those areas, I have little, if anything, intelligent to say about them. That being the case, discretion is the better part of valor.

My organizational goal is coherence. The law can be a jigsaw puzzle at times and you may need to pull pieces from several chapters together to look at certain situations. Whenever a more detailed analysis of a particular issue exists elsewhere in these materials, I try to refer you to its location. Even with that jigsaw puzzle quality, you may note that the book can be divided roughly into three parts, each with five chapters: (i) conflict resolution, common claims, and defenses; (ii) substantive legal issues; and (iii) the interplay among people, law, and ministry in special situations. These areas and issues all interrelate, though, making further organizational efforts fairly ineffectual. In the midst of these parts and chapters, I use sequential end notes. The text notes frequently used in legal writing tend to distract readers who are unfamiliar with lengthy, confusing citations in the middle of a paragraph. As I said, my goal is coherence, not a foolish consistency to conventions.

I frequently use abbreviations when referring to entities or laws, typically by first stating a full, formal name, followed by the abbreviated form. I purposely use an abbreviated form of citation to legal authorities, with apologies to *Uniform System of Citation* and *Texas Rules of Form*. Unless otherwise noted, all scriptural references are to *The Holy Bible, New International Version* (American Edition), © 1973, 1978, 1984 by the International Bible Society, used by permission of Zondervan Publishing House.

The text often refers to a hypothetical church, but certain portions of these materials may have a wider application, offering insights for associations, conventions, or related ministries. Further, while I am most familiar with Baptist denominations, I am passingly familiar with other evangelical churches which face similar, if not identical, legal issues on a daily basis. My aim is for these materials to benefit as broad a spectrum of denominational, independent, hierarchical, and congregational churches as possible. Thus, I use the terms "clergy," "staff member," "minister," "priest," and "pastor" somewhat interchangeably. Likewise, the terms "deacon" and "elder" should be read broadly. I do not intend to define any correct church structure, to interpret Greek or Hebrew words, or to offend any person or church with my choice of terms in describing anything. I do so primarily to disguise my own ignorance concerning these terms' precise meanings and secondarily to make these materials as relevant to as many believers and churches as possible.

You will note that I use alternating gender pronouns. Doing so goes against my grammatical instincts, but I consider the restrictions which some advocate toward women in ministry an important enough issue to make whatever small statement that I can about that topic. Thus, you will read about men and women confronting each other on more or less equal footing without much regard for gender. May we continue in submission to one another and stay focused on bigger issues, many of which we still have not quite managed to conquer.

Introduction

My first memory of church involves painting Noah's ark animals with watercolors and eating cookies, no doubt at Sunday School. I do not remember life without a church in it and I always have been active in my church, even before I professed my faith in Jesus as my savior at the age of sixteen. I went on to pursue my formal education and courted my wife of many years, Kimberly, at Houston Baptist University. We were married in 1984, shortly before I started attending law school at the University of Houston.

Kimberly is a minister's daughter with her master's degree in psychology and a slightly higher collegiate grade point average than mine. She worked with Children's Protective Services for several years as a sexual abuse case worker before working with me for five years and doing everything in my practice that did not require a law license. She now is Vice-President of Administration at Trilogy Systems Corporation, an industrial manufacturer and my biggest client. More than anyone else, she has provided valuable insight for and made many contributions to these materials. More than any other client, Trilogy Systems Corporation has contributed to this book by entrusting many of its affairs to me. To it and its owners I owe a debt of personal and professional gratitude.

My practice has consisted primarily of civil work since I began practicing in 1987. I occasionally have meddled, as my grandfather would put it, in church affairs by advising churches and staff members on various legal issues. Mostly, though, my practice has been a general practice focused on the civil side of the law. That has included helping individuals and businesses with personal injury, corporate, real estate, employment, tax, insurance, and estate matters, as well as representing them in prosecuting their claims and defending them when they have been sued.

It is true that some plaintiffs are simply opportunistic and greedy. It also is true that other plaintiffs suffer real loss and tragedy when they are injured in accidents or hurt in commercial dealings. Defendants and their insurers struggle with these claims. They must determine whether or not a claim is real and, if so, whether or not to pay, whether or not they can pay, and how much to pay.

These perspectives, plaintiff and defendant, form the polarized extremes of our adversarial system. These extremes, encouraged by our present system, also play havoc with our mandate to be a peaceful, dispute resolving people. Thus, some of my favorite work consists not in prosecuting and defending claims, but in advising clients about actions which they can take to prevent such claims in the first place. Staying away from the courthouse, for both plaintiffs and defendants, is a small victory itself.

Some attorneys and judges carry a deep love of our judicial system and will defend it vigorously. I am not one of those people. I carry a carefully mixed sense of respect and wariness for our judicial system. While the framers of our federal and state constitutions, our legislators, and our judges have done a better job than any group of men and women ever has done, the system is imperfect and we should not place our faith in it or those who run it. The Lord warns us in Jeremiah 17:5: "[c]ursed is the one who trusts in man, who depends on flesh for his strength, and whose heart turns away from the Lord."

When men seek their own wisdom and trust their own creation, as many do with the law, they place their faith in a flawed system. The writer of Hebrews made a parallel observation, asserting in Hebrews 7:28 that "the law appoints as high priests men who are weak." If I place my faith, trust, and loyalty in weak men and a system which ultimately will fail me, then I have accepted a lie. Thus, when people start to speak of the glories of our judicial system, I cannot listen very seriously. I may not be alone in this perspective, either. One of our former pastors joked in a sermon that his view of heaven does not include attorneys, at least not practicing attorneys. I hope that he intended it to be a lighter moment.

Prior to writing this book, I represented a client who sued a religious institution. As that case progressed, three things constantly confronted me: the defendant's negligence and subsequent indifference toward my client, my client's suffering, and my own reluctance to take such an institution to task. I became increasingly convinced in dealing with that situation that there was a better way to handle claims like that, for the potential benefit of all involved.

That the defendant had been negligent was an inescapable conclusion to me. No matter how well-meaning some of its employees and staff were and no matter how noble its mission statement sounded, something terrible happened and it completely ignored my client after the incident. There was no ministry, compassion, or communication. There was simply avoidance. Other churches have behaved similarly in comparable circumstances. Nonetheless, it is an ill-advised course of behavior, in addition to being a one hundred eighty degree swing away from scriptural guidelines. Jesus gave us legal advice, if not also advice concerning eternity and forgiveness, in Matthew 5:25–26 upon which no lawyer has improved.

> Settle matters quickly with your adversary who is taking you to court. Do it while you are still with him on the way, or he may hand you over to the judge, and the judge may hand you over to the officer, and you may be thrown into prison. I tell you the truth, you will not get out until you have paid the last penny.

Matters were settled by the defendant almost two years after the incident. However, the costs involved in attorney's fees and settling a case like this can be much more than the last penny for many churches. Consider the millions of dollars being paid by or adjudicated against Catholic churches and dioceses arising from charges of sexual abuse by their own priests. As Karol Jackowski relates in *The Silence We Keep*, "[t]he Church Fathers with the most to hide and the most privilege to lose are likely to consider then pursue the escape route of bankruptcy (moral, spiritual, and financial) as the only way out of the mess they created."[1] That is already happening.

It is more than a matter of dollars and cents, then, as the last penny is not necessarily reflected on a bank statement. In any dispute, there are non-economic costs, such as negative public perception, tension in a church's fellowship, divisiveness, and time and energy spent away from the church's mission and ministries. The last penny could be spent well before the first check is written. Would it not be more productive instead to turn our attention to seeking ways to prevent such incidents and disputes before they occur?

Having confessed that I sued that organization on my clients' behalf, I obviously am not the one to tell the church that it is always right. When confronting legal issues, the church needs candor much more than a cantor. That candor includes embracing the notion that actions and, sometimes, inaction have consequences. We tell our children this from the time when they can think concretely enough to connect cause and effect. The same concept applies to the church and that is why we need to study our actions, to modify them where advisable, and to accept the potential consequences which our actions and inaction may bring, regardless of whether or not we intend those consequences. To do so gives us credibility and allows us to bear witness to a lost world which looks for ways to shirk its responsibilities whenever it can.

Most ministers are aware of the church's increasing role as a target. Further, as we find the bull's-eye being placed on our sanctuary doors, the law is becoming more complex than ever and it is difficult for attorneys, much less staff members with other demands on their hands, to maintain the church on steady legal footing. This book intends to raise legal issues meriting your personal and corporate consideration, to discuss whether or not your church is doing what it should do to protect itself and its members, and to provide a general reference for those in the church who are responsible for its legal affairs. May its flaws not detract from those goals.

PART ONE

CONFLICT RESOLUTION, COMMON CLAIMS, AND DEFENSES

CHAPTER 1

The Church, the Law, and Attorneys

SCOPE OF THE MATERIALS

These materials are designed to familiarize you with general legal issues which may arise during the course of a church's ministry. They are not, however, a substitute for legal advice rendered by a qualified attorney who is informed of the specific facts of any given situation. Thus, taking these materials as the answer to any given legal scenario makes as much sense as scuba diving in a water soluble shark cage. Not that I fail to appreciate a good shark/attorney reference, but every legal situation has different facts which a good attorney will recognize either as great white sharks or red herrings.

As such, please take the following disclaimer seriously. Do not assume that the information provided in these materials is suitable for dealing with any particular legal situation. If you are faced with a specific legal problem, then consult an attorney. A corollary disclaimer is that you should not use any legal forms without consulting an attorney. My experience has been that clients with forms will use those forms without an attorney's advice. That is exactly why I always ask unwelcome questions when a client asks to use one of my forms. "It's just a simple form," is the usual plea. Yes, but that simple form may or may not do the job which you intend for it to do. There probably are issues which the form does not address or which you have not considered. Thus, my intention in this book is not to render legal advice. Using the observations in this or any other book to address unique, real life situations is a recipe for trouble. Once again, if you are faced with a specific legal problem, then consult an attorney.

Another aspect of the law that most people do not appreciate is that some of this material may be obsolete, perhaps even before it is published. Is that aggravating? Yes, but the Texas Legislature meets every other year and changes the law in each of those sessions. State and federal courts are open for business almost around the clock and may be overturning what a legislative body has done, may be fine tuning the law according to the cases presented to them, or may be dealing with disputes which statutes and prior cases have never contemplated. Added to these factors are the relatively constant meetings of legislative committees and state and federal administrative agencies. Some of these entities promulgate new rules and regulations, effectively implementing what amounts to new law.

The wheels of justice may grind slowly in a particular case, but society's concept of justice can change very quickly when driven by political winds, social currents, or economic forces. Like it or not, these are exactly the forces which give momentum to man's incessant refining of just what justice means in any given situation. The Supreme Court of Texas or the Texas Legislature could decide tomorrow that a certain injury, although deserving of justice in the past, no longer deserves either a trial or a remedy, no matter how seriously you may have been injured by another's actions.[2] Those same political bodies also could decide to recognize a new cause of action next year that relates back to conduct occurring prior to its creation, *i.e.* someone could sue your church next year for an action which was lawful for your church to have taken today.[3]

Such instances may be rare, but the *Boyles* case involved a claim for negligent infliction of emotional distress, a person seeking the protection of that law, and the supreme court abolishing that cause of action well after the misconduct occurred. The *McCamish* case evolved from a person's attempt to sue another person's attorney for negligent misrepresentation, a cause of action against attorneys that was previously unrecognized by Texas courts. The supreme court allowed that claim to proceed against an attorney who did not even represent the plaintiff. Why did the court expand one negligence claim and abolish another within a very short time frame? Was the court following the lead of other states' courts in doing so? Did changing political and social mores dictate the results? Did it have more to do with the unpopularity of plaintiffs and their lawyers than with justice? I do not pretend to know the answers to those questions, but there is more at work in many, if not most, cases than an objective, unadulterated search for justice. In short, the protection and privileges which we enjoy today could be gone tomorrow. Thus, we must guard them carefully.

THE CHURCH DEALING WITH THE WORLD

Chapter 3 will discuss standards for how Christians should deal with one another in the context of resolving conflict. These standards will not necessarily work in situations in which we are dealing with the world. Jesus spoke to the apostles as He was sending them out to testify to the Jews. He warned them in Matthew 10:16–17 and His warning resonates with us today. "I am sending you out like sheep among wolves. Therefore be as shrewd as snakes and as innocent as doves. Be on your guard against men; they will hand you over to the local councils and flog you in their synagogues."

Jesus issued much the same warning in the parable of the unjust steward in Luke 16:8. "The master commended the dishonest manager because he had acted shrewdly. For the people of this world are more shrewd in dealing with their own kind than are the people of the light." The parable's point is one of contrasts. The steward acted shrewdly and sinfully, gaining what he had not earned and, by doing so, depriving his master of the same. That same master, although he had been cheated, commended the steward because the steward had acted wisely, albeit dishonestly, in taking care of himself, even to the master's detriment.

However, people of the light, Christians, are to act shrewdly and innocently. We do not always do so. We tend to focus more on the innocent part of the equation and to ascribe our mistakes to something other than our lack of shrewdness. Not so, said Jesus, commanding us to be shrewd. This is not just another "it would be nice if . . ." item on a wish list. We are commanded, immediately after being told that we are being sent out "like sheep among wolves," to "be as shrewd as snakes." We are to approach everything that we do obediently and with working, planning, knowledge, and wisdom, as instructed in Ecclesiastes 9:10. That is being a shrewd sheep. Instead of working on ourselves, though, we condemn the world for its cunning and trickery. We must turn from that unproductive behavior and contemplate what Jesus meant when He told us to be shrewd sheep. One thing is certain in that regard: we have at our disposal all that is necessary to be good stewards of the Gospel and every other asset with which God entrusts us.

THE CHURCH DEALING WITH ATTORNEYS

You may or may not have an attorney in your congregation. Ideally, you should have several whose areas of practice overlap. When you are faced with a situation in which the church should retain counsel, these attorneys should be consulted first regarding their suggestions. They should have the church's best interests at heart, should understand the legal issues of the situation, and should be happy to refer you to an experienced attorney.

Another good source for locating an attorney is your church staff's contacts within and outside of your denomination. Your church will not be the first to need an attorney and you should consider taking advantage of the experiences which other churches have had with specific attorneys. Your church's business leaders' contacts may be helpful, also. Another source for finding an attorney is the State Bar of Texas' referral service. Your local county's bar association also may operate a referral service. From that point on, though, the reliability of the information which you receive about a particular attorney decreases. Any attorney with money or credit can advertise in a telephone company's directory, buy thirty seconds of time during the late night movie marathon, surf the net with his own stylized web page, or market himself in even more creative ways. That does not mean that he is the attorney for your church or that you should contact him. Further, some attorneys utilizing those media are not especially attuned to the needs of the church. While the State Bar of Texas has taken measures aimed at elevating the tactfulness and reliability of advertisements and has limited attorneys' ability to contact prospective clients directly, my experience has been that word of mouth advertising is still any attorney's and any potential client's best friend.

A church should be considerate of many issues when asking a member attorney to represent it. First, its request may put the attorney in an awkward position. He may be uncomfortable with charging a fee, even a reduced fee, or with the idea of negotiating with his church over fee arrangements. Yet, like any other professional in the community, he is being asked to undertake a serious duty in reliance on his ongoing business operations, education, experience, and license. Another attorney may feel perfectly comfortable representing the church on a *pro bono* or reduced fee basis and may view that as part of his ministry. If you have such an attorney in your congregation, then use his services wisely. Burnout comes in many forms and, just as you would be considerate of Sunday School workers who take offerings, mow the grass, sing in the choir, serve on four committees, and eventually complain, three years later, about being at the church whenever the door is open, you should not take undue advantage of such an attorney.[4]

This discussion assumes that your church will retain an attorney in private practice. Some attorneys, like those representing federal, state, and local governments and certain non-profit institutions, are prohibited from representing clients other than their respective employers. Corporate attorneys also may have restrictions on any outside work which they do, although they sometimes are allowed to represent a limited number of private clients. Further, even attorneys in private practice usually must gain the consent of the firms for which they work prior to accepting any client. Sole practitioners, on the other hand, have the greatest freedom in accepting new clients and matters. Thus, there are some practical restrictions regarding any attorney's ability to represent your church.

Most attorneys specialize in one or more areas. You may find that your particular problem is best served by a specialist, who may or may not be "board certified." That simply means that an attorney has practiced long enough, devotes a certain minimum percentage of his practice to a specific area, and has passed an examination in that area. Having raised this issue, there are attorneys, although not "board certified," who are just as capable, if not more so, in a given area of law than a recognized specialist. Conversely, the State Bar of Texas' stamp of approval does provide some objective verification of an attorney's level of expertise.

Factors which generally affect the amount of legal fees are as follows:

- the time and labor required
- the novelty and difficulty of the questions presented
- the skill requisite to represent the church properly
- the likelihood that accepting an assignment will prevent the attorney from representing other clients
- the amounts charged by other attorneys in the same area for similar service
- the amount involved and results obtained
- the time limitations which a church or the circumstances impose
- the nature and length of the attorney's relationship with the church
- the attorney's experience, reputation, and ability[5]

However, these factors only address the amount of the fee to be charged. Determining how the fee is structured is a different issue.

Generally, the type of fee charged will be determined by the type of case or the nature of the legal matter. Some of the more customary fees are hourly fees, in which a certain amount is charged for each hour or partial hour of work, contingency fees, in which the attorney charges a percentage of the amount recovered, and flat fees, in which the attorney charges a predetermined amount for the work to be performed, regardless of the amount of time which he must invest to perform that work. It will be rare that a church will have legal work to be performed on a contingency basis, but it is possible. Thus, you probably will encounter flat fees and hourly fees more often.

Perhaps the primary factor evaluated when setting the fee is the amount of time anticipated to be spent on a matter. A lawyer may hesitate to set a flat fee, perhaps because he cannot control all or a portion of a matter or because he is uncertain of all of the facts. Understandably, clients always want to know how much representation will cost at the beginning, wanting to avoid the specter of the case (and bill) that simply will not end. However, even with all of these considerations in mind, attorneys can be flexible in reaching fee agreements that work for both parties, perhaps combining elements from two or more of the standard arrangements. If both your church and its attorney demonstrate some creativity, then both may benefit from an unconventional arrangement.

Attorneys base their fees not only on court appearances, but also on time spent while talking with a church's representatives, opposing parties and attorneys, insurance adjusters, court clerks, court reporters, witnesses, government clerks, and others with whom the attorney may need to speak in order to represent a church effectively. In addition, the attorney must respond, almost always in writing, to documents and correspondence from the opposing party, its attorney, or the court and draft his own letters, pleadings, and other documents. In order to represent any client properly, he must review the file and make any necessary notes before he speaks or corresponds with anyone concerning that file. He also may need to research the law in order to determine a church's particular rights and duties. That may involve as little as reviewing a book in his office or as much as reading and briefing cases in a law library for hours. His fees also may include the time during which he is forced to travel, if an assignment requires him to drive or to fly elsewhere.

If a church is involved in litigation, then there may be court costs for filing various pleadings. There also may be travel expenses and exhibit and deposition costs, which include paying for a court reporter to transcribe a deposition. In almost every case or matter, there will be copying and postage expenses. Another potential expense involves a settlement procedure, mediation, which has gained favor with courts. However, this is only an overview of expenses and fees, as it is impossible for me to describe every situation. Any matter may involve any of these expenses or even expenses which I have omitted.

If you are worried about attorneys' fees and expenses, then we share a mutual concern regarding the church becoming entangled in disputes. We insulate electrical wiring to prevent fires. We put child locks on cabinets to prevent children from hurting themselves by playing with the items inside those cabinets. We audit financial records regardless of whether or not any wrongdoing is suspected. We take these measures because we have learned that to do so is more responsible than not to do so. We have learned that property damage, personal injuries, and financial irregularities should be avoided and that, if we can study situations and find better, safer ways to go about our business, then it makes sense to exercise a little caution. Thus, if an ounce of prevention is truly worth a pound of cure, then let us look at our legal house with an eye toward prevention before the cure burns it down.

ATTORNEYS DEALING WITH THE CHURCH

A church is an attorney's client in any matter which affects that church. Although exceptions may exist, a church's attorney generally should not represent its staff members, deacons, trustees, or any of the church's other agents in connection with a matter pertaining to that church. To do so invites a conflict of interest. Further, while the attorney may be a member of the church which he represents and may represent individual congregation members, staff members, or church employees in connection with unrelated matters, his duty of loyalty should rest with the church alone in connection with any matter which affects the church. This requirement is based on several factors, including the principle that, in creating a church, its charter members created a new "person" under Texas law, a person which potentially may have conflicting interests with its members and ministers. Most Texas statutes containing definitions of the word "person" include not only individuals, but also corporations, nonprofit corporations, partnerships, and other recognized business and governmental entities.[6] Thus, when a church's charter members file its articles of incorporation, they create a legally recognized person which can maintain its own attorney/client relationship with an attorney.

As such, an attorney takes his instructions from a church and, more specifically, from the person or committee appointed by that church through its governing documents to speak for it. In the business world, the attorney's liaison usually is a company's president or another corporate officer appointed to that duty by the president. A church's governing documents may or may not address this issue. If they do not, then the attorney's liaison should be the person responsible for a church's business decisions. That may be the pastor, a business administrator, or the chairman of the deacons or board of trustees, among others. If these documents do not specify whom that should be, then some agreement should be reached within the church to appoint that person. Following these suggestions should ensure that the action which an attorney takes on behalf of a church truly reflects the wishes of those whom the church has called to speak for it.[7]

These restrictions may seem to be overly legalistic. However, consider the potential problems posed when a deacon attempts an end around play and directs an attorney to take action on a church's behalf without informing anyone. In these situations, a clear problem arises if an attorney takes action pursuant to the direction of someone who lacks authority. To avoid this, an attorney should make clear from the beginning that he represents only the church in connection with any matter which affects the church. Similarly, a church has an obligation to make clear the identity of those authorized to confer with and to direct the attorney.

If an attorney learns of any unprivileged information, regardless of its source, which he has a duty to disclose to a client, then he must disclose that information. A typical situation occurs when a member confides something to an attorney which affects his church and which the member wants to keep secret. However, if the attorney represents the church, not the individual, then his duty of loyalty must be directed toward that church and he may be obligated to disclose the information to that church, despite the protests of the member who revealed the information. Keeping the attorney's role as counsel for the church well-defined in this process helps to reduce the possibility of a member thinking that the attorney represents him individually.[8] For further protection, I also recommend that churches retain attorneys outside of their own membership. This also tends to minimize the invariably negative consequences for the attorney when his advice conflicts with someone else's opinion and lends a somewhat desirable degree of formality in the relationship between church members and the attorney.

Finally, when you ask an attorney to represent your church, remember that you are asking first and foremost for his professional opinion. An attorney is trained to put his personal opinions aside and will do so, perhaps sitting silently by while wanting to speak either from a personal or spiritual viewpoint. Conversely, some attorneys are comfortable limiting their role to strictly professional advice, not wanting to share their morals and personal opinions. Lawyers generally receive little guidance in this area from their clients or during their professional training. In fact, one treatise on Texas corporate law opines that lawyers' ethical guidelines speak "very little of attorneys as having . . . responsibility for their clients' morality."[9] Thus, if you want to know what an attorney thinks about a particular issue as a person, then specifically ask him the difference between his legal opinion and his personal opinion. The church may benefit from doing so, as the best advice is not always strictly legal advice.

THE TENSION BETWEEN LAW AND MINISTRY

As church members, we often are leery of becoming entangled in the law's snares. We feel vulnerable and under attack. We are wary of those who would sue the church and its members. Our feelings make us question how we should respond to the law's encroachment into the church's territory. For example, there are some legal matters over which an element of debate should not exist. Your church should avail itself of tax-exempt status when possible. It also should avoid delinquencies and shortfalls on any payments due to the Internal Revenue Service (the "IRS") and, if incorporated, should comply with Texas' non-profit corporation reporting requirements. However, the black and white of life blur when we move away from the extremes and toward the middle of the legal continuum.

In any youth activity there is the potential and, perhaps, probability for horseplay, exuberance, inexperience, and lack of foresight to collide violently at one intersecting point. While writing this book, our church held an event in which the entire youth group spent the weekend at various church members' houses in groups of eight to ten. When the Bible study sessions were over on Saturday night, some boys from another house visited our house, wrapping our only tree and engaging our girls in a water balloon fight of historic proportions. Injuries are a predictable result in these types of activities. If you doubt this, then talk to your youth minister. If you doubt him, then I can attest to winding up on crutches after church events which I attended, years apart, as a youth group member and sponsor. Among the questions which these situations raise are:

- Should your church seek to limit its liability for accidents?
- Should your church acknowledge the risk and purchase insurance in order to protect itself, its members, and its assets and to provide a source of recovery for the losses which a young person and his family may suffer in an accident?
- Should your church seek to have the parent of a young person sign a written authorization or release in order for their child to participate in youth activities?
- Is a written release enforceable if a dispute arises and someone seeks to hold the church responsible for any loss?
- Should such documents be worded to apply to all youth activities or just to the dangerous ones?
- Should all such documents be signed by one parent or both?
- What if one parent is unavailable, as is the case in many of our children's homes today?
- Should all such documents be acknowledged by a notary public, because one young person in particular has been known to forge his parent's signature?
- Should a release contain language releasing the church and its members for their own negligence?
- Will a release designed to protect your church and its members from their own negligence render your church's insurance coverage unavailable, thus removing what may be the only source of recovery for medical bills available to the young person?

If these questions made you progressively more uncomfortable, then you understand how the seemingly black and white question of "Should your church seek to limit its liability for accidents?" becomes very gray toward the end of that line of questioning. It is exactly this continuum, however, with which every church must deal in analyzing its response to such issues. There usually will not be a fluorescent "X" marking the spot where the correct answer rests and your church may struggle to find its comfort zone between the black and white extremes.

Lawyers are supposed to represent their clients zealously.[10] Thus, I might advise your church to require both parents to execute a written release applicable to each youth activity, whether held on the church's premises or off-site, with an attached listing of all scheduled youth events, to be acknowledged by a notary public, containing a conspicuously printed express negligence clause relieving the church and its members of their own negligence and an indemnity clause with a penalty provision against the parents for bringing a claim against the church in violation of the release. I also might advise your church to purchase several insurance policies, including liability, errors and omissions, property and casualty, and umbrella policies, making each issuer of an insurance policy aware of the existence of the releases. Finally, I might advise your church to cancel all youth events, because the probability of an injury or loss far outweighs any financial or legal benefit which could accrue to the church. That would be zealous representation.

To review this issue from another perspective, though, does the prospect of the church becoming a legalistic corporation with its collective eye focused only on its own protection bother you? Would you, as a Christian parent, have concerns about the staff member who approves the all-encompassing release requiring both parents' signatures, two witnesses, the acknowledgement of a notary public and including a provision warning you that the church will not be liable for anything which happens at the activity, even if what happens is the church's fault? Would you be concerned that you should have your own attorney review such a document? Would you be concerned that the church had lost any sense of its mission?

Your church must find the level of risk which it deems appropriate when legal issues confront it. One church may be more comfortable with less risk, while another church may be more comfortable with more risk. However, I believe that we must fight an increasing tendency to isolate the church from all risk. It may surprise you to hear an attorney say that. I am not advocating that common sense, preparation, and risk analysis be ignored and that we encourage the youth group to perform a mass "Bungee Jump for Jesus" off a short bridge. The church needs to minister first and to insulate itself from legal liability second. That is the Jesus' example in Luke 15:4 in which He describes the shepherd who left ninety-nine obedient sheep, putting many sheep and his next quarterly performance review at risk, to find one lost sheep. To man, it may be unreasonable to place ninety-nine at risk to save one. However, we are called as Christians to do exactly that. Thus, our primary consideration in ministry decisions should not be the business rules of the world and the rule of law. We should work on and plan out our ministries, seeking knowledge and wisdom, as commanded in Ecclesiastes 9:10, but we should not necessarily let the law dictate the confines of our ministries.

It is precisely this tension which can force two wise, reasonable Christians to oppose each other with a fullness of conviction seldom seen. While the intrusion of the law into your church's ministry may be a molehill of inconvenience, there is no reason to let it become a mountain. Paul exhorted Euodia and Syntyche, fellow believers with a history of good works for the church, to agree with each other on a contested matter in Philippians 4:2–3. That is our example. We should seek to agree with each other when these issues arise, even while acknowledging that finding a consensus may be difficult.

The decision-making process and autonomy levels of individual churches within different evangelical denominations vary drastically. Independent churches obviously have the greatest autonomy. Texas Baptist churches also cherish their independence, as it is each church's prerogative within that denomination to make its own decisions on virtually every issue which it faces.[11] Each church has its own circumstances and may react differently to a similar issue. However, regardless of your denomination or affiliation, seek agreement on your church's chosen course of action. Jesus promised in Matthew 18:19 "that if two of you on earth agree about anything you ask for, it will be done for you." May we have the faith to claim that promise for the decisions which we make in the legal arena, as well as others.

THE NEED FOR LEGAL PLANNING

There are those in church circles who do not like attorneys, even attorneys who profess to be Christians, and do not like the prospect of attorneys meddling in the church's affairs. Having said that, I do not like vegetables. I grudgingly admit that they seem to make people healthier when they are eaten, though. The necessary evil argument applies to attorneys and vegetables. Both may be unpalatable, but, when taken in their proper context, both may serve you well.

The law has become extremely complex. The church must not only take its collective head out of the sand, but it also must wipe the sand from its eyes and keep those eyes wide open. Your pastor and other staff members wisely opted for seminary or other training. No matter how knowledgeable or discerning a staff member is, he probably does not have the training necessary to deal with most legal issues. Fortunately, there are Christian attorneys who view the defense and support of the church as part of their ministry in a world which would like nothing more than to attack the church in any vulnerable area which it can find. Being the shrewd sheep which Jesus commands us to be in Matthew 10:16 may be difficult to accomplish, but it is within our reach. Ignoring the law will not assist the church. Maligning lawyers will not assist the church, either, fun as it may seem. Education, preparation, and prayerful action will assist the church in reaching that goal, though.

For example, many people are unaware that pedophiles sometimes attend church because it provides them with easy access to children. Others are unaware that the church can be a tremendous source of recovery for claims as diverse as an unfulfilled promise of a fresh start at life to food poisoning from the cafeteria during Wednesday night supper. Claims such as these are being made against churches and we must stop ignoring reality. As Jesus promised in John 16:33, trouble will find us. That is not only a promise, but an ever-present reality. Once we have acknowledged these facts, we need to look at preventing these claims when possible, minimizing the damage when probable, defending them when inevitable, and accepting responsibility when culpable. That is not negative thinking. It is simply a realistic assessment of the church's place in our society as we enter the twenty-first century. William V. Arnold humorously expressed the underpinnings of this need for planning very succinctly in *Pastoral Responses to Sexual Issues*: "[a]nyone who believes in the doctrine of original sin has to be a bit paranoid - and rightly so."[12] Thus, since there may be some small truth in the trite warning that "they're out to get us," we should be preparing for "them."

God commands us to be good stewards of His creation and the resources with which He entrusts us. To do so, we must understand the ground rules of the world in which we live. In many cases, those ground rules are the law. Engaging in any activity, whether business, sports, or otherwise, without knowing the rules is a certain recipe for disaster. When the world engages us in a game which we do not understand, we put the resources with which we are entrusted at risk. Thus, why would we engage as a church in ministering to the world without familiarizing ourselves with its ground rules? It is simply bad stewardship to do so.

I am not advocating that we turn our churches into fortresses with written entrance tests and criminal background checks for membership. I simply am advising the church to be wise, to make note of the points along the way where problems have surfaced, and to be careful of those points before they become swordtips upon which we impale ourselves. We have received the following command in Ecclesiastes 9:10: "[w]hatever your hand finds to do, do it with all your might, for in the grave, where you are going, there is neither working nor planning nor knowledge nor wisdom." Have we really embraced that command? Are some of the problems confronting our churches a direct consequence of our dereliction? When we look specifically at our responses to the law's impact on our churches, is it obvious that we have imbued those responses with working, planning, knowledge, and wisdom?

Why should we concern ourselves with the law? After all, Jesus commands us in Matthew 6:34 not to "worry about tomorrow, for tomorrow will worry about itself." Will God not protect us from lawsuits if the work which we are doing as a church is in His name? II Thessalonians 3:3 specifically tells us that "[t]he Lord is faithful, and He will strengthen and protect you from the evil one." Further, why should we pay attention to a government which establishes laws that allow sin to flourish, which sometimes persecutes the church, and whose leaders are often corrupted by the very power they wield? Facing such contemporary difficulties, we sympathize with the Israelites, who complained in Hosea 10:4 that their kings "make many promises, take false oaths, and make agreements," leading to lawsuits that "spring up like poisonous weeds."

The best reason for respecting the law is found in Romans 13:1–2. "Everyone must submit himself to the governing authorities, for there is no authority except that which God has established. Consequently, he who rebels against the authority is rebelling against what God has instituted, and those who do so will bring judgment on themselves." While this command does not justify absolute submission to anything that a government may require, it guides us to a pattern of civil obedience and, sometimes, disobedience, consistent with our convictions and principles. Daniel 6:8–16's story of his faithful obedience in the face of oppression makes that clear. My desire is to follow God's direction and to protect, to educate, and to strengthen the church and its members as we encounter the governing authorities, all without compromising our mission and ministries.

CHAPTER 2

Conflict in the Courthouse

LITIGATION - THE PLAYERS

Your church will deal with several governmental entities during its legal life. Through constant media exposure, we perhaps are most familiar with the courts. While we hope to avoid becoming a featured litigant on any courtroom drama series, disputes do arise and, when they do, the Constitution of the State of Texas guarantees its citizens the right to petition its courts to address their complaints.[13] Thus, Texas courts resolve disputes for churches by enforcing applicable state and federal law, whether or not you believe that they do that wisely or correctly.

The lowest level state courts are municipal, justice of the peace, and small claims courts. Municipal courts generally deal with traffic tickets, violations of city ordinances, and minor criminal offenses. Justice of the peace and small claims courts differ primarily in that they have some distinctive civil procedural rules. Criminal and civil cases are heard in these courts, but these disputes generally will be of a minor nature.

County court is the next higher court. These courts usually handle probate matters and other criminal and civil matters. County courts hear appeals from the justice of the peace and small claims courts. Civil cases with larger amounts in controversy and more serious criminal cases are generally tried in district courts. Some counties have county and district courts which deal with either criminal matters or civil matters and some have courts which deal with both types of cases. Some larger counties may have a district court dedicated to family matters. More populated counties may have many district courts.

However, sparsely populated counties may share a single district court and the judge may hold court in several different county seats. All of the courts previously mentioned are referred to as courts of original jurisdiction because they can try cases which have not been heard before in another court.

There are fourteen courts of appeal scattered in Texas' larger cities to which civil and criminal cases may be appealed from the county and district courts. From these fourteen courts, civil cases may be appealed to the Supreme Court of Texas and criminal cases may be appealed to the Texas Court of Criminal Appeals. Taken together, none of these sixteen courts conduct trials, as they only hear appellate cases. Their written decisions are published in books known as "reporters." These decisions, called opinions, not only interpret the statutes and codes promulgated by the Texas Legislature, but also contain rulings on common law, which is the body of law created by courts, as well as procedural rules.

Federal trial courts, aside from special issue courts such as bankruptcy, patent, and governmental claims courts, are the district courts. These courts deal with both civil and criminal matters. Most states have several district courts and segregate these geographically into districts and divisions. Appeals from these courts are directed to a circuit court of appeals, of which there are twelve. Texas cases proceed to the Fifth Circuit Court of Appeals, with New Orleans being the courthouse site. Appeals from the circuit courts and state supreme courts are taken to the Supreme Court of the United States in Washington, D.C.

The government's dealings with the church are not limited to courts, though. The State of Texas maintains several offices which may affect churches in one way or another. The Secretary of State (the "Secretary of State") is the elected official who, through a staff, receives, rejects, approves, and maintains all corporate filings. The Comptroller of Public Accounts (the "Comptroller") also receives certain filings and applications, but deals mostly with state tax issues. Tax information and forms are available at the Comptroller's Austin office and at thirty-four regional offices throughout the state. The Texas Workforce Commission (the "TWC") also regulates certain aspects of employment in Texas and maintains local offices in many major Texas cities.[14]

In addition to the courts and various state government agencies, the federal government can involve itself with your church through the IRS.[15] Few of us need an explanation of this entity's duties. The IRS issues your church's employer identification number and approves your church's application for tax-exempt status, if it chooses to file one. It also receives the social security and federal income tax payments and various forms which the church may forward for its employees, as well as passing judgment on tax-deductible contributions to the church and auditing returns. Your church may find itself in dispute and dealing with any one or more of these entities.

LITIGATION - THE PROCESS

A civil law suit formally begins with the plaintiff filing a document with the court's clerk. State courts call that document a petition and federal courts call it a complaint. The court's clerk charges a filing fee and may issue a citation, which can be served on the defendant by a law enforcement officer (usually a constable's or sheriff's deputy) or a private process server authorized by the courts to serve citations. In some cases, opposing attorneys may agree to accept or to waive service of citation. If your church is served with a petition or complaint and does not have counsel advising it about the situation, then retain counsel immediately, as there will be a deadline which your church must meet in filing its answer to the petition. This deadline may vary, so the immediate retention of counsel after being served, but preferably as soon as you even suspect a problem, is imperative. After your church's attorney reviews the petition, she then will draft and file an answer, which will contain a brief description of your church's position and may set forth any defenses to the claims set forth in the petition.

The defense attorney will review the petition and will advise your church concerning various defenses and strategies. She may contact the plaintiff's attorney and discuss what settlement options may be available prior to undertaking what may become an expensive defense. If the suit is without any merit whatsoever, then she may advise your church not to settle and to fight the suit. She may speak to witnesses, inspect physical or personal property, and review documents related to the suit. In short, she should want to know almost everything about anything at the beginning because even the tiniest fact or perspective may influence the eventual outcome. If that is the case, then it is wise to cooperate with your church's attorney, even though doing so may be time-consuming and frustrating for your church's staff. Remember that your church's attorney is there to help your church. You should help her in that task, because an equally frustrated attorney seeking to withdraw from representing your church in the middle of a case, based on your church's failure to cooperate, is a bad thing for everyone involved.

At some point during the case, the judge probably will ask the attorneys to come to the courtroom for a status conference. The judge sometimes attends these conferences, but the judge's clerk often oversees them and sets various dates and deadlines for the progress of the case. The result of this conference is a piece of paper, usually called a docket control order. That order usually (i) lists deadlines and other parameters for adding parties, conducting discovery, and naming witnesses and expert witnesses; (ii) states whether or not and by what date mediation will occur; and (iii) sets dates for pretrial conferences and the trial. The flexibility inherent in these dates and deadlines varies from court to court and may be extended in some cases by the agreement of all of the attorneys involved. Thus, your church's attorney may advise you that these dates and deadlines will be strictly enforced or that there is some wiggle room. It just depends on the circumstances. More detailed discussions of mediation occur later in this and the next chapter.

Discovery usually begins shortly after or even simultaneously with the filing of the petition and answer. It is the process in which parties request information from the other parties and even third parties and divulge information, sometimes grudgingly, to the other parties. When a petition is filed, the plaintiff may not know everything that he needs to know in order to try the case. Likewise, the church may need more information from the plaintiff in order to support some of its defenses. A court is likely to allow discovery to go on for several months, even years in complicated cases or cases with several parties.

I intentionally do not address many of the subtleties involved in discovery because it is a vast topic. However, it generally takes three distinct forms. The first, perhaps most efficient, and most common form of discovery is paper discovery. It involves the following:

- requests for disclosure - requests for basic information about parties, potential parties, witnesses, expert witnesses, theories supporting or disputing certain claims, and damages
- requests for production - requests for the other party to produce certain documents or other information contained on other types of media
- requests for admission - requests for the other party to admit or to deny specific allegations
- interrogatories - requests for the other party to identify information or documents or to explain claims, facts, or issues

A second form of discovery is the deposition, which can either be oral or written. While the public is perhaps more familiar with the concept of an oral deposition, written depositions are often used by parties to obtain information from third parties, especially in cases in which business or medical records must be obtained to develop certain claims or defenses. Oral depositions more commonly involve the parties or witnesses. All parties and their attorneys can attend oral depositions and they can be just as emotional and demanding as trials. They also can become pivotal in the determination of a case, because the testimony taken at a deposition can be used in trial to impeach a party or witness or to provide testimony if that party or witness is unavailable. Thus, while the facts of each case will determine how much preparation should be given to a particular deposition, it is a good idea for an attorney and her client to be well-prepared for an oral deposition.

Another form of discovery which is not used as commonly as the preceding forms is inspection. This might become particularly important in premises liability or other negligence cases, in which the condition of a piece of real property or personal property is at issue. Both parties might be very interested in inspecting whatever tangible property gave rise to the claim.

Motions and hearings on motions can be an important part of any case. A motion simply is a request by one of the parties for the judge to make a ruling on how the parties should proceed with one or more issues, either before, during, or after the trial. It might be as trivial as forcing one of the lawyers to supply information which he is withholding for no apparent reason or it might be as conclusive as a motion for summary judgment, which is a request for the court to issue judgment on the case even before the trial, thus obviating the need for a trial. It also might be a motion from the victorious plaintiff for the church to turn over financial records so that he can see how much money is available to satisfy that judgment. Motions can be very simple, yet momentous in their effect. Therefore, your church and its attorney should take them seriously.

After (i) the petition and the answer have been filed, (ii) the parties have conducted all necessary discovery, (iii) all of the pretrial motions have been filed and hearings have been held, (iv) the parties have attended mediation and failed to settle the case, and (v) the judge has determined at the pretrial conference, if one has been held, that the parties are ready to go to trial (or should go to trial, even if they are not ready), then the trial may begin. Do not hold your breath, though, because the trial at that very moment may be postponed for several months. This can happen when (i) one of the parties or attorneys requests a continuance, (ii) older or preferentially set cases take up more time than expected, or (iii) one of the parties or attorneys has a scheduling conflict. If and when your church finally finds itself about to go to trial, it could be over in less than one day or it could take several weeks.

Judges always manage the procedural flow of trials, but decisions as to liability and damages can be made either by a judge or a jury. Your church's attorney will assist you in determining which is best for your church, but you should remember that either party is entitled to try the case before a jury. Thus, even if your church would prefer to try the case before a judge, that may not occur if the other party has demanded a jury trial.

If a jury hears the case, then the attorneys must select a jury from a larger pool of potential jurors. That process is called *voir dire*, which means to speak the truth. In *voir dire*, attorney question potential jurors about various aspects of their experiences and biases in order to determine if they would make acceptable jurors. Naturally, each party's attorney may have a very different view of just who would be an acceptable juror, so the law allows each party to approve of and to object to certain jurors in a somewhat complicated, but reasonably fair, process.

At trial, each party is allowed to give an opening and closing statement of what the case is about and what the parties think that the evidence will be. After the opening statements conclude, the plaintiff is allowed to present his case through the testimony of witnesses and other evidence. The plaintiff's attorney and defense attorney will be given an opportunity to question all witnesses about their knowledge and opinions and, if appropriate, about tangible evidence. The attorneys may object to certain questions and the judge will rule on those objections. After all of the testimony is over and other evidence has been entered, the attorneys will make closing statements, in which they hope to persuade either the jury or the judge that the evidence presented and the applicable law should result in a decision favoring their respective clients. If the case is tried to a judge, a decision may be immediate or may be issued after the judge gives it some thought. If the case is tried to a jury, the jury leaves to deliberate in another room and answers a series of questions about the case which will determine liability, and, if liability exists, then the amount of damages. If the decision is obvious, the jury may return in an hour. It may take days to decide more complicated or difficult cases. Another possibility is that the jury may not be able to agree about what its verdict should be, leading to what has become known as a "hung jury," also leading to what has become known as "starting over."

ALTERNATIVE DISPUTE RESOLUTION

Lawyers refer to alternative dispute resolution as "ADR." You may find more formal definitions, but ADR essentially is any process that does not rely on litigation to resolve disputes. Among the more popular types of ADR used by lawyers are mediation and arbitration. There are others, but their use is comparatively infrequent. Mediation is the most popular form of ADR, especially when it comes to disputes involving individuals. Its format encourages dialogue and involves a neutral third party, the mediator, who often can be helpful in diffusing the emotion of the situation. I shall say much more about mediation later.

Arbitration is perhaps most common in labor disputes (in which unions and companies desire to resolve their disputes efficiently and promptly) and disputes involving sophisticated commercial transactions (in which judges and juries may not be experienced enough to grasp the issues). One well-known example of labor arbitration is the high / low form used in professional baseball's major leagues. The player, picking a "high" number, and the club, picking a "low" number, submit those numbers to a neutral decision-maker, called the arbiter. They then attempt to persuade the arbiter as to which of the two numbers is the more reasonable salary figure for the player, the arbiter being limited in his decision to picking one of the two submitted numbers. In theory, high / low arbitration encourages each party to be more reasonable than the other party. This contrasts with conventional negotiation theory, which encourages parties to start with progressively more unrealistic positions in the hope that starting higher will result in a higher result or, conversely, starting lower will result in a lower result.

Other forms of arbitration allow the arbiter more latitude, ranging from accepting any number proposed by the parties to a number somewhere in the middle. As long as the parties can fashion arbitration rules on which they can agree, arbitration provides an extremely flexible, expedient, and final tool for resolving disputes.

Perhaps surprisingly, both arbitration and mediation have scriptural bases. The world has discovered and exploited these tools to its advantage and, to a great degree, the church has ignored them. Nonetheless, when conflict confronts us, our instructions are simple: in most cases we should go directly to our sister when we have a problem with her or when we know that she has a problem with us. We simply have ignored that instruction for far too long. To correct that problem, each church should work toward having a scriptural ADR program in place, either independently or in association with other churches or umbrella organizations, and encouraging its members to engage in that process. ADR can address vital needs in our churches and can fulfill scriptural admonitions for us to be a conflict-resolving people. We shall look at ADR in a church context more specifically in Chapter 3.

Alternative Dispute Resolution - Mediation

Many, if not most, Texas litigants mediate their cases. While those that do not settle at mediation go forward in the litigation process, some actually are settled before trial based in part on the work accomplished at mediation. Judges love settlements and refer cases to mediation with three purposes in mind. First, the parties are free, at least in theory, to fashion their own settlement at mediation. Next, cases resolve without further time, energy, or attorney's fees being expended. Finally, resolved cases are removed from the courts' dockets.

Essentially, mediation is a settlement conference presided over by our mediator, Ann. She assists the parties in analyzing their positions, the strengths and weaknesses of their respective cases, and their settlement offers. The first and foremost goal of mediation is settling the case. A distant, secondary goal may be facilitating communication and better understanding among the parties. However, once the parties have engaged in the adversarial nature of litigation, they usually remain adversarial, even if they resolve their immediate problem. They do not desire to communicate with the other party or to preserve any prior relationship. As Robert Bush and Joseph Folger put it in *The Promise of Mediation*, "[i]n the world of practice today, mediation is generally problem-solving mediation."[16] Problem-solving mediation rarely concerns itself with restoration and reconciliation.

As Bush and Folger note, "problem-solving mediation translates into a kind of four-step version of practice, in which the mediator 'hears the case,' diagnoses the problem, formulates what he or she sees as a good solution, and tries to persuade the parties to accept the solution."[17] Is this approach inherently wrong? The answer to that depends in large part on your priorities and values. If you value settlement above all, then this approach cannot be wrong. However, problem-solving mediation probably has little place within the context of conflict among believers, as it does not create an atmosphere conducive to the parties' appreciation of God's presence, sensitivity to the Spirit's leading, and focus on peace, forgiveness, restoration, and reconciliation. The goal, instead and bluntly, is the cutting of a deal that seemingly resolves the problem.

Problem-solving mediation is sometimes described, perhaps innocently, but certainly misleadingly, as non-binding. That description is misleading because, if the parties choose to settle at mediation, then they have bound themselves to the deal which they cut. While mediation differs greatly from binding arbitration in its potential for the parties to walk away without an agreement or decision, it certainly can be and in most cases is very binding.[18] Thus, mediation is only non-binding in the sense that the parties can choose to withdraw from the process at any time, living to fight another day if they desire to do so. If they settle, though, then mediation is binding.

The process usually begins with an opening session attended by the mediator, whom we shall call Ann, the parties, and their attorneys. Ann explains the ground rules of mediation and ensures that all present understand the process. She asks the plaintiffs to present an abridged version of their case and their last settlement offer. She then asks the defendants to present an abridged version of their case and their last settlement offer. At any point during these presentations Ann can interrupt and ask questions of the attorneys or their clients, if she feels that it is appropriate. However, it is usually considered inappropriate for the attorneys and their clients to do so, unless the mediator suggests that the parties engage in a less structured, more conversational, discussion of the issues.

After this joint session is over, Ann usually will ask the parties to separate into groups in different rooms, with the attorneys joining their respective clients. Without disagreeing in the least with Bush's and Folger's four step analysis, she then will go from group to group:

- asking questions to ensure that she understands the facts of the case and the parties' respective legal theories
- reinforcing the stronger elements and bringing into question the weaker elements of each party's case
- suggesting possible positions which a party may take in reaction to the other party's position
- communicating the respective counteroffers made by each party
- encouraging further counteroffers and, ultimately, agreement

Ann is bound in performing these tasks to strict rules of confidentiality, which are explained to all participants in a set of rules which she may have forwarded to the parties prior to the mediation. One of the most important of these rules deals with confidentiality. She cannot reveal any communication to anyone, unless a party or its attorney authorizes her to do so. Further, she cannot testify later regarding any aspect of the mediation, except to confirm that she mediated the case and whether or not the case settled at mediation. Thus, she cannot inform the court or anyone else of what was said at mediation or of anything else that she learned at mediation.[19]

Mediation usually lasts between four and eight hours, but can take weeks or even months in some extended contexts. It can end with Ann calling an impasse, meaning that Ann does not believe that further work will bring the parties any closer to an agreement, or it can end with one or more of the parties walking out. Fortunately, it has been my experience that it usually ends with the parties agreeing to settle their dispute. That does not mean that they walk away hand in hand, but they do agree to settle the dispute and to bring some closure to the process. Some lawyers even have remarked that a good settlement is one in which neither side is happy, which is a fairly cynical way of saying that both sides were just greedy or obstinate enough to offset each other into settling the matter.

If a case does not settle, then Ann will inform the court of that fact. If a case settles, then Ann will assist the parties in fashioning a written settlement agreement reflecting specific terms and, again will notify the court of the mediation's outcome. In either case, though, she should not inform the court of anything other than whether or not the case settled and the amount of her fee. The terms of that agreement may or may not remain confidential, depending on the parties' agreement, and there may be some paperwork to file with the court reflecting the case's dismissal, but a settlement in mediation, followed by compliance with the settlement agreement, effectively ends the case and, usually, the relationship.

ALTERNATIVE DISPUTE RESOLUTION - ARBITRATION

Arbitration is used less often in civil litigation than mediation, although it certainly is a viable tool in the appropriate case. Arbitration also consists of the parties meeting at a predetermined time and place to air their differences. However, the arbiter, Mark, has a different role from Ann's role. Instead of attempting to fashion a settlement between the parties and conducting private sessions, Mark listens to each side's presentation and makes a binding decision based on the evidence presented to him.[20] Absent misconduct by Mark or a party, such as fraud, duress, *et cetera*, there is no appeal, which is certainly more comforting if you prevail than if you do not.[21]

The formats of arbitration differ quite extensively. In arbitrated cases, the parties can fashion the rules somewhat based on the unique characteristics of the dispute. The parties also can limit the amount of time and money spent and the number of testifying witnesses at an arbitration. The parties' creativity in fashioning a procedure which best fits their dispute is an attractive benefit of any ADR process, especially arbitration.

As in mediation, there are few, if any, mandatory or formal rules of evidence or procedure which must be followed. While privileged communications should remain privileged, lawyers tend not to object as much, lending to a smoother and more efficient presentation of evidence. Each side normally is allowed to make an opening and closing statement and to examine and to cross-examine witnesses. Mark also may interrupt the proceedings and question a witness or attorney directly about a point of law or fact. Finally, while the parties may make persuasive arguments and may suggest the correct decision to Mark in opening and closing statements, he is free to make his own judgment. After Mark does so, it is enforceable just as if a court had rendered a judgment.[22]

THE CASE AGAINST LAWYERS

Kim and I had agreed before going into Sunday School one morning that we would not say anything controversial. We had just started attending this church. No one yet knew that I was a lawyer, so people were still treating us nicely. It was in this setting that the teacher asked the following question at the very end of the class: "Has anyone here had training in dispute resolution"? It was an innocent, seemingly non-spiritual question. He was curious, because he had just been through a mediation with an employee at his job. Without thinking, my hand shot up. It was a Baptist church, so the teacher knew that I was responding to the question in an orderly manner and not attempting to engage in worship.

"Have you had dispute resolution training?"

"Yes." Immediately sensing the danger to which I had exposed myself, I adopted a popular legal strategy, *i.e.* be arguably truthful, yet evasive and indirect.

"How much training?"

"Three years."

"What kind?"

"Well, I wrote a paper on arbitration." I was still doing everything that I could to avoid confessing my lawyer status and was regretting my lack of impulse control.

"What kind of paper takes three years?"

"Well, the paper didn't take three years."

"Well, what took three years?" There was no more avoiding the issue. This man should have been a lawyer.

Following a very pregnant pause, "law school." Audible gasps escaped from the crowd.

"Oooooohhhhhhh, you're a lawyer!"

The next few minutes consisted of the teacher cross-examining me concerning exactly how being a lawyer qualified me to resolve disputes. My answer was that law school equips students to resolve disputes through litigation. The teacher clearly saw a lawyer's role as more of dispute instigator, though, and certainly did not mind sharing that with the class.

Was my teacher's opinion, that lawyers start or at least encourage conflict, accurate? Many people would shout an adamant "Amen" and they would have ample ammunition to support that view. Advertisements for lawyers' services can sound more like "get rich quick" schemes than a search for justice. Words like "reconcile," "forgive," and "mercy" just do not make it onto the billboard very often. Yet, should these words be equally or even more important to Christians when it comes to resolving disputes, especially among themselves? The teacher had a fair, albeit debatable, point.

Are all lawyers worthless as dispute resolvers? The answer is an unequivocal no. Some of the finest mediators whom I have met are attorneys. I know other attorneys who think that they provide no better service to their clients than keeping them out of trouble in the first place, rather than resolving problems for them after the fact. We simply have placed a heavier burden on lawyers as dispute resolvers than they deserve. It is, in fact, God's people who have abdicated dispute resolution on a grass roots level. We need to repent and to accept responsibility for admitting, confronting, and resolving our own conflict and broken relationships, instead of laying all of the blame at the lawyers' doorsteps.

CHAPTER 3

Conflict in the Church

THE CASE AGAINST YOU AND ME

If you think that lawyers are not effective dispute resolvers, then who should pick up that gauntlet? You should. I should. Our brothers and sisters should. It should not always take a law degree or mediation credentials to do so. The only requirement should be that we actually read the Bible and have the faith to follow fairly simple instructions about how we should relate to each other and resolve disputes among ourselves when we inevitably fail to get along. We do not do that very well, though.

Being human, we are going to have conflicts with one another. Eve grabbed hold of a lie and indulged her pride and envy. Adam was right there, at first aiding and abetting and, later, blaming his partner. Cain then gave a poor effort, became jealous, killed Abel, and lied to God. That summary of the first family just about covers the spectrum of conflict which we face on a daily basis. James 4:1–3 puts it this way.

What causes fights and quarrels among you? Don't they come from your desires that battle within you? You want something but don't get it. You kill and covet, but you cannot have what you want. You quarrel and fight. You do not have, because you do not ask God. When you ask, you do not receive, because you ask with wrong motives, that you may spend what you get on your pleasures.

We are proud and envious. We hide, lie, and steal. We reject God, indulge ourselves, chart our own course, blame others for our sin, and kill them when they get in the way. In our sophisticated, politically correct, post-modern world, we are nothing more than what we always have been. Do we really look like we want to resolve conflict?

If we are not ready to resolve our conflict and the pain has become too much, then we look elsewhere for relief. We look to lawyers to sue those who abuse us. We look to therapists to rationalize away our guilt. We look to pastors to justify our righteousness. We look to doctors to relieve our physical symptoms. We look to virtually anyone who can mask our pain or, if it cannot be masked, anyone who will make the other person suffer more than we are suffering. In rejecting the reconciliation which would be a balm for our souls, we heap burning coals and ashes on ourselves.

It is time that we start casting aside the stumbling blocks which we have created, clearing the courts' dockets of *First Faction of First Church v. Second Faction of First Church*, and putting an end to the Hatfield and McCoy relationships in our churches. To accomplish those goals, though, we also must start thinking of those toward whom we cast sideways glances as being worthy enough for us to invest the effort to resolve the dispute. We have to value that relationship. We have to love our friends *and* our enemies. We have to submit to each other, to acknowledge our fault, to repent of our sin, and to forgive our brothers, sisters, and selves, finally finding peace in the process. Too many of us are just not ready to do that because reconciliation is not a priority.

I often reflect on I Corinthians 12:20 in regard to church conflict. Was Paul speaking to the church at Corinth or, perhaps, all churches? "For I am afraid that when I come I may not find you as I want you to be, and you may not find me as you want me to be. I fear that there may be quarreling, jealousy, outbursts of anger, factions, slander, gossip, arrogance and disorder." Paul knew what he would find in Corinth. We know what we find in our own churches.

BUILDING BLOCKS AND THREE MODELS

You understandably may be surprised to find these topics addressed in a book about the law. You even may doubt that I have the background to address these issues. You very well may be correct about that, as there are many others far more qualified in this area than me, both from an educational and experiential perspective. What I can confirm, though, from being around law offices for two decades, is that any church or believer who relies on the law to resolve conflict associated with the church usually is engaging in an unscriptural, destructive, and wasteful exercise.

Reconciliation is a spiritual, not legal, process.[23] It is possible only among believers because, without Christ having reconciled us to God, we have no ministry of reconciliation with our brothers and sisters or even any concept of what that is. It is our ministry and we understand it only because of what Jesus did for us on the cross. Reconciliation with God already has occurred. Reconciliation with our brothers and sisters is within our grasp, if we have the faith to be obedient. Paul tells us in II Corinthians 5:18–20 that God:

> reconciled us to himself through Christ and gave us the ministry of reconciliation: that God was reconciling the world to himself in Christ, not counting men's sins against them. And he has committed to us the message of reconciliation. We are therefore Christ's ambassadors, as though God were making his appeal through us. We implore you on Christ's behalf: Be reconciled to God.

Our sin against God creates the need for reconciliation with Him. Our sin, as Isaiah 59: 2 warns us, separates us from Him, causing Him to hide His face from us. Further, we know that there are no exceptions, as Paul tells us in Romans 3:23 that "all have sinned and fall short of the glory of God." God did not leave us in our sin and isolation, though, as Romans 5:10–11 informs us.

> For if, when we were God's enemies, we were reconciled to him through the death of his Son, how much more, having been reconciled, shall we be saved through his life! Not only is this so, but we also rejoice in God through our Lord Jesus Christ, through whom we have now received reconciliation.

This ministry of reconciliation includes three New Testament models. Those are Matthew 5:23–24 (resolving a charge against you), Matthew 18:15–17 (presenting a charge against your brother), and I Corinthians 6:1–8 (taking your brother to court, submitting disputes to the church, and overlooking offenses). Of somewhat more infrequent application are Paul's instructions for unique situations in I Corinthians 5:1–5 (open, unrepentant sin) and I Timothy 5:19–21 (a charge against an elder). These models are best understood by first discussing some foundational verses, building blocks within the models, if you will. Other building blocks, such as prayer, are just as important as any of these discussed. They all have a vital place in every conflict and we all need to engage in and to explore them fully as we seek to resolve conflict. By conforming our attitudes, intentions, and actions with these building blocks, we place ourselves in a better position both to avoid conflict and, when necessary, to be reconciled in obedience to these models.

BUILDING BLOCKS - OFF WITH THE OLD

We know what we do to each other in church in regard to conflict. We have, perhaps, more in common with the churches to which Paul wrote than we admit. Before we begin to apply conflict-resolving scripture among ourselves, though, we need to take seriously Paul's command in Ephesians 4:22–25:

> You were taught, with regard to your former way of life, to put off your old self, which is being corrupted by its deceitful desires; to be made new in the attitude of your minds; and to put on the new self, created to be like God in true righteousness and holiness. Therefore each of you must put off falsehood and speak truthfully to his neighbor, for we are all members of one body.

This is the big paradigm shift. Our priorities should be different: His kingdom, not ours. Our behavior should be different: truth, not lies. Our focus should be different: others first, not self. Our very natures should be different: living, not dying. The new self must understand, embrace, and act on these foundational verses because the old self can make no sense of what we are commanded to do.

These new emphases are expressed throughout the New Testament. These writers acknowledge, in deference to the fact that we are in the process of putting on and learning about our new selves, that we will continue sinning and that conflict will exist. They also teach us first how best to behave ourselves and, as a corollary, how best to react to the presence of conflict and sin. Colossians 3:12–15 expresses this.

> Therefore, as God's chosen people, holy and dearly loved, clothe yourselves with compassion, kindness, humility, gentleness and patience. Bear with each other and forgive whatever grievances you may have against one another. Forgive as the Lord forgave you. And over all these virtues put on love, which binds them all together in perfect unity. Let the peace of Christ rule in your hearts, since as members of one body you were called to peace. And be thankful.

We shall discuss some of these aspects of Christian conduct separately in order to gain some sense of how they impact the processes set forth in Matthew 5 and 18 and I Corinthians 6.

BUILDING BLOCKS - LOVING

Paul assures us in I Corinthians 13:13 that love is the greatest among faith, hope, and love. Jesus tells us in Matthew 22:34–40 that the action verb in the greatest two commandments is love. We are to love God with all that is within us and we are to love our neighbors as ourselves. If all of our heart, soul, and mind goes into this effort, then what part may be left that is withheld from God? The obvious answer is nothing. The thrust of the greatest commandment is a consuming, exclusive love of God, out of which arises the second greatest commandment, to love those whom God also loves. John gives some form to the concept in II John 1:6, stating that "this is love: that we walk in obedience to his commands. As you have heard from the beginning, his command is that you walk in love."

Jesus adds to that description, telling us in John 13:34–35 that we are to love each other as He loved us and that people will know us, will know that there is something different about us, and will know to whom we belong by the fact that we demonstrate love to each other. Further, our love is not simply to be words, feelings, and such sentiment. Our love is to be constructive, expressive, and tangible. We see in I John 3:17–18 that we are not just to "love with words or tongue but with actions and in truth." If we see a brother in need and do not respond as God has enabled us to respond, then we simply are not acting in love. The logical extension of this carries us to the extreme. Just how deeply are we to love? The simple, profound answer which we all know is found in John 15:13. "Greater love has no one than this, that he lay down his life for his friends."

We are to love each other as He loved us. We know what that means. Can we really do that? Do we really do that? Those are, of course, two entirely different questions. Of course we can do that through His strength, but do any of us really ever sacrifice that deeply for another because of love? This is exactly what John is saying when he tells us how to recognize love in I John 3:16. "This is how we know what love is: Jesus Christ laid down his life for us. And we ought to lay down our lives for our brothers." We see the salutary effects of love vanish when we cease loving our brothers and sisters with a sacrificial love. Since we regularly fail to do that, we should not be amazed when conflict increases.

BUILDING BLOCKS - FORGIVING

Do you want to do something really nice for yourself? Then forgive someone or ask someone to forgive you. In either case, forgiveness really is not about the other person. It is about your relationship with God. Holding on to anger and resentment or guilt about any issue is a stumbling block in your relationship with God. Jesus' words in Matthew 6:14–15 are instructive. "For if you forgive men when they sin against you, your heavenly Father will also forgive you. But if you do not forgive men their sins, your Father will not forgive your sins." Forgiveness is all about what we learn in our relationship with God. If we understand the value and place of forgiveness in our lives and understand the significance of the sacrifice which God made for us, then we will understand the necessity of forgiving and asking for forgiveness and be compelled, out of love, thanksgiving, and conviction, to forgive others and to ask for forgiveness. If we cannot do that, then we essentially are telling God that we do not appreciate His ceaseless and boundless acts of forgiveness toward us. This is the message of the parable of the unmerciful servant in Matthew 18:23–35.[24]

Jesus died for the sins of the world. That means all the sins ever committed by anyone anywhere, at any time; past, present, and future; venial and mortal; intentional ones and neglectful ones; *et cetera*. Has someone committed a sin against you that does not fit into this category? Is someone's sin against you so much more significant than what each of us has done in rebelling against God that it does not deserve to be forgiven? Are you holier than God and, therefore, worthy of saying that there is no atonement for this or that sin committed against you? Putting it into the proper perspective, "the moral gap between God and ourselves is far greater than it is between the worst of us and the best of us. Consequently, the price that Jesus paid is far greater than we will ever have to pay in order to forgive others."[25] Colossians 3:13 tells us to "[b]ear with each other and forgive whatever grievances you may have against one another. Forgive as the Lord forgave you." The Lord's forgiveness in our lives, seventy times seven and more, is immeasurable. Has our forgiveness of others' sins against us, in addition to our requests to be forgiven, met the same standard?

BUILDING BLOCKS - REPENTING

We all are more than happy to acknowledge that repentance is necessary for conflict resolution. We usually disagree over the most minor point, though: just who needs to repent of what. Jesus acknowledged this problem in Matthew 7:1–5.

> Do not judge, or you too will be judged. For in the same way you judge others, you will be judged, and with the measure you use, it will be measured to you. Why do you look at the speck of sawdust in your brother's eye and pay no attention to the plank in your own eye? How can you say to your brother, "Let me take the speck out of your eye,"

when all the time there is a plank in your own eye? You hypocrite, first take the plank out of your own eye, and then you will see clearly to remove the speck from your brother's eye.

We see the need for repentance all too plainly with our brothers' circumstances. Jesus cautions us, however, to check the cause of our own myopia and to watch ourselves, ensuring that we have engaged in some critical self-examination prior to examining others' lives. Further, as II Timothy 2:25–26 tells us, without repentance, there is "no knowledge of the truth" and no escape from the "trap of the devil." Without repentance, there is no reconciliation.

BUILDING BLOCKS - ENCOURAGING

Hebrews 3:13 directs us to "encourage one another daily, as long as it is called Today, so that none of you may be hardened by sin's deceitfulness." That sounds fairly straight-forward and simple. Encourage! Who? One another! When? Daily! Why? So that our brothers and sisters are not "hardened" by sin. "Hardened" is a wonderfully descriptive word of what happens to people in conflict. Curiously, it also is a word that describes bunkers used in nuclear war, bunkers that can both take and deliver a lethal blow.

When in conflict, do we encourage our adversary? No. We gossip. Whenever we hear the phrase, "it's nothing personal, but . . ." we are assured that whatever comes next will be extremely personal. We criticize. Whenever we have an opportunity to persuade someone, especially when our sister is not within earshot, we are sure to utter our most objective, caring observations about the stupidity of her opinions. In short, when we are in conflict, we engage in every one of the behaviors which Paul feared that he would find in I Corinthians 12:20. Guidance comes from Ephesians 4:29–32:

> Do not let any unwholesome talk come out of your mouths, but only what is helpful for building others up according to their needs, that it may benefit those who listen. And do not grieve the Holy Spirit of God, with whom you were sealed for the day of redemption. Get rid of all bitterness, rage and anger, brawling and slander, along with every form of malice. Be kind and compassionate to one another, forgiving each other, just as in Christ God forgave you.

God's forgiveness and Jesus' death remind us, poignantly, of just why we should encourage one another. In I Thessalonians 5:10–11, Paul reminds us that our duty to encourage one another rests on Jesus' sacrifice. "He died for us so that, whether we are awake or asleep, we may live together with him. Therefore encourage one another and build each other up, just as in fact you are doing." Our encouragement is not only from one another, though, as we see Paul instruct us in II Thessalonians 2:16–17. "May our Lord Jesus Christ himself and God our Father, who loved us and by his grace gave us eternal encouragement and good hope, encourage your hearts and strengthen you in every good deed and word." Thus, encouragement is not just some lofty goal. It is a grass roots, street level, "heart to God" and "hand to man" service issue.[26] It is an integral part of our relationship with God, by whom we are encouraged, compelling us to encourage fellow Christians, even those who discourage us. The only possible conclusion is that encouragement is not only a preventative, but also a curative, element in church conflict.

BUILDING BLOCKS - SEEKING PEACE

For those of us who have been accused of liking confrontation a little too much, peace can be challenging. We even may think of peace as boring and justify our behavior by saying that we are just trying to spice things up a bit. We know a couple of things about peace, though. First, Paul tells us in Romans 12:18, in relation to conflict, that "[i]f it is possible, as far as it depends on you, live at peace with everyone." Paul acknowledges that our sister may not be quite willing to be reconciled, i.e. "if it is possible." The burden is on us, though, perhaps even the ones wrongfully charged with an offense, to start the reconciliation effort, i.e. "as far as it depends on you." If I have not done all that I can do to be at peace with my sister, then what business do I have offering a gift to God?

Next, we know from Galatians 5:22–23 that peace is one of the fruits of the Spirit and that "there is no law" against it, a reassuring thought from Paul, lest anyone ever think that peace is illegal. We also know that the unity of Spirit, spoken of in Ephesians 4:2–3, is kept through "the bond of peace." Paul again chooses words which stress the motive and the effort, not the result. As in Romans 12:18, in which he acknowledges that peace is to be desired "if it is possible, as far as it depends on you," he urges us in Ephesians to "make every effort" toward peace. If we do so, then we have been obedient, regardless of whether or not peace reigns immediately.

In dealing with our brothers and sisters, Colossians 3:15 reminds us that "as *members of one body* . . . [we] are called to peace." We see in I Thessalonians 5:10, 13 that Christ died for us so that "we may *live together* with Him" and "[l]ive in peace *with each other*" (emphasis added). With Christ's death and our effort, peace is possible. However, peace is meant for community, not for isolation. Thus, we "live together" and are commanded "as members of one body" to be "at peace with everyone." II Timothy 2:22–23 issues a similar calling, *i.e.* that we are to "pursue righteousness, faith, love and peace, along with those who call on the Lord with a pure heart." Again, peace is not to be sought apart from our communities of faith. Peace is not saying "I am at peace with myself, for I have no further use for those with whom I disagree." Instead, peace is to be sought where we always find each other, in and out of conflict.

BUILDING BLOCKS - OVERLOOKING OFFENSES

As a society, we are quickly offended. Some of us interpret every unintended turn of the head or failure to say hello as a deliberately orchestrated snub. As Christians, though, we have options. We do not have to take offense at every little thing that does not go our way. We can forgive without confrontation. We can patiently endure the little things without letting them get to us. Proverbs 17:9 instructs us that one "who covers over an offense promotes love, but whoever repeats the matter separates close friends." Thus, when we cover over an offense, we promote love, without which, Paul says in I Corinthians 13:1, we are nothing but "a resounding gong or a clanging cymbal." When we repeat the matter, *i.e.* when we gossip (even if we are telling the truth), we separate "close friends." The conflict does not exist because of the original offense. It exists because the offended one "takes" offense.

Similarly, Proverbs 19:11 tells us that "man's wisdom gives him patience; it is to his glory to overlook an offense." Wisdom and patience are cultivated over time and are marks of spiritual maturity. They enable us to do the seemingly impossible: "to overlook an offense." I can offer no bright line test for when it is appropriate to overlook an offense *versus* when it is appropriate to confront, except to say that we usually err toward confrontation or, worse yet, simply writing another name on our black list. Yet, scripture plainly states that we promote love and glorify Him when we can overlook an offense. When we should overlook, but do not, we separate friends and create conflict, perhaps even where none existed.

BUILDING BLOCKS - CONFRONTING

Many attorneys have what some would describe as the spiritual gift of confrontation. It is, perhaps, better described as a professional skill, as attorneys with an aversion to confrontation never seem to last very long on the front lines. Focusing on the adversarial nature of confrontation is not at all how God intends for us to confront, though.

For Nathan, confrontation was part of his prophetic calling. He did not confront a relative, someone sitting next to him in the pews, or his neighbor. He confronted a king with the power to kill him. He spoke the truth in love and confronted David with robbery, adultery, and murder. He stood there, uncertain of David's reaction and immersed in risk. Repentance came immediately in David's brief, but contrite reply in II Samuel 12:13: "I have sinned against the Lord."

Confrontation is hard work. It always involves love, the task of truth telling, and an element of risk. The confronter never truly knows how the confronted will react. Many are the times when a brother will accuse his confronter of being judgmental and not minding her own business. At best, we hope for a Davidic reaction, but those seem rare. Perhaps they are rare because we are not confronting our brothers and sisters as Nathan confronted David. Perhaps we are not obeying Jesus in Matthew 18:15 when He tells us, if your brother has sinned against you, then "go and show him his fault, just between the two of you."

There are certain aspects to scriptural confrontation that we are ignoring. First, we must absolutely confront ourselves about what we are doing before we confront others. Our attitudes, selfishness, and myopia make confronting others about their mistakes a delicate proposition at best. As the artist Bryan Duncan sings, "[t]he perfect motive has another, ulterior . . . Check yours twice when you're feeling superior."[27] Jesus relates this cautionary message in Matthew 7:1–5, which I repeat from an earlier section.

> Do not judge, or you too will be judged. For in the same way you judge others, you will be judged, and with the measure you use, it will be measured to you. Why do you look at the speck of sawdust in your brother's eye and pay no attention to the plank in your own eye? How can you say to your brother, "Let me take the speck out of your eye," when all the time there is a plank in your own eye? You hypocrite, first take the plank out of your own eye, and then you will see clearly to remove the speck from your brother's eye.

Paul warns us, not specifically about being blind to our own sin, but about our attitudes in Galatians 6:1–5. Notice that Paul implicitly links confrontation with the act of restoring a person caught in sin.

> Brothers, if someone is caught in a sin, you who are spiritual should restore him gently. But watch yourself, or you also may be tempted. Carry each other's burdens, and in this way you will fulfill the law of Christ. If anyone thinks he is something when he is

nothing, he deceives himself. Each one should test his own actions. Then he can take pride in himself, without comparing himself to somebody else, for each one should carry his own load.

Too often we think of confrontation as having to be done boldly and aggressively. Not so, says Paul: "restore him gently." In II Timothy 4:2b, Paul reiterates his emphasis on how we approach this issue, telling us to "correct, rebuke and encourage—with great patience and careful instruction."

We simply cannot carry an air of spiritual superiority into confrontation. If we are not guarding our hearts and watching ourselves, then we may find that we are the ones in need of some confrontation. Paul understands that we all have a tendency to think too highly of ourselves, especially when we think that we are being spiritual big brothers. "Watch yourself." These are words worth repeating and remembering, just as Luke recorded Jesus saying them in Luke 17:3–4. "So watch yourselves. If your brother sins, rebuke him, and if he repents, forgive him. If he sins against you seven times in a day, and seven times comes back to you and says, 'I repent,' forgive him."

Finally, there is a preventative aspect to confrontation. We cannot forget that we are talking about sin in this context and that sin is always to be weeded out from the church. Paul makes this abundantly clear in the example of I Corinthians 5:1–5. Further, the writer in Hebrews 12:11–15 speaks to the fruit of discipline accompanying confrontation, as well as weeding out sin from the church's garden.

No discipline seems pleasant at the time, but painful. Later on, however, it produces a harvest of righteousness and peace for those who have been trained by it. Therefore, strengthen your feeble arms and weak knees! "Make level paths for your feet," so that the lame may not be disabled, but rather healed. Make every effort to live in peace with all men and to be holy; without holiness no one will see the Lord. See to it that no one misses the grace of God and that no bitter root grows up to cause trouble and defile many.

James echoes these thoughts in James 5:19–20. "My brothers, if one of you should wander from the truth and someone should bring him back, remember this: Whoever turns a sinner from the error of his way will save him from death and cover over a multitude of sins." As we see from a variety of scriptural sources, confrontation, when carried out in harmony with scripture, is not only curative for the person being confronted, but also preventative for her church.

BUILDING BLOCKS - TRUTH TELLING

Paul instructs to speak truthfully to our neighbors. Doing so is an act of integrity. Acting with integrity is a spiritually mature and considered act, because when we finally arrive at the place where we can begin speaking the truth, we also understand that our brothers and sisters do not necessarily like hearing the truth. Certainly there is much more to be said about the how, when, and to whom of speaking the truth that can be said here, but Paul sets out some of it for us in Ephesians 4:14–16.

> Then we will no longer be infants, tossed back and forth by the waves, and blown here and there by every wind of teaching and by the cunning and craftiness of men in their deceitful scheming. Instead, speaking the truth in love, we will in all things grow up into him who is the Head, that is, Christ. From him the whole body, joined and held together by every supporting ligament, grows and builds itself up in love, as each part does its work.

Thus, spiritual maturity is both a precursor ("then we will no longer be infants") and a consequence ("we will . . . grow up into Him") to this truth telling. Any conciliatory efforts must grab hold of this truth. Its presence in all stages is necessary for God to be glorified through the reconciliation of His people.

BUILDING BLOCKS - BEING PATIENT

We have seen Paul's emphasis on patience in II Timothy 4:2b, where he admonished us to "correct, rebuke and encourage—with great patience and careful instruction." Other verses apply as well. In Ephesians 4:2–3, Paul tells us to be "completely humble and gentle; be patient, bearing with one another in love. Make every effort to keep the unity of the Spirit through the bond of peace." This is not simply a New Testament concept, though.

In that regard, Proverbs 14:29 advises that a "patient man has great understanding, but a quick-tempered man displays folly." Similarly, Proverbs 15:18 advises that a "hot-tempered man stirs up dissension, but a patient man calms a quarrel." Who is preferable in a mediation in which the future of a church is at stake? Regardless of my role in the matter, I prefer someone with patience to someone prone to hasty decisions. I prefer someone with understanding and appreciation of what is at stake to someone who is clueless about what he is doing and the consequences of the decisions which he is making. Conflict feels uncomfortable in most circumstances, but we cannot allow that discomfort to short-circuit the scriptural processes of conflict resolution. Patience helps us to avoid doing exactly that.

BUILDING BLOCKS - BLESSING THOSE WHO CURSE YOU

What happens when you put forth the effort to be reconciled, but cannot achieve the desired result? Sadly, there will be some situations in which the other person stares at you and refuses to reconcile. Proverbs 18:19 states what should be obvious to us by now: "[a]n offended brother is more unyielding than a fortified city, and disputes are like the barred gates of a citadel." A sister may reject your apology. She may acknowledge her actions, yet be unrepentant. She may simply say, "I do not like you, have never liked you, and never want to have anything to do with you." Because we are dealing with humans, the possibilities for an inappropriate response are almost limitless.

Lacking any control whatsoever over our sister, how do we react when she refuses to be reconciled? First, if we already have not forgiven her, then we forgive her. She has done nothing worse to us than we have done to others. We see her as a person, just like us, for whom Jesus died. We reflect on the fact that we have made mistakes and have failed to ask for forgiveness, just like her. As Ronald Dunn wrote in *Surviving Friendly Fire*, we share not only a common grace, but also a common guilt with everyone who has hurt us.[28] We understand her weakness and her humanity and we take those partial steps which are appropriate, given her continuing rejection, to reconcile ourselves with her.

Directly and plainly, so that we can understand it, Jesus tells us what we should do in Matthew 5:43–44. "You have heard that it was said, 'You shall love your neighbor and hate your enemy.' But I say to you, love your enemies, bless those who curse you, do good to those who hate you, and pray for those who spitefully use you and persecute you." (*New King James Version*). Peter echoes Jesus' hard words in I Peter 3:8–9. "Finally, all of you, live in harmony with one another; be sympathetic, love as brothers, be compassionate and humble. Do not repay evil with evil or insult with insult, but with blessing, because to this you were called so that you may inherit a blessing."

Jesus' and Peter's words run directly counter to our old natures. We want justice and vengeance. We want our enemies in stocks in the town square. God wants us to let go of those desires, though, and to see the bigger picture, where without His mercy, grace, and forgiveness we would not have the breath to utter our selfish thoughts. Having been so blessed, we should be willing to continue extending a hand of reconciliation to our brothers and sisters, even after they have bitten that hand, by blessing them.

BUILDING BLOCKS - SPIRITUAL MATURITY

Almost all of these building blocks point to one thing: spiritual maturity. In almost every instance, whether we are reading the words of Jesus, Paul, or someone else, the qualities or actions being heralded usually exist in spiritually mature people. Regardless of the role which we and others play, when we are in conflict we want and need everyone around us to be spiritually mature. We want the mediator or arbiter to have been through the process a few times and to grasp not only the import of the issues, but also the map showing us the way out of the forest. We want to think of ourselves as seeking God's kingdom first and letting all else go by the wayside. We want the bystanders to be spiritually mature so that they will be praying and making good decisions in light of how the conflict affects the church. Finally, deep down, we should want anyone with whom we are in conflict to be spiritually mature, because the ultimate resolution of any conflict will depend in some degree on how spiritually mature all of the parties are or can become through the process.

THREE MODELS - A CHARGE AGAINST YOU

George saw Al do something and recoiled in horror. Now George has something against Al, but decides to tell Bill, not Al. George told Bill that Al is a drunk. If George had bothered to talk to Al directly, he might have found that the word "beer" on the bottle that Al was drinking was preceded by the word "root" and that it could not be seen from his vantage point. Now George and Bill have something against Al and they tell two people. The wildfire then begins to spread. Al has no idea that he is being set up for a fall.

George's initial problem was one of perspective. He did not see the situation for what it was. He had incomplete information, he did not care enough about Al to ask a simple question or to lend a helping hand, and he judged a man. His second mistake was that he spread his false judgment and infected Bill and others, who foolishly listened and accepted George's judgment. One of those infected tells Al that he is no longer qualified to teach Sunday School. Conflict is now rampant.

We never find conflict, though, without instructions on how to resolve it and a command to resolve it. Directly and plainly, so that we can understand it, Jesus tells us what we should do in Matthew 5: 23–24:

Therefore, if you are offering your gift at the altar and there remember that your brother has something against you, leave your gift there in front of the altar. First go and be reconciled to your brother; then come and offer your gift.

When exactly do I offer "a gift at the altar"? What does that mean? Although I am just a lawyer, I shall play theologian for a while. I think that we offer gifts at the altar through our praise, worship, and service. This does not place our relationship with our brother above our relationship with God; it simply means that Al may have something that he needs to do first in order to be able to worship God as God intends that to occur, a condition precedent in legal terms. It does not matter that George is wrong. It does not matter that George lied about Al. It does not matter that George may continue to gossip about Al after they speak. George's response is irrelevant to Al's responsibility, which is quite simple: to try to reconcile with George. Why should we do this? Because Jesus commanded us to do so and because our obedience is thanksgiving for the grace, mercy, and forgiveness that we have received. If Al knows that George has something against him, then Al's charge is to "go and be reconciled."

THREE MODELS - A CHARGE AGAINST YOUR BROTHER - GOING TO YOUR BROTHER

Suppose that Barbara does some work for Al. For reasons which he does not share, Al decides that he does not want to pay her, even after they had agreed on a price and Barbara had done everything that she had promised to do. Is Barbara angry with Al? What does she do about it, though, beside complain to everyone who will listen?

Directly and plainly, so that we can understand it, Jesus tells us what we should do in Matthew 18:15–17.

> If your brother sins against you, go and show him his fault, just between the two of you. If he listens to you, you have won your brother over. But if he will not listen, take one or two others along, so that every matter may be established by the testimony of two or three witnesses. If he refuses to listen to them, tell it to the church; and if he refuses to listen even to the church, treat him as you would a pagan or a tax collector.

After minutes of intensive Bible study, Barbara's reaction might be something like this:

> That last part, the part about writing off Al and treating him like a pagan or tax collector, sounds really good. I especially liked the part about exposing how he has mistreated me by taking along witnesses. If two witnesses are good, then several probably would be that much better. Maybe I even should share what this guy did to me with my Sunday School class as a prayer request. After all, the class needs to learn how to protect themselves by

hearing what Al did and he certainly needs the prayer. I'm going to follow this advice to a 't.' Getting even can be fun and scriptural!

There are a couple of problems with that reaction. The first is that Barbara is not focusing in any way on efforts that will lead to reconciliation. She does not have any bent toward forgiveness or toward righting her own perspective. She has a vindictive attitude that will never have a resolutory role in the peace-making process. The second problem is that confidentiality, at least at this stage, is important. Her desire to spread the word about her victimization accomplishes the opposite goal: spreading the bad news about Al. That is gossip and slander.

The entire approach set forth in Matthew 18:15–17 is a four-step process. Jay E. Adams contends in *Handbook of Church Discipline* that it is, in reality, a five step process and offers some persuasive arguments for that proposition.[29] To distinguish, though, his analysis takes a broader cast than this chapter. Lynn R. Buzzard and Laurence Eck maintain in *Tell it to the Church* that "our Lord suggests a three-step process" in these situations.[30] Thus, without disagreeing with any of them in the least, I shall rest on Proverbs' convention that three are good, four are better, and on my conclusion that there is not any significant meaning in the number of steps, as long as the substance is consistent with scripture.

How comfortable are any of us with this process? Based on the number of times which I have witnessed it being followed *vis a vis* the amount of conflict which I have seen among Christians, the answer must be not very comfortable at all. Why do we have such an all-encompassing aversion to following Jesus' command in this area? Could it be that we simply do not care enough about the other individual to want to restore that relationship? Could it be that our pride gets in the way every time and that we are loathe to admit that someone has hurt us, someone whom we may even have considered to be a friend? Admitting to either of these propositions forces us to admit our vulnerability and the reality that we have been hurt. There is not much, if any, encouragement in our society or in our churches for us to acknowledge these feelings. Only the dependent, weak, and helpless would confess to having those feelings. The body of Christ has bought into these cultural talismans hook, line, and sinker.

Jesus spoke to these conditions in Matthew 5. He did not say that those who are strong are blessed. He did not say that those who can inflict or withstand great pain, the hardened, are blessed. Instead, He introduced such radical ideas as exalting those who are poor in spirit and meek. He promised in Matthew 5:3, 5 that "theirs is the kingdom of heaven" and that "they will inherit the earth." He promised that peacemakers would "be called sons of God" in Matthew 5:9. He also said that we would be blessed when we "are persecuted" because of righteousness and when we are insulted, persecuted and lied about because of Him in Matthew 5:10, 11. When we achieve these goals, He calls on us to "rejoice and be glad" in Matthew 5:12. This is the foolish message of which Paul speaks in I Corinthians 1:18. These "counterintuitive paradoxes . . . alert us to the fact that Jesus' new community is a contrast society, out of synch with the 'normal' order of the world."[31]

Jesus first calls for a private meeting. This is the optimal and primal place in which to resolve a brother's sin. As Richard B. Hays notes in *The Moral Vision of the New Testament*, "[T]his rule, if followed would eliminate much gossip and backbiting in the church. It also provides the offender with the opportunity to receive the word of admonition and repent without public scandal."[32] This step is not optional and there is no appropriate alternative. "Whenever an unreconciled condition exists between two believers, there is no option left: discipline must be pursued."[33] These instructions are not contradictory to Matthew 5:23–24. Instead, they are complementary. Scripture places an obligation on both the offended and the offender to seek reconciliation.

If that is unsuccessful, then Jesus calls for another meeting, this time with "one or two others" in attendance. Of what possible help could they be? Neil T. Anderson and Charles Mylander in *Blessed Are the Peace Makers* list the following five roles for "one or two others." First, "[t]hey verify the facts." "He said, she said" has become a catch phrase in our society. Verifying the facts is an important role, as people in conflict sometimes are not very careful with the truth. Next, the others "calm the hostility." All of us tend to behave better when there are witnesses. If the objective witnesses are present, then we are encouraged to be on our best behavior. Third, "[t]hey clarify communication." In the heat of battle, subtleties, especially opportunities for recognition and even outright apologies, may be missed. Someone who has the ability to call time out and to ask Barbara if she just heard Al apologize is vital to the process. The others also assist in the "search for possible solutions." Those in conflict can suffer from tunnel vision and a "win at all costs" mentality. This restricted thinking is a tremendous hindrance to seeing the possibilities for creative problem solving that always exist within conflicted situations. The others have clearer heads and can guide the parties toward possible solutions which may not occur to them. Finally, "[t]hey provide accountability." The witnesses can hold the parties to agreements and, if church discipline becomes an issue, report to the church on the steps taken toward reconciliation.[34]

If Barbara is unsuccessful with the first two steps, then she should "tell it to the church." What does that mean? Should we call a special session and gather the congregation? Should the matter be placed on the business meeting agenda? That certainly would liven things up, but I doubt that it is what Jesus intended. I think that the church in this sense means the elders, deacons, staff, or other authority in a particular church.[35]

It is an uncertain interpretation, at best, but I do not see the publication of a private matter to the entire church body as being consistent, even at this stage, with Jesus' admonition against gossip and slander. Thus, Barbara should take it to some person or group in authority at the church, not to the entire church. However, there are good arguments favoring the elders' involvement first and, if those efforts are unsuccessful, then the involvement of the entire church.[36] Regardless of this particular issue's resolution, though, much greater care must be taken in the handling of the matter as the number of people increases.

There can be exceptions to this model, though. There is a situation in I Corinthians 5:1–5 in which Paul discusses a man whose sin is well known in the community. He discusses the situation openly in his letter and directs the church to remove the man from its fellowship. This was an ongoing, notorious refusal to repent which affected not only the sinner, but the entire church. Thus, sins which could affect or are known to the church should be brought before the church as a body and dealt with in that fashion.

A similar situation is contained in I Timothy 5:19–21, where Paul directs us not to

> entertain an accusation against an elder unless it is brought by two or three witnesses. Those who sin are to be rebuked publicly, so that the others may take warning. I charge you, in the sight of God and Christ Jesus and the elect angels, to keep these instructions without partiality, and to do nothing out of favoritism.

Who is an elder? I leave the exact definition to the theologians, but it could encompass clergy members, deacons, and lay leaders serving in comparable offices. Several other verses shed light on this issue, which different churches interpret differently.[37] Nonetheless, sins committed by "an elder" should be brought before the church as a body and dealt with in this fashion.

While Matthew 18:15–17 arguably could include public sin or an elder's sin, it deals specifically with a brother who has sinned against you. Unless that brother's sin is public or he is an elder, I believe that Jesus calls for a method of resolving the conflict that does not involve every member of the congregation, at least initially. I cannot support that position authoritatively with scripture, though. Therefore, you should regard it skeptically and approach the matter with an open heart and mind. My reasoning relies simply and, perhaps, misguidedly, on believing that the goals of the process are best served and reached in a context which expands cautiously. That is the example of the first two steps and the third step should not depart from that paradigm, unless the sin involves the two exceptions specifically mentioned by Paul. Credible arguments exist, however, which advocate that telling it to the church should be read more broadly and that every member of the congregation (which certainly does not mean every person who happens to be in the sanctuary) should hear the matter upon reaching the third step.

Finally, we come to the fourth step. How should the church treat a pagan or a tax collector? This is a very straightforward piece of advice which finally gives us a shot at the justice that we so richly deserves, allowing us to bask in the justness of the wrongdoer's deserts. That, again, is usually our first reaction, which by now we should realize is usually wrong. Jesus, in telling the church to treat the wrongdoer as an enemy, is telling us that we have to love him and to forgive him, just as Jesus did with Matthew and Zacchaeus. Surely there is more to this story, though.

There are, as promised in other situations, some practical consequences to a wrongdoer's continuing rejection of a sister's conciliatory gestures and his church's attempts to impose discipline. At this level, these consequences have just as much to do with church discipline and removing one who refuses to repent from the church's midst as they do with reconciliation. The reasoning behind this is perhaps as much for the church's and its members protection as for the wrongdoer's eventual restoration and reconciliation. The matter, thus, is no longer a private matter. It is a matter between the wrongdoer and his church. As such, if the wrongdoer persists in his present conduct or will not repent of past conduct, then he "is to be treated exactly as one would treat other unbelievers."[38] This means that the local church judges his conduct and "in all her relationships to him functions as it does toward an unregenerate person."[39] The consequence of this is that the wrongdoer is to be removed from the membership of the local church and from fellowship unique to its members. However, his removal does not justify abuse or call for the members to shun him.[40] "[U]nless he is acting divisively he should be allowed to hear the preaching of the Word and should be witnessed to by the members, treating him like any unbeliever who enters."[41] Thus, even though he may have confessed Jesus as Lord in the past, he is to be treated like any other unbeliever at this point, since he has scorned the church's discipline, among other entreaties to right fellowship.

The goal of Matthew 18:15–17 "must always be the restoration of the sinner to fellowship."[42] How many of us have ever gone through just the first part of that process, much less the second stage of bringing in witnesses or the third stage of telling it to the church? How many of us have ever witnessed or participated in a church voting to put a member out of fellowship? I am sure that the silence is staggering, such that we should wonder just how we ever accomplish anything with all of the unresolved conflict in our churches.

THREE MODELS - A CHARGE AGAINST YOUR BROTHER - GOING TO THE LAW

Do you want to sue your brother? Paul has some advice in I Corinthians 6:1–8.

If any of you has a dispute with another, dare he take it before the ungodly for judgment instead of before the saints? Do you not know that the saints will judge the world? And if you are to judge the world, are you not competent to judge trivial cases? Do you not know that we will judge angels? How much more the things of this life! Therefore, if you have disputes about such matters, appoint as judges even men of little account in the church! I say this to shame you. Is it possible that there is nobody among you wise enough to judge a dispute between believers? But instead, one brother goes to law against another — and this in front of unbelievers! The very fact that you have lawsuits among you means you have been completely defeated already. Why not rather be wronged? Why not rather be cheated? Instead, you yourselves cheat and do wrong, and you do this to your brothers.

Is Paul suggesting intramural arbitration in this passage? It seems so to me, especially when combined with Jesus' instructions in Matthew 18:18–19 on the power of the church to bind and to loose matters on earth. If we have the faith to believe that we will judge the world and angels and that "the church effectually acts as God's agent in this world," then does it not make absolute sense to think that we are more than capable of judging disputes among ourselves?[43] We simply have never done what Paul is suggesting on a wholesale basis. I am unaware of any church to which I have belonged ever having appointed "even men of little account" as judges. I also have not experienced any group appointing an arbiter in reliance on Matthew 18:20's promise that "where two or three come together in my name, there I am with them."

Paul simply is directing some well-earned sarcasm toward us when he uses the word "even." His point is not necessarily that we should seek out "men of little account" to arbitrate disputes: his point is to say that even those new to the faith or of little repute are better-suited to resolve conflict among believers than the courts. Disputing parties, if they have the faith to follow Paul's advice and Jesus' words, should seek out a respected church member upon whom they can agree or, if they cannot agree, seek guidance as to whom they should select to judge their dispute. Perhaps the church even should anticipate conflict, since we acknowledge that it exists and will continue to exist, and should designate believers gifted, trained, and willing to serve in this capacity. Jesus' point is that doing so is both within the church's power and authority and under His guidance.

This much is clear: the victory is in peace-making, not in winning. We lose sight of the truly priceless thing, kingdom relationships, when we pursue the trivial. If we need to pursue matters against our brothers, then we have a scriptural path set in front of us. May we have the faith to take the first step, may we do so with working, planning, wisdom, and knowledge, and may the Holy Spirit guide the rest.

SPECIFIC PROCESSES

According to Blake Coffee in *One Body: Experiencing Unity in the Church*, conflict rarely, if ever, appears without a prior breakdown in interpersonal relationships among church members.[44] Those breakdowns easily occur when the parties ignore the building blocks discussed earlier in this chapter. The apparent conflict may easily be resolved, *e.g.* something as silly as whether peanut butter sandwiches or jelly sandwiches should be served to the children or it may be more serious, *e.g.* search committee members remaining at odds with each other and bringing that committee's work to a grinding halt. Whatever it is, though, you can be fairly sure that the apparent conflict is deeply rooted and is merely a symptom of the disease. The writer even describes such conflict in Hebrews 12:15 as a "bitter root [that] grows up to cause trouble and defile many." You also can be sure, without proper weeding, that this bitter root will resurface without true reconciliation. The conflict may not be seen in the same context, but it will grow again. Thus, in addition to resolving the apparent conflict, dispute resolution processes in a church context will attempt to mend the broken relationships and to reconcile those in conflict in conformity with our mandate to be peacemakers.

In addition to the traditional mediation and arbitration processes discussed in Chapter 2 and complementary to the specific verses discussed in this chapter, there are several unique dispute resolution processes. These processes may be as simple and direct as a short meeting between two mature Christians whose hearts already are attuned to kingdom issues or as complicated as a lengthy, multi-session, hybrid mediation / arbitration session involving many facilitators and factions consisting of individuals, churches, and umbrella organizations. However, suggesting that one or another of these processes is better or more appropriate than another, without careful consideration of the unique circumstances involved in each situation, simply is unwise. I list a few of them below, along with a brief description, in order to allow you to assess them and to provide references for further exploration of resolving disputes in the church.

SPECIFIC PROCESSES - PROBLEM-SOLVING MEDIATION

The predominant, secular model for mediation may not be appropriate for resolving church conflict. It may be sufficient for some type of agreement to be reached and, in this regard, may leave the appearance of having been successful. However, it focuses on solving superficial problems quickly and efficiently. It is, in many senses, simply a dispute resolution tool which businesses and people have come to see as preferable to litigation for financial and practical reasons. This is not, though, the bull's eye of our focus. As such, problem-solving mediation rarely reaches moments when people reconcile. While it can be used as a process to resolve conflict in the church, it probably is not the best process choice available.

SPECIFIC PROCESSES - TRANSFORMATIVE MEDIATION

This is a form of mediation in which "conflict is first and foremost a potential occasion for growth in two critical and interrelated dimensions of human morality": strength for self and compassion for others, culminating in a quality which this process' proponents describe as "compassionate strength."[45] Joseph P. Folger and Robert A. Baruch Bush describe this process and its orientation and compare its efficacy to problem-solving mediation in their works, *The Promise of Mediation: Responding to Conflict Through Empowerment and Recognition* and *Designing Mediation: Approaches to Training and Practice within a Transformative Framework*. Transformative mediation is not necessarily aligned with any religious movement, although you will find Christians and Jews, if not others, among its proponents. While seemingly secular in nature, I have been impressed with its emphasis on moral growth for the parties. It does so through emphasizing (i) empowerment, "achieved when disputing parties experience a strengthened awareness of their own self-worth and their own ability to deal with whatever difficulties they face, regardless of external constraints," and (ii) recognition, "achieved when, given some degree of empowerment, disputing parties experience an expanded willingness to acknowledge and be responsive to other parties' situations and common human qualities."[46] To the extent that it recognizes and stresses the relative importance of relationships *vis a vis* resolution in disputes, it is an improvement over problem-solving mediation in the church context.

SPECIFIC PROCESSES - ARBITRATION

Lynn R. Buzzard and Laurence Eck tell us in *Tell It to the Church* that "Matthew 18 and I Corinthians 6 contemplate the authority of the church to render judgments on the matters at dispute."[47] While the process must be modified from secular arbitration, Buzzard and Eck describe an arbitration in which they were involved which exemplifies how conflict in the church can and should be resolved at times through arbitration.[48] Paul's admonition in Matthew 18:18–20 for us to agree about judges over the disputes in which we find ourselves embroiled, together with our agreement to allow that to happen, make arbitration an extremely viable process for the right church conflict situation.

SPECIFIC PROCESSES - SEVEN STEPS TOWARD BIBLICAL RECONCILIATION

This process, developed by Neil T. Anderson and Charles Mylander and explained in detail in *Blessed Are the Peace Makers*, differs somewhat from traditional mediation, in that the steps "depend upon the Lord to be the mediator, and one or two mature Christians to facilitate the process."[49] Roughly, the seven steps include (i) recognizing the other parties' good qualities; (ii) recounting good aspects of the relationship; (iii) recounting painful aspects of the relationship; (iv) seeking forgiveness; (v) making commitments to the relationship; (vi) entering into a covenant based on new agreements and understandings; and (vii) praying for God's blessings for the other parties.[50]

SPECIFIC PROCESSES - CHRISTIAN CONCILIATION

Developed by Peacemaker Ministries and Ken Sande, its President, and further explained in *The Peacemaker: A Biblical Guide to Resolving Personal Conflict*, Christian conciliation essentially involves three steps.[51] These are (i) individual counseling followed, if necessary, by (ii) mediation, followed, if necessary, by (iii) arbitration.[52] While Peacemaker Ministries has developed these three steps into quite detailed procedures, it essentially is the Christian equivalent of a secular ADR process called med / arb, meaning that the parties will engage in mediation and, if that mediation is unsuccessful, then the mediation transitions into arbitration, thereby taking the resolution of the conflict away from the parties and placing it in the hands of an arbiter. Despite apparent similarities to secular forms of ADR, Peacemaker Ministries stresses that Christian conciliation is driven by four convictions: the centrality of Christ, the responsibility of the church, the necessity of Biblical counseling, and the comprehensiveness of God's word.[53] As such, it reflects modifications to problem-solving mediation and secular arbitration which are appropriate for Christian communities.

SPECIFIC PROCESSES - CONGREGATIONAL INTERVENTION

Utilized by Lombard Mennonite Peace Center in Illinois and Blake Coffee of Christian Unity Ministries in Texas and specifically designed for use in congregational settings, this approach emphasizes unity in the body through the process of (i) defining expectations for the church in conflict; (ii) instructing church members concerning Biblical interpersonal relationships and equipping them for personal reconciliation; (iii) receiving the stories of conflict reported by church members in small groups, interviews, and written responses; (iv) reporting back to the congregation concerning the information learned in the previous phase; (v) leading the congregation in the healing process through structured dialogues and mediation, reconciling relationships, and neutralizing past pain; (vi) resolving issues by building consensus, first in small groups and then throughout the congregation; and (vii) closing, in which a written report is submitted, a reconciliation service occurs, and subsequent contacts with leadership are maintained in order to ensure the effectiveness of the process.[54] As the name implies, this approach targets conflict at the church-wide level, although with modifications certain aspects surely can be applied to conflict among individuals.

CHAPTER 4

They've Sued Us For What?!: Common Claims

BREACH OF CONTRACT

I know of no better way to describe a contract except by building the definition layer by layer. First, a contract is an agreement. Contracts can be unilateral or can have several parties. An example of a unilateral contract would be Hilary's offer to pay $20.00 to Al for mowing her yard. Al, as long as he does not commit himself to cutting the yard, may choose whether or not to cut the yard. If Al chooses to cut the yard, then he has performed under a unilateral contract and Hilary has obligated herself to pay $20.00 to Al.

A bilateral contract might consist of an agreement between Hilary and Al for Al to cut Hilary's yard for $20.00. Other terms which probably should be in that contract are missing, but the very seed of a contract exists, which brings us to the next point. In order to be enforced, a contract must have enough material terms of sufficient definiteness and certainty for a judge or jury to determine exactly what it was that the parties agreed to do. For instance, what happens if Al waits ten days to cut Hilary's yard, but Hilary wanted the yard cut within seven days? A court probably would impose, in the absence of an agreement on this point, a reasonableness requirement, inquiring as to whether or not it was reasonable for Al to have waited ten days under the circumstances, perhaps excusing Al if bad weather intervened. Will Hilary be entitled to a cash discount if she pays Al's bill early? Can Al ask Bill to cut Hilary's yard for him, promising $15.00 to Bill and keeping $5.00 for himself? Can Al use a riding lawnmower, even though Hilary hates the noise and it disrupts her nap? What if Al's equipment breaks because of a manufacturer's defect and he cannot mow the yard in seven days, even though he wants to do so? Hypothetical examples can become ridiculous, but they raise issues which typically appear when the parties to a contract have not put in enough thought to address all or even some of the "what ifs" that lawyers see on a daily basis. For a practical example, consider Chapter 9, in which I suggest that there are approximately twenty different major issues which should be considered in a real estate lease. Some lawyers would argue that twenty issues are overkill; others would insist that twenty are not enough.

Another related layer in the anatomy of contracts is the concept of offer and acceptance. Some contract cases revolve around whether and to what extent one party offered and the other party accepted. If Hilary offers to pay Al $20.00 to mow her yard and Al accepts the job, but says that he will mow her yard for $25.00, does a contract exist? The answer is probably not, as Al has made a counteroffer, *i.e.* he has agreed to mow the yard, but not for Hilary's price. Since Al's acceptance of Hilary's offer must conform to all material terms, Al has not accepted Hilary's offer. Al and Hilary may negotiate the final deal through a series of counteroffers, ultimately leading them to an agreement on all material terms, or they may walk away, having rejected the other's offers and counteroffers. That is the essence of offer and acceptance.

While we all hate to put in the work up front on contracts, you should remember one thing, if nothing else, from this chapter. All contracts of any significance or complexity require hard work. You can either work on them while putting them together or work on them after they fall apart. The contracts which usually withstand all of the unforeseen developments and the application of Murphy's law are the ones which receive the most work in the investigation and negotiation process. That process takes time and a commitment at exactly the point at which the parties may be unsure about committing. However, there is no better time to test that commitment than before it is made. You may think of it simply as "ironing out the wrinkles," but a neatly pressed contract should wear well for a long time.

When disputes arise, the words "breach of contract" cannot be far behind. Most bilateral contracts carry with them an obligation for both of the parties either to do something or not to do something. When contracting with another party, your church usually is promising to pay money or to do something. In some cases, though, your church may promise not to do something. The law views such a forbearance as having value and will enforce a contract in which your church or the other party agrees to forego doing something. The majority of our focus will be on affirmative duties, though. These duties, sometimes generally called the duties of payment and performance, are the backbones of most agreements. In some contracts, these duties are very complex. In others, they are simple and easily identified.

If Hilary promises to pay for Al's performance and Al performs, but Hilary does not pay, then Hilary has breached her contract with Al. If Hilary pays Al, but Al does not perform, then Al has breached his contract with Hilary. This is the most basic of analyses. It is the parties' expectation that one party will pay and the other party will perform for each other's benefit. Again, these expectations must be so definite that, if the contract is breached, a court can understand and enforce the agreement, determine what damages exist, and award a judgment to the innocent party.

We may not think of the church as a party to many contracts, but a little reflection will do wonders. Each employment relationship is a contractual agreement. While many, if not most, employment relationships are "at will" relationships, as discussed in more detail in Chapter 8, the analysis of that relationship is still a contractual analysis. Why is the word "terminate" used to describe the process of firing someone? An employer really is terminating a contract, even though the contract may be terminable at a moment's notice.

Other examples are contracts for the purchase of raw land, leases for temporary facilities, and construction contracts for the building of permanent facilities. Will the church need insurance for its real property and buildings? The answer is affirmative, but the answer requires the church to obtain an insurance policy, which really is an insurance contract, despite being called a policy. Will the church use a consultant to assist it in raising money to build its facilities? If so, then that consultant will want to contract with the church for his services. Will the church require financing for its real estate projects? The future will be filled with contracts of every type and description.

Even something as mundane as arranging for water, power, and telephone services involves a contract. In requesting utilities, the church obligates itself to pay for the utilities according to certain terms and by certain deadlines. If the church fails to abide by those terms, then utilities can be terminated. A final example is the simple act of writing a check. Your church may be writing that check to fulfill a contractual obligation, *e.g.* the payment of money to someone who has performed a service, but that check also is a part of a contract with the bank. Your church has promised its bank only to write checks in amounts which cumulatively are less than its deposits. As we come full circle in the payment and performance analysis, the bank is performing a service, honoring the church's checks, in exchange for the church's payment, the deposits in the church's account. Written into that contract, among other terms, are a penalty for writing an insufficient funds check and an option for the bank to terminate the contract if it happens too frequently.

Contracts are all around us and can be breached very easily if we do not understand our obligations. We sometimes even breach contracts when we understand our obligations. This can occur through inadvertence, unexpected inability to pay or to perform, bad decisions, or even decisions which we might classify as sharp dealing. In any of these situations, the law allows the party which feels that the contract has been breached to file suit in order to obtain a judgment determining that party's rights and damages.

NEGLIGENCE

Many claims filed against churches are based on negligence. They may be called something else, but when they are taken apart and analyzed, they are simply saying that someone inadvertently did something that they should not have done or failed to do something that they should have done, in either case injuring the plaintiff. Depending on which book or case that you consult, there are generally three or four separate parts to a negligence case. First, a party must owe a duty to another party. Second, there must be a breach of that duty.[55] Next, the plaintiff must suffer damages. Finally, those damages must be proximately caused by a breach of the applicable duty. The law defines proximate cause as consisting "of cause in fact and foreseeability."[56] We shall discuss many types of claims in this chapter, most of which will be based on a negligence theory. Please note that the claims which I choose to discuss in this chapter are not the only claims which can be made against churches. I believe that they are some of the more likely claims, but this is by no means an exhaustive list.

NEGLIGENCE - PREMISES LIABILITY

Premises liability cases merit special consideration in connection with the law's application to the church. The theory behind a premises liability case is that a property owner owes a duty to keep his property in a certain state of repair and to warn visitors of the property's current condition. These cases range from the classic "slip and fall," where a store patron slips on a wet substance on the floor, falls, and hurts himself, to the more recent inadequate security case, in which a visitor to a place of business is criminally assaulted, perhaps robbed, and sues the property owner for failing to provide adequate security for the visitor's protection.

To assess the duty owed by a church to a visitor, it is necessary to determine the visitor's status under the law.[57] These types of plaintiffs are classified as trespassers, licensees, or invitees. Texas Pattern Jury Charges § 66.06 provides the following definitions, which I have abridged:

- A trespasser is a person who is on the property of another without any right, lawful authority, or express or implied invitation, permission, or license.

- A licensee is a person who is on the premises with the permission of the possessor but without an express or implied invitation.
- An invitee is a person who is on the premises at the express or implied invitation of the possessor of the premises.

Many churches maintain an implicit open door policy. Thus, it is likely that any visitor to church property will claim to be an invitee, *i.e.* being on the property at the church's implied or explicit invitation. If an invitee is on an owner's property, then the owner owes to that invitee a duty of reasonable care.[58] When an owner has actual or constructive knowledge of a condition on its property which poses an unreasonable risk of harm to invitees, then that owner must take whatever action is reasonably prudent under the circumstances to eliminate or to reduce the unreasonable risk, including warning invitees of that risk.[59] We all know what actual knowledge means, but constructive knowledge is knowledge which is imputed to an owner or knowledge which the owner does not necessarily have, but should have. Combined, actual and constructive knowledge form the "knew or should have known" test. Thus, in order to prevail on the liability portion of a case, an invitee must prove, among other things, that:

- There was something posing an unreasonable risk of harm that caused her injuries.
- The church knew or should have known about that risk.
- The church should have taken reasonable steps to reduce or to eliminate that risk or to warn her of the danger, but did not do so.

The standard of care which a property owner owes to a licensee is slightly lower, but still significant. An owner has a duty not to injure a licensee willfully, wantonly, or through gross negligence. Further, an owner also "has a duty either to warn a licensee of, or to make reasonably safe, a dangerous condition of which the owner is aware and the licensee is not."[60] An interesting point to note about the duty to warn licensees is that it only arises when the owner has actual, not merely constructive, notice of the dangerous condition or defect.[61]

Lower still is the duty owed to trespassers. A property owner must only "refrain from injuring him wilfully, wantonly, or through gross negligence."[62] However, because of the church's unique position in the community, it may have a difficult time challenging a trespassing plaintiff's inevitable claim of invitee or licensee status.

NEGLIGENCE - PREMISES LIABILITY - SPECIFIC AREAS OF CONCERN

The duty of reasonable care requires that you take steps to eliminate or to reduce any unreasonable risk of which you are aware or of which you should be aware. The "knew or should have known" requirement places a difficult burden on a property owner. If you do not know about a problem, then how can you correct it or warn visitors to avoid it? While you will never know about every problem immediately when it occurs, there are steps which you can take to reduce the risk of being told that you should have known about a problem.

You should always keep your eyes open for potential problems with your property. Further, everyone on staff at a church should be briefed about premises liability issues and they should be responsible for noticing and reporting problems to the appropriate person. I am not suggesting that everyone fill out an inspection report every time that they leave their desk. However, if a staff member sees a problem while attending to his other duties, then he should not ignore it.

Your church should have a set procedure for inspecting its premises and visibly marking any suspect item or equipment as needing further inspection, repair, and/or replacement. This includes making a specific person or persons responsible for carrying out that duty. There also should be a set procedure for notifying those responsible for tending to an item so that a clear path of accountability is established. Securing or marking pieces of equipment or property, such as a piece of furniture with a broken leg or an electrical outlet which emits a shock, provides a visible reminder to church staff to do something about a problem as soon as possible and a visible warning to invitees and licensees to avoid a potentially dangerous situation.

When, what, and how to inspect are questions that must be determined with respect to all of your church's particular circumstances and property. I recognize that this vague instruction does not give you much practical guidance. If your church is conducting regularly scheduled inspections, then it already has demonstrated concern about the condition of its premises and is a step ahead of most property owners. However, if your church's inspection schedule is once every year for playground equipment that is used daily by hundreds of children, then it has not done much good. Certainly a much more frequent inspection schedule is appropriate in these circumstances. Further, if an incident, such as a lightning strike, high winds, flooding, vandalism, or mechanical system failure, gives you any cause to believe that a specific part of the premises may have been adversely affected, then do not wait for a regularly scheduled inspection to take place. Visit that part of the premises immediately.

Following these procedures demonstrates your concern for your church's assets and members, assists you in keeping the premises in good repair, and minimizes the risk of occurrence of and damage from future incidents. Conversely, your failure to inspect the premises on a regular basis or even at all eventually may land you in hot water. If an invitee is injured and he demonstrates that a reasonably careful inspection would have revealed the risk, then his claim may succeed, even if you had no actual knowledge of the risk.[63]

There are predictable areas and activities from which many claims arise, some of which are listed below. Paying particular attention to the condition of the premises involved may pay dividends for you and your members in terms of reducing injuries and potential claims.

- playgrounds and recreational facilities - where people are physically active and injuries are likely to occur
- cafeterias and kitchens - chairs and tables are constantly moved, creating trip and fall risks; people are carrying trays of food, rendering them off-balance; food and beverages are spilled on the floor constantly, creating slip and fall risks
- day-care facilities - children are being dropped off and picked up in parking lots; parents and children are carrying bags, books, backpacks, lunches, clothing, and other items, keeping them off-balance
- youth group activities - see Chapter 15
- community and church sports leagues - see Chapter 5
- restrooms and water fountains - spilled water creates a slip and fall risk
- stairs and steps - handrails, height differences in steps, frayed carpet, worn tile, gravity, and other hazards carry the potential for severe injuries during falls
- parking lots - the combination of cars in reverse and pedestrians is always a problem
- doorways - corners of mats are overturned, creating trip and fall risks; dirt, water, mud, and other debris are tracked in and out, creating a slip and fall risk

NEGLIGENCE - PREMISES LIABILITY - ATTRACTIVE NUISANCE

When I was growing up, I remember the state of church playground art as being the four "S"s: swings, seesaws, slides, and St. Augustine grass. Times have changed. Churches have schools and some even have recreational and athletic facilities located on the campuses. These facilities can be simple, *e.g.* a basketball goal on a cement slab and a set of swings, or elaborate, *e.g.* go-kart tracks, swimming pools with diving boards, volleyball courts, covered basketball courts, game rooms, dormitories, soccer fields, softball / baseball fields, reflection ponds, manicured paths, landscaped gardens, and team building center facilities with ropes and climbing equipment.

I am not criticizing any church for constructing these attractions. However, I have concerns when these facilities are not adequately safeguarded by security measures and warning signs. For example, if your church has a facility containing even one-half of the attractions mentioned in the first paragraph and these attractions always are accessible to the general public, including unsupervised children, most of us would agree that your church has a potential problem. Any child could make his way easily from the surrounding community into your church's very visible, unguarded recreational area without seeing any warning signs, without having to scale a fence, and without being seen by a security guard or church personnel. In short, there would be no obstacles between that child and, for instance, the pond with the cute ducks swimming in it. If you think that examples like this do not exist, then you simply need to look around your community, for I have seen them in mine.

The attractive nuisance doctrine is problematic for churches. We want to welcome people, but sometimes the law encourages us to build fences between our churches and the community and to add disclaimers to distract from what we would like to be a genuine "welcome." Our greeting does not seem very genuine when the attorneys are finished with it. We want to attract people by having nice facilities, yet those same facilities expose us to risk. We want to attract families by having equipment on which children play, yet there are few people, if any, to monitor that equipment after services are concluded. Again, we face the continuum. Complete safety rests in not having any facilities worthy of being deemed an attractive nuisance. Complete risk rests fairly close to the earlier example.

As noted earlier, property owners usually owe to trespassers only the duty to avoid injuring the trespasser willfully, wantonly, or through gross negligence. An exception to that rule is the attractive nuisance doctrine. Under this doctrine, children who otherwise would be trespassers rise to the level of invitees.[64] The duty which the property owner owes to these children rises correspondingly, thus forcing property owners to eliminate the risk and, if they do not eliminate the risk, then to protect the children from the risk.

The elements in a claim for attractive nuisance are as follows:

- the place where the condition exists is one upon which the possessor knows or has reason to know that children are likely to trespass
- the condition is one of which the possessor knows or has reason to know and which he realizes or should realize will involve an unreasonable risk of death or serious bodily harm to such children

- the children because of their youth do not discover the condition or realize the risk involved in intermeddling with it or coming within the area made dangerous by it
- the utility to the possessor of maintaining the condition and the burden of eliminating the danger are slight as compared with the risk to children involved
- the possessor fails to exercise reasonable care to eliminate the danger or otherwise to protect the children[65]

Many of these cases eventually focus on two specific elements: whether the child appreciates the risk and the exact nature of the risk. Again, we face the continuum. As a child matures, the likelihood of his appreciating a given risk grows, such that it is very unlikely that a seventeen or eighteen year old child could bring a successful attractive nuisance claim. Children in the three, four, and five year old range, however, usually will not be considered able to appreciate a given risk. To complicate this gray area, the dissenting opinions in two Supreme Court of Texas cases indicate a willingness to consider individual factors, *e.g.* relative intelligence levels and special knowledge of a particular risk, in evaluating whether or not a particular child appreciates a particular risk.[66] Thus, as to the former element, some judges seem willing to apply a more subjective ("did this particular child appreciate this particular risk") standard, while others prefer a more objective ("would a normal child of average intelligence have appreciated risk of this type") standard. Thus, courts struggle with the ever present special circumstances in these cases.

The latter element tends to be complicated, also. In *Timmons*, an intoxicated fourteen year old boy climbed a twelve feet high fence topped with barbed wire, ignored a warning sign, ignored verbal warnings from his relatives, and scaled an electrical utility tower which supported electrical wires. After his death, his mother argued that, while he might have appreciated the risk of actually touching the electrical wires while at the top of the tower, he did not appreciate the risk of what actually killed him: being too near an electrical wire which caused an electrical arc to hit him. The Supreme Court of Texas did not buy that argument, instead holding that a general appreciation of the dangers of electricity was sufficient to take that case out of the attractive nuisance doctrine. Perhaps bolstering that finding was the utility company's placement of warning signs and securing the facility so that all but the most determined members of the general public did not have access to the facility.[67]

While this type of risk seems extreme and while *Timmons'* facts did not make a particularly sympathetic case for the plaintiff, it does not take a great deal of foresight to anticipate a persuasive argument on this element in many attractive nuisance claims. Consider, for example, the church with the wonderful recreational facility. A ten year old girl who lives in the neighborhood wanders into the facility and no one is there. She did not have to climb a fence and there were no warning signs. She has seen teenagers climbing on poles and walking on tightropes and none of them ever fell. She tries it and falls. At least one Texas case holds that a six year old child can appreciate the risk of falling from heights and consequently suffering an injury.[68] Does that affect the resolution of this hypothetical case? Does the fact that this girl has seen older children complete this same task safely, under the encouragement of church officials, mean anything? Does the absence of a warning sign and an entry obstacle change your mind? Does the church's failure to install any nets under the thirty feet high tightrope help or hurt its defense? Attractive nuisance claims can be very gray cases on the continuum.

NEGLIGENCE - PREMISES LIABILITY - PUBLIC OR PRIVATE NUISANCE

The law defines a private nuisance as a "nontresspassory invasion of another's interest in the private use and enjoyment of land."[69] Thus, the attractive nuisance theory and the public or private nuisance theory have at their core the allegation that a property owner is doing something inappropriate with the property. One of the main ways in which they differ, though, is that an attractive nuisance claim usually will involve a person physically entering your property, with resulting personal injuries. That is not true with a public or private nuisance claim. There usually will not be any entry onto your property and damages may tend to be more economic than personal.

A person becomes liable "for an intentional invasion [public or private nuisance] when his conduct is unreasonable under the circumstances of the particular case."[70] While I would love to be more specific about what reasonableness is, the law intentionally defines it very vaguely so as to allow a judge and jury great latitude under whatever circumstances present themselves. Thus, the same circumstances, *e.g.* the noise and traffic emanating from Vacation Bible School, might appear reasonable to one jury and unreasonable to another jury. That lack of preciseness, especially in light of the pre-formed attitudes which we all bring to work with us every day, greatly hinders an attorney's ability to forecast the results of a particular public or private nuisance claim.

What is the difference between a public and private nuisance? One court put the issue this way:

> A nuisance is said to be private when the injury resulting therefrom violates only private rights and produces damage to only one person or to not more than a few persons. On the other hand, a public nuisance is one which disturbs or injures the inhabitants of an entire community or a considerable portion thereof.[71]

That test obviously does not give us very much guidance as to how to distinguish between the two claims. The ends of that continuum seem apparent enough, but churches facing such claims may find themselves in the middle, again. Many churches are located in residential areas with blocks of houses surrounding the church's property. Whether a court would define an affected group as "not more than a few persons" or "a considerable portion" of a community seems to be as in the middle of that continuum as possible.

All of this begs the question as to how much an aggrieved property owner may recover if he chooses to assert a claim against your church for a public or private nuisance. One court has said that, where injury to land is temporary, "the plaintiff may recover damages measured by the loss of the reasonable rental value of the property."[72] As injunctive relief is available to those filing these types of claims, any finding that a nuisance exists probably also will merit the issuance of a permanent injunction banning the nuisance's continued existence. Thus, cases in which a court finds permanent damages probably will be rare, as the court should order the offending property owner to terminate the offensive activity. I would assume that where the injury is permanent, though, the measure of damages might be the difference between the property's fair market value before the nuisance began versus the property's fair market value after the nuisance began, although I can find no authority to support that view.

Negligence - Premises Liability - Inadequate Security

Perhaps surprisingly, the duty of reasonable care has been extended to include the intentional, even criminal, acts of third parties, if it is reasonably foreseeable that such acts are likely to occur.[73] What does this mean? Several Texas cases have concluded that evidence of prior criminal acts in the same vicinity, especially on the same premises, constitutes foreseeability. Thus, your interest in this subject should increase proportionally according to the amount of crime in your church's area, just as a plaintiff's lawyer will certainly argue that foreseeability increases exponentially with each reported incident.

If your church is located in an area in which it is reasonably foreseeable that a crime will occur, then it must take reasonable measures to protect its invitees from criminal conduct.[74] Each church has different environmental, geographical, sociological, demographic, and physical plant circumstances. All of these factors, among others, potentially affect security. If your circumstances alert you to security problems, then you should think about and take reasonable steps to reduce the risk of criminal conduct.

Many of us regard the imposition of liability on a third party for the criminal act of an unrelated party to be somewhat contrary to the way things should be. However, these cases should provide a wake up call for you, if you already were not aware of this trend. Taking reasonable steps to reduce potential criminal activity should reduce the potential for claims and, more importantly, should reduce the chances for one of your members or visitors to become a statistic. This topic receives much more attention, especially *vis a vis* prevention, in Chapter 11.

NEGLIGENCE - NEGLIGENT HIRING AND NEGLIGENT RETENTION

While each of these distinct claims involves the employment relationship, I shall discuss them together. The difference between these claims is one of timing. In a negligent hiring claim, the claimant will argue that the employer should never have hired the bad actor as a result of past conduct about which the employer knew or should have known. Alternatively, if the employer knew about the conduct and hired the bad actor anyway, then the employer should have placed the employee under some restrictions after hiring him. In a negligent retention claim, the claimant will argue that something happened during the employee's employment, which the employer knew or should have known and which should have caused the employer to have fired the employee or, again, to have placed the bad actor under some restrictions before the events giving rise to the suit occurred. In either case, the argument goes, if the employer had taken the appropriate action, then the employee would not have been in a position to injure the claimant. Therefore, if there is a sufficiently foreseeable relationship between the injury and the employee's responsibilities, then the employer will be responsible.

That should be confusing enough for a starting point. Thus, let me address the duty which an employer owes to the general public in relation to its employees. Put succinctly,

> an employer has a duty to adequately hire, train, and supervise employees. The negligent performance of those duties may impose liability on an employer if the complainant's injuries result from the employer's failure to take reasonable precautions to protect the complainant from the misconduct of its employees.[75]

Does the employee have to be in the course and scope of his employment to sustain a negligent hiring / negligent retention cause of action? The answer is apparently not.

> While the issue has not been directly addressed by a Texas court, we hold that liability for negligent hiring and supervision is not dependent upon a finding that the employee was acting in the course and scope of his employment when the tortious act occurred.[76]

However, there must be at least some relation between the bad actor's employment and the injury of which the claimant complains.

> [W]hen the servant turns aside, for however a short time, from the prosecution of the master's work to engage in an affair wholly his own, he ceases to act for the master, and the responsibility for that which he does in pursuing his own business or pleasure is upon him alone."[77]

A more recent opinion put it this way:

> [I]n order to impose liability upon an employer under the doctrine of negligent hiring, there must be evidence that the plaintiff's injuries were brought about by reason of the employment of the incompetent servant and be, in some manner, job-related. Stated another way, the negligence in hiring the employee must be the proximate cause of the injuries to the plaintiff.[78]

I cited many cases and facetiously used the word "succinctly" to emphasize one thing: courts seem to use a rather imprecise approach in these cases, instead of a bright line test, to determine liability. Such an approach is inherently more unpredictable, leaving more than enough wiggle room for different courts to reach different results in similar cases. The emphasis of one fact over another in these types of cases can lead to the scales of justice tipping the wrong (or right) way. Thus, care must be given to weighting those scales before an incident occurs.

Negligence - Failure to Report Child Abuse or Neglect

As suggested in Chapter 14, a person has a duty to report known or suspected child abuse or neglect to the appropriate authorities. There are two different scenarios in which criminal penalties can be assessed for a person's failure to comply with that duty. First, a knowing failure to report a known or suspected case of abuse or neglect is a Class B misdemeanor.[79] Second, knowingly or intentionally making a groundless report under this statute is also a Class B misdemeanor.[80]

Criminal liability is not our only concern, though. If a person is required to make a report, but does not make that report, then the affected child may have a civil claim against that person. A claim might even exist against that person's employer, if the employee's duty to report is connected somehow to his employment duties. The concept of negligence *per se* consists of a simple negligence claim, with a statutory twist. If you owe a statutory duty to a protected class of people and the plaintiff is a member of that class, then the standard of care which you owe to that person is the standard of care set forth in the statute.[81] Outside of proving the existence of the statute and the child's membership in the class of people protected by the statute, there will be no argument regarding whether or not you owed a duty to the child and what a reasonably prudent man would have done under similar circumstances. You simply face the consequences if you fail to report.

Damages in abuse and neglect cases run the gamut. You may be faced with a child who survives an incident with no physical injuries and with minimal psychological consequences. On the other hand, death, severe injuries, and/or permanent emotional scarring are equally predictable. As juries love children, especially those who have suffered, these claims have the potential to yield tremendously high verdicts.

NEGLIGENCE - CLERGY / COUNSELING MALPRACTICE

The good news about clergy malpractice is that Texas does not recognize that cause of action. The bad news is that some of the conduct which otherwise might be characterized as clergy malpractice can be characterized and usually is characterized as counseling malpractice.[82] Courts are consistently holding that the First Amendment's free exercise clause, while prohibiting ecclesiastical claims against ministers and churches, does not provide ministers with a "get of out jail free" card with respect to conduct that may have some secular aspect to it, *e.g.* counseling. As Jim Smith observes in *Mastering Pastoral Counseling*, "[t]he counseling room, once a safe haven where a pastor could simply counsel and pray with a troubled parishioner for an hour, has become a source of moral anxiety and legal liability."[83] These types of claims are discussed in much more detail, along with related issues involving privileged communications, in Chapter 13.

NEGLIGENCE - HAZARDOUS ACTIVITIES

Churches generally do not sponsor hazardous activities. However, I have seen churches turn their parking lots into skateboard and roller blade parks, complete with obstacles, ramps, jumps, *et cetera*, and that type of activity strikes me as bordering, if not crossing over the border, on being hazardous. The proliferation of extreme sports and their occasional carryover into youth group activities should make us pause and consider exactly what we are doing. Companies offering activities such as bungee cord jumps, high-speed miniature race car tracks, sky diving, rock climbing, and paint gun wars recognize the hazardous nature of these amusements and utilize comprehensive releases to limit their liability. These releases generally will not assist the church in avoiding a claim if an accident happens during one of these activities, though. They protect only the operator and, if an accident occurs, then the church may find itself in the unenviable position of being the more attractive defendant.

The church sometimes involves itself in sponsoring activities which go beyond their intended scope or which may be on the edge of being termed hazardous. If, for example, a beach trip turns into a body surfing contest or tossing the football turns into a game of Australian rules football, these activities could be deemed to be hazardous. As such, the law may require that the church exercise a higher level of supervision than you might expect in order to meet the reasonably prudent man standard.[84] I am not advocating that these activities be abandoned, only that you understand the extent to which your church's conduct may be scrutinized if an accident occurs. Thus, depending on the circumstances, it may be appropriate to discuss the church's concerns with any group which regularly engages in these activities and to make suggestions as to limiting the church's involvement.

NEGLIGENCE - AUTOMOBILE ACCIDENTS

General negligence principles are applied in automobile accident cases. A plaintiff usually will plead that the defendant was negligent *vis a vis* specific conduct, *e.g.* failing to keep a lookout, failing to apply brakes in a timely manner, failing to yield the right-of-way, failing to control speed, *et cetera*. Almost everyone has been involved in and has experience with an automobile accident. Starting with the time when my head created several cracks in my grandmother's car's windshield in the 1960s, I have been involved in several wrecks. If your church has a vehicle or if your staff drives their own vehicles on church business, then your church may experience these claims, also.

They range from dented fenders to the tragedy which we witnessed in 2002, when Garland's Metro Church lost four students in a terrible bus crash. When tragedy strikes, though, legal advice pales in comparison to meeting immediate needs. Fortunately, the vast majority of automobile accidents do not approach the loss which Metro Church experienced. For relatively minor accidents, we should respond appropriately to the situation, which should include courtesy to the other drivers involved, regardless of fault, and may include notifying law enforcement officials, insurance company representatives, and others. I have included in this chapter a modified version of the instructions which I carry in my glove box. These instructions are not strictly legal advice about what to do when you are involved in a wreck; they are practical pointers, as well. To confirm your suspicions, though, I have not followed these instructions to the letter in my accidents, either. Accidents can be trying times in which to remain focused, rational, and practical, which is why I made the list.

The Metro Church crash haunts us all. As you might expect, there were allegations about the bus driver's qualifications, lack of sleep, and use of drugs, as well as the sufficiency and / or accuracy of any background checks undertaken by his employer. This recent example proves Dr. William Arnold's advice, quoted earlier in this book, that "[a]nyone who believes in the doctrine of original sin has to be a bit paranoid - and rightly so."[85] Will I ever drop my daughters off again for a bus trip to camp without hesitation? No. Should you? No. We must remain vigilant in every area of our responsibility in order to protect our churches' members, mission, and ministries.

NEGLIGENCE - AUTOMOBILE ACCIDENTS - NEGLIGENT ENTRUSTMENT

Imagine that Hilary, a college student, has been helping you in the youth ministry and she asks you if she can borrow the church's van to assist her in moving from one apartment to another. You know that Hilary probably does not have the money to rent a vehicle, so you slip the keys to her and tell her to have the van back in its parking place by early Sunday morning with a full tank of gas. You smile to yourself, knowing that you have helped a person in need and that the church will not be financially affected by having to pay for the gas that will be used. All is well.

What you did not know and what you did not bother to find out is that Hilary's license was suspended a few months ago for driving under the influence. That only hastened her losing her license, though, as several of Hilary's unpaid moving violation tickets were slowly winding their way through the wheels of justice and were coming up for trial in another few weeks. In short, Hilary was a menace behind the wheel, the church's wheel. Imagine your surprise on Saturday night when the police call to ask why such a strong smell of alcohol permeates what is left of the church's van. They go on to describe the damage to other vehicles and you hear ambulance sirens screaming away in the background as the officer asks you to come down to the accident scene.

Under conditions like these, your automobile liability policy may provide coverage. Then again, it may not. Hilary is not quite old enough to meet the minimum twenty-five year old driver requirement in your church's insurance policy. Your insurance company may decide that a coverage issue exists and that it will defend you under a reservation of rights letter, as discussed in Chapter 10. Even if coverage exists, though, will it be enough to satisfy the amount of the claims?

In order to prevail on a claim for negligent entrustment, a claimant must plead and prove five elements:

- that the vehicle's owner entrusted the vehicle to another person (the "driver")
- that the driver was an unlicensed, incompetent, or reckless driver
- that the vehicle's owner knew or should have known that the driver was an unlicensed, incompetent, or reckless driver
- that the driver was negligent on the occasion in question
- that the driver's negligence was a proximate cause of the claimant's damages[86]

In the hypothetical case which I described above, the claimant probably can plead and prove all five elements necessary to hold the church responsible for the damages caused by Hilary. How helpful do you feel now?

If an employee or volunteer will be driving a vehicle for the church, ensure that she has a valid driver's license and at least ask her if she has received any tickets or been convicted of any traffic-related offenses. Ensure that she meets any age requirements placed upon the church by the insurance policy. If the church learns that she has (i) has no license or that it has been revoked; (ii) has received multiple traffic tickets; (iii) has been convicted of any traffic related offenses; or (iv) has a reputation for reckless driving, then the church should prohibit her from driving the church's vehicles. If you follow these suggestions, then you are being helpful.

NEGLIGENCE - AUTOMOBILE ACCIDENTS - IN CASE OF AN ACCIDENT . . .

- Stop the vehicle at or as close as possible to the scene of the accident.
- Do not move the vehicle, unless the accident site is on a main lane, ramp, shoulder, median, or adjacent area of a freeway in a metropolitan area and the vehicle can be driven normally and safely, in which case you should move the vehicle to a cross street, frontage road, accident investigation site, or other suitable location.
- Set your parking brake, even if the slope is level, and engage your hazard lights, even in daylight.
- Turn off the engine, extinguish any tobacco products, and check for leaks.
- Notify law enforcement officials through their non-emergency telephone numbers of the accident: the police department if you are within city limits and the sheriff's department if you are outside of city limits. Dial 911 if you suspect that anyone has been injured or if the accident has created any dangerous conditions. Notify law enforcement officials of any fuel leaks immediately upon their arrival.
- Assist the injured by reporting the accident to law enforcement officials and/or notifying emergency medical response personnel to arrange for their transport to appropriate medical facilities.

- Do not move any injured people or attempt to render medical assistance unless you have appropriate medical training.
- Be courteous to law enforcement officials and the other people involved in the accident. Remember that your church's name may be printed on your vehicle and your post-accident conduct is still a witness, regardless of whether or not you are at fault.
- Provide your name, address, telephone number, driver's license, vehicle's license plate number, vehicle's identification number, church's name, church's address, church's telephone number, insurer's name, and insurance policy numbers to law enforcement officials and the other parties.
- Do not make any statement about the accident except to law enforcement officials, your insurer, and church officials.
- Note the date, time, and location of the accident. Although law enforcement officials should make a report, everyone makes mistakes and your version of the accident is just as important as anyone else's version.
- Diagram how the accident occurred, including the vehicles involved, the directions they were traveling, the approximate speeds they were traveling, the lanes in which they were traveling, which vehicle hit which vehicle, and a description of the roads, intersections, and other landmarks involved in the accident. Include in your diagram a north directional arrow, description of weather and road conditions, the existence and status (if known) of any traffic control devices, and the existence and length of any skid marks.
- Identify the other vehicles by manufacturer, model name, model year, and license plate and note which passengers and drivers were in which vehicles.
- Obtain personal information, such as names, addresses, and telephone numbers, for all people involved in or witnessing the accident and note how they were involved (driver, passenger, pedestrian, witness, *et cetera*).
- Note whether any of the people involved in the accident claim to be injured or obviously are injured.
- Note what kind of property damage occurred to your vehicle, others' vehicles, and other personal or real property. If other property or unattended cars were damaged in the accident, then take appropriate steps to identify and to notify those owners of the damage to their property.
- Identify the law enforcement officers involved, noting their names and agency affiliations.
- Note whether any charges are filed against or citations are issued to any of the drivers involved in the accident.
- Describe in your own words how the accident occurred.

- Do not share the notes which you make with anyone other than your insurer and church officials.
- Contact a staff member or other church employee as soon as possible and report the accident.
- If a law enforcement official does not investigate the accident and file a report and if the property damage exceeds $500.00, then you are required to file a report of the accident with the Texas Department of Public Safety within ten (10) days after the accident.[87]

INTENTIONAL TORTS - MALICIOUS PROSECUTION

It is a rare occasion when a church is sued for malicious prosecution. However, statutes discussed elsewhere in these materials require the church or its members to report potentially criminal conduct to law enforcement agencies. If the church is placed in the criminal justice loop, then it is entirely conceivable that the church could be sued for malicious prosecution at some point. While defenses exist in connection with our duty to report certain conduct, you should be aware of this potential claim.

To recover under a malicious prosecution claim, a plaintiff must prove the following elements:

- criminal action was commenced against him
- the church instituted that criminal action
- the criminal case against him was terminated in his favor
- the church did not have probable cause to file a complaint
- the church acted maliciously in filing the complaint
- he suffered damages.

In these types of cases, a rebuttable presumption exists that the church has acted in good faith and with probable cause. A plaintiff must overcome that presumption in order to prevail. One court has defined probable cause as "the existence of such facts and circumstances as would cause the belief in a reasonable mind, acting on the facts within the knowledge of the complainant that the person charged was guilty of the crime for which he or she was prosecuted."[88] As malicious prosecution is a common law cause of action, there is no applicable statutory definition of malice. Thus, I look to the statutory definition of malice, which is either a specific intent to cause substantial injury or an act or omission which meets the definition of gross negligence.[89] Gross negligence, in turn, must involve an act or omission involving an extreme degree of risk, considering the probability and magnitude of potential harm to the plaintiff, and the church's actual subjective awareness of the risk involved, with the church nevertheless proceeding in conscience indifference to a plaintiff's rights, safety, or welfare.[90]

As you would imagine, these types of cases are seldom prosecuted because the plaintiff must prove that the person who pressed charges pursued an incredibly malicious course of behavior against him. Even if ill will exists between a church and someone else, it hopefully will be difficult for a plaintiff to prove that a church acted maliciously toward him and had no probable cause for reporting his conduct to the authorities.

INTENTIONAL TORTS - DEFAMATION

Tex. Civ. Prac. & Rem. Code Ann. § 73.001 states that a claim for libel exists when a person makes a written or graphic expression that

> tends to blacken the memory of the dead or that tends to injure a living person's reputation and thereby expose the person to public hatred, contempt or ridicule, or financial injury or to impeach any person's honesty, integrity, virtue, or reputation or to publish the natural defects of anyone and thereby expose the person to public hatred, ridicule, or financial injury.

A claim for slander exists when a person makes a spoken statement "that tends to injure a person's reputation, exposing her to public hatred, contempt, ridicule, or financial injury" or that "tends to impeach that person's honesty, integrity, or virtue" and "is communicated or published to a third person without legal excuse."[91]

These claims can be made against churches, just like any other claims. That we should watch both our tongues and what we write about others is advice which we have received elsewhere. James 3:8 tells us that "no man can tame the tongue. It is a restless evil, full of deadly poison." He also instructs us in James 1:26 that "[i]f anyone considers himself religious and yet does not keep a tight rein on his tongue, he deceives himself and his religion is worthless." There is no good reason for a church ever to be involved in a defamation case, which means that it probably will happen.

STATUTORY CLAIMS - SEXUAL EXPLOITATION

After you read this section, you will understand why I go to such lengths in Chapter 13 in discussing sexual misconduct. The Texas Legislature created a cause of action to address the growing number of cases of sexual misconduct by mental health professionals and the clergy. This statute provides for a private cause of action against any person, with or without a license, who purports to render mental health services. It covers the following professionals:

- social workers
- physicians
- professional counselors
- marriage and family therapists
- clergy members
- chemical dependency counselors
- psychologists
- mental health officers[92]

The statute defines mental health services and sexual contact very broadly.[93] After stating that the statute covers mental health service providers ("MHSPs") and describing exactly what MHSPs normally should be doing with patients (providing mental health services), it tells us what MHSPs should not be doing: engaging in sexual misconduct with the people whom they supposedly are helping.

Sexual misconduct can take three different forms under the statute. It can be sexual contact, sexual intercourse, or deviate sexual intercourse, all as defined by the Texas Penal Code, or even a request for any of those three behaviors.[94] Further, it can be sexual exploitation, meaning "a pattern, practice, or scheme of conduct, which may include sexual contact, that can reasonably be construed as being for the purposes of sexual arousal or gratification or sexual abuse of any person."[95] It even can be therapeutic deception, meaning that the MHSP represents "that sexual contact with, or sexual exploitation by, the mental health services provider is consistent with or a part of a patient's or former patient's treatment."[96]

In the five churches of which I have been a member in my adult life, staff members have had affairs at three of those churches while we attended. I am not saying that any one of these situations would or would not have qualified as sexual exploitation under the current statute. Quite frankly, that is the least of my concerns. My concern is the absolute epidemic of sexual misconduct that plagues the church and the world and how we can find ways to stop it. If criminal sanctions are needed to help the clergy and others to keep their pants on, then so be it.[97]

Fortunately or unfortunately, there is an escape hatch for the clergy.[98] It states that the statute's definition of "[m]ental health services" "does not include religious, moral, and spiritual counseling, teaching, and instruction." While some ministers will plead this defense and will try to prove it, it will be a tough row to hoe in front of a jury of very unsympathetic peers.[99]

The cause of action is simply stated. If a MHSP engages in sexual misconduct with a patient, then the patient can sue the MHSP.[100] A jury may award past and future actual damages, which should look something like the following list (also applicable to many of the other claims discussed in this chapter), set forth with a $_____ beside each item for the jury to fill in.

- mental anguish
- physical pain
- lost earning capacity
- lost wages
- physical impairment
- loss of consortium
- medical and counseling expenses
- disfigurement

What will the jury do? No one knows before it returns with its list. It does not end there, though. Important additions to this list of actual damages are punitive damages and attorney's fees, making a former president's settlements look cheap.[101] Well, you might say, anyone who does that should pay for the damage that they have caused. It is only right. Here comes the surprise, though. The Texas Legislature reasoned that, if it is only right for the offending MHSP, then it may be only right for the church who initially hired the offending MHSP, too.

The organizational liability section of the statute is long and complex. I shall summarize it in this manner, but it is just a summary. The devil, as they say, is in the details. Your church will be held just as responsible for any misconduct as the offending MHSP if it:

- failed to check an MHSP's references before the alleged misconduct occurred
- knew about the alleged misconduct and failed to stop it or to report it
- knows about the alleged misconduct and fails to disclose the misconduct to a subsequent potential employer who requests a reference regarding the MHSP

Liability for churches generally will be limited under the disjunctive elements of this statute to the local church, unless it can be shown that some umbrella organization with authority or control over the local church knew or should have known about the alleged misconduct and did nothing to stop it.[102]

When the defense section in any statutory scheme starts off with "it is not a defense," then you know that the Texas Legislature has had enough and wants a pretty tough law in place. That is exactly what happens when the statute declares that the following are not defenses to misconduct:

- that the patient consented
- that the misconduct occurred outside of formal sessions
- that the misconduct occurred away from the church[103]

There is one defense, *i.e.* that the patient was no longer "emotionally dependent" on the MHSP at the time of the alleged misconduct.[104] However, if you are defending yourself on this basis, then you have made some poor choices in your personal and professional life.

If you are a MHSP or you employ a MHSP and you know of, have been notified of, or suspect conduct which meets this statute's definitions, then you have a duty to report that information to "the prosecuting attorney in the county in which the alleged sexual exploitation occurred" and "any state licensing board that has responsibility for the mental health services provider's licensing."[105] Note the conjunctive language. You cannot pick and choose. You must report the information to both offices.

Additionally, you must inform the alleged victim of your intention and duty to report and you should inquire if the victim wishes to remain anonymous.[106] In the report, you should identify yourself and the alleged victim, if anonymity has not been requested, and state that you suspect that an act of sexual exploitation has occurred.[107] This statute also contains an immunity clause very similar to the immunity clause applicable to the good faith reporting of child abuse or neglect.[108]

CHAPTER 5

What Do We Do Now?!: Defenses

CAN THEY SUE US FOR THAT?

Most clients who feel strongly about a particular matter will approach me, explain their situation, and indignantly demand justice. Occasionally, though, a client will approach me rather furtively and ask me if he can sue somebody over some act by which he feels wronged, an act over which he suffered nothing but personal chagrin and which invariably is fairly minor. The first half of my answer is always "yes." In Texas any person can sue any other person over anything. The Texas Constitution guarantees that "[a]ll courts shall be open, and every person for an injury done him, in his lands, goods, person or reputation, shall have remedy by due course of law."[109] The Interpretative Commentary to this section states that "[i]n a free government it can be said that the doors of litigation are wide open and must constantly remain so."[110] Thus, a correct answer to that client's question is "yes."

However, better and more complete answers to that question may start with "yes, but" and end as follows:

- You should forgive and, in this case, try to forget about it.
- The person did not realize that he was wronging you.
- There are more appropriate methods by which to settle this dispute.
- You are trying to take undue advantage of a situation.
- You will have to pay an attorney to prosecute your claim.

- You may have to pay the other party's attorney's fees and, perhaps, a fine when the judge learns how silly you have been in filing suit over such a trivial and groundless matter.
- I strongly advise you not to file suit and, if you do so, you will need to find another attorney because I shall not take part in any of this nonsense.

Procedural rules also provide a counterweight to the constitutional provision in this balancing test. They state that the signature of attorneys or parties on any document filed with a court constitutes a "certificate . . . that to the best of their knowledge, information, and belief formed after reasonable inquiry the instrument is not groundless and brought in bad faith or groundless and brought for the purpose of harassment."[111] That rule also allows judges to penalize an offending party or attorney by awarding a wide range of sanctions, ranging from restricting the offender's ability to participate in the suit in some manner to the dismissal of the suit and the payment of the opposing party's reasonable expenses and attorney's fees. A further restraint on the constitutional provision is found in the ethical guidelines set forth for attorneys. A lawyer must refrain from engaging in any matter "unless the lawyer reasonably believes that there is a basis for doing so that is not frivolous."[112] Additionally, a lawyer should not file a pleading for an improper purpose, which includes filing a pleading to harass someone else, to delay a matter unnecessarily, or to increase litigation needlessly.[113] Thus, although some people are reckless in filing suits and do so in unwarranted situations, the system has some safeguards.

Other than these restraints, the types of claims which can be filed are limited only by the imagination of a plaintiff's attorney. I say that because the law is designed to be flexible and to respond to society's ever evolving attitudes toward certain forms of behavior. There were not criminal laws against stalking until recently. They evolved in response to a perception that this particular form of misbehavior warrants criminal sanction for the punishment of the wrongdoers and a stronger deterrent for the protection of the potential victims. Concurrently, while criminal statutes may be expanding, civil claims may be contracting. Within the past few years, the Supreme Court of Texas has become very conservative and leery of new causes of action. The Texas Legislature has not been in a very civil mood toward plaintiffs, either, and passed sweeping tort reform measures in the last decade, making it more difficult for plaintiffs to succeed in almost every area of negligence, insurance, and consumer law. While this may be good news for defendants in general, it simply forces plaintiffs' attorneys to look elsewhere for target defendants. Fewer traditional targets or smaller recoveries force attorneys to be creative and to seek non-traditional targets, like the church, in order to sustain their practices and to recover settlements for their clients. If one well dries up, then it is an entirely logical consequence that those who are thirsty will look for another well.

Before going on to more specific areas, one point bears repeating. If your church is sued, then retain an attorney immediately. Serious mistakes can be made when a well-meaning staff member calls the plaintiff's attorney and says something that he should not have said, even if only in an attempt to make things right or to make things go away. Service of citation in a suit and, in some cases, demand letters from attorneys start deadlines running.[114] Neglecting those deadlines may mean forfeiting valuable legal rights, paying additional attorney's fees to repair the damage, or, in the worst case, a default judgment. While it may seem superfluous, a corollary to this advice is that staff members should not attempt to represent their churches in court, even in justice of the peace or small claims court. Texas law requires a licensed attorney to represent any corporation, whether for profit or nonprofit, in its courts in almost all cases.[115] As most churches operate as nonprofit corporations, attorneys must represent them in court.

CONTRACTUAL PROTECTION - INSURANCE

If you are concerned about claims and lawsuits, then you likely will take as much action as you can to avert their occurrence. However, you can never foresee everything and unanticipated accidents do happen. Further, when accidents happen, those injured invariably believe that someone else is responsible for the occurrence. These are some of the best reasons that I can think of to have insurance. Having acknowledged the need for insurance, I sometimes resist following my own advice and I wince every time that I write a check for a premium, internally noting that my insurance agent probably does not appreciate just how careful I really am. It was with this perspective that Kimberly dragged me kicking and screaming into a meeting about a decade ago with an insurance agent. I walked out of that meeting having bought both life and disability insurance policies.

I told my agent that, although my accidents were a family joke, they had been fairly minor. I always had rebounded in a day or two and it was inconceivable to me that I could ever do anything to disable myself. The agent's argument about the potentially disastrous consequences of a serious accident finally persuaded me, though. The financial burden that could be placed on my family by my not working and not covering the expenses to which we had committed ourselves in running a law practice convinced me that I should exercise a bit of prudence and make another insurance company richer. One year later, my left hand became too closely acquainted with my table saw during my pursuit of a former hobby, carpentry. After extensive surgery, a lengthy hospitalization, and an introduction to the joys of physical therapy, my disability policy paid a claim that helped to support my family when I was recovering.

That same argument applies to churches. What happens to an uninsured church if a significant claim is made against it and it eventually is found liable? The same thing happens to it as happens to any other business. A judgment is taken against it and, if it cannot or does not pay that judgment, then its bank accounts can be garnished and a sheriff can levy on and sell its assets, such as land and buildings, at public auction to pay the judgment. How would you like to be a member of a church which no longer owns or can meet in its own sanctuary?

Insurance eventually comes down to a stewardship argument. How much to purchase, from whom to purchase, and what type to purchase should be decided on a case by case basis. Shopping for the best rates and widest scope of coverage is also a smart idea, as there can be a significant disparity in premium amounts, coverage exceptions, and reputability of your agent and company. Consideration should be given to whether or not your association or other governing body, if applicable, is likely to be an additional target of potential claims, as well as to the types of potential claims which are likely to arise from your church's ministries. Other considerations entail your church's ability to meet the monthly, quarterly, or annual premiums and any deductibles, in the event of a claim. More detailed information on insurance is contained in Chapter 10.

While some have said that you can never have too much insurance, I disagree. Your church definitely can be overinsured. There are insurance salesmen who will sell a policy to your church with more coverage than your church needs, with coverage duplicating coverage in another policy, or with premiums which your church cannot meet. These decisions should be analyzed carefully, preferably with help from church members who have significant business experience and, better yet, who have been through the claims filing process.

What does insurance do? It protects your church's assets, ministries, and members. It protects your church's assets because, depending on the type of claim and policy, the insurer either must pay you for your loss or indemnify you for claims made against you. In other words, if a plaintiff makes a claim against you, then your insurer must convince the plaintiff to dismiss his claim or must pay money to the plaintiff to settle that claim. If the case does not settle and an adverse judgment is rendered, then your insurer must pay the judgment amount, to the extent that the judgment is within your policy limits.

It protects your church's ministries because it allows the church and its members to continue concentrating on those ministries in the face of a claim. If staff members are scrambling around trying to figure out how to defend a suit, how to pay the attorneys, and how to pay a potential judgment, then they cannot focus on what their church has called them to do. As a result, some aspect of that church's ministries will suffer.

Finally, it protects your church's members from some of the inevitable finger-pointing which goes on when a claim is made. "If you know who had not been so careless, then we all would not be in this mess." This type of behavior and its destructive consequences are much less likely to occur when the church has insurance to cover any potential claim than when the members are thinking about the special offering which will be taken to settle a case or to pay a judgment.

CONTRACTUAL PROTECTION - INSURANCE - NOTICE OF AN INCIDENT

Most churches designate a staff member who is responsible for gathering information relating to an incident on the church's behalf. This person should be acquainted with the issues in these materials and should be thoroughly familiar with any applicable insurance coverage which the church has in place. Notice of an incident does not have to come in the form of a letter from an attorney representing someone. Assume that you have notice if an incident occurs and someone could claim to have been damaged by or injured in that incident.

After learning of an incident, you will need to notify your insurance company of the underlying circumstances. Before embarking on any investigation by yourself, though, you should speak to your agent or the adjuster assigned to the claim regarding just how much and what type of information, if any, you should gather. Among the more pertinent facts needed, if someone anticipates a claim or litigation, may be the following:

- the names, addresses, and telephone numbers of any witnesses
- the basic facts surrounding the incident, such as place, date, time of day, witnesses, weather conditions, items of personal property involved, a sketch of the location, action taken by anyone in connection with the incident, claimed injuries, identity of health care providers consulted by the person claiming to have been injured, *et cetera*
- any statements made by the potential plaintiff, church members, and/or others involved in the incident

Taking pictures or video (be sure to use reproducible media, not instant film) of the incident scene and the items involved in it also is a good idea. Where the size of an item cannot be determined readily by the picture, place an object with a recognized size, such as a briefcase, next to it. Further, be sure to set aside any items involved in the incident so that they can be identified, inspected, and/or tested if a claim is made. If someone claims that a chair gave way when he sat on it, then you should have that chair inspected to determine if it is broken or defective and, if so, to prevent other incidents arising from its continued use. Finally, put all of this information in a file and keep that file in a place where the information can be used if the plaintiff files a lawsuit one year and three hundred sixty-four days later without ever having complained to the church that he was hurt.

CONTRACTUAL PROTECTION - INSURANCE - DUTY TO COOPERATE WITH INSURERS

The duty to cooperate with insurers may be difficult to accomplish at times. An example is when a church member is hurt at your church and the church is legitimately at fault. For its own reasons, your church's insurer probably will direct the church and its members not to discuss the matter with the plaintiff, his family, and, especially, his attorney. This includes giving statements concerning what happened, especially before your insurer and any attorney whom it retains become involved. It is difficult to minister to someone and to avoid discussing his problems with him, though. I do not have any suggestions to resolve this dilemma, except to hope that the claimant understands the restrictions which you are under and that violating those restrictions could place the insurance coverage upon which all of you rely at jeopardy.

In any such situation, your insurance company will assign an adjuster or claims representative to handle the claim. Your insurer also may retain an attorney to represent you, but generally only after suit is filed. Your concerns regarding ministering to or speaking with an injured church member should be explained to the adjuster or attorney. Their response may not be what you expect or want, but you should at least address the situation and make an attempt to explain yourself.

The duty to cooperate with insurers encompasses several distinct areas. First, you must cooperate with your insurer by making those employed or otherwise controlled by the church available for investigative and strategic discussions with the adjuster or attorney. Second, those employed or otherwise controlled by the church should avoid discussing any aspect of the incident with anyone not affiliated with the church or the insurance company. Next, the church should forward a copy of any investigative materials which it has to the insurance company to assist it in evaluating the claim. The church also must allow the insurer to inspect any premises or items involved in an incident. Finally, if the claim proceeds to litigation, the church must make itself, those employed or otherwise controlled by it, its premises, and certain of its records available to its attorney to aid the attorney in defending the church.

It is vital to remember that the insurance company is paying the attorney and any settlement or judgment. These are sometimes referred to as the insurance company's duties to defend and to indemnify you, respectively. It also is vital to remember that the insurance company has no relationship with the plaintiffs and wants to keep as much of its own money as possible, regardless of whether or not you believe that the plaintiff has a worthy claim. Thus, your church's attorney, who probably receives business from the insurer on a regular basis and whom your insurer is paying, will be attempting at every turn to minimize or even to destroy the value of the plaintiff's claim. That is your church's attorney's objective. The duty to cooperate contained in the insurance policy for which you paid forces you to cooperate with that very objective. Your failure to do so may void the coverage extended by that policy and make the church's assets viable targets for the plaintiff's recovery. Thus, if you desire for your church and, potentially, for any claimants to receive a benefit from the premium dollars which you paid to the insurer, then you should take heed of your duty to cooperate.

CONTRACTUAL PROTECTION - RELEASES

Releases have two (2) primary functions: they attempt to relieve you of liability for an incident which already has occurred or might occur. As to the former, you probably will have to pay something to persuade a third party to sign a release. As to the latter, you probably will prohibit someone from going forward with a specific activity without the tender of a signed release. Let us look at hypothetical examples for each of these scenarios.

Keith Klutz, a litigious, volunteer youth worker, is walking through the church carrying a television. He borrowed the television without permission from the pastor's office in order to show a music video to some of the youth and he is in a hurry to return it before its absence is noted. In his haste, Keith decides to take a shortcut through the church's kitchen during the senior women's guild's fruit salad exposition. The ladies traditionally throw banana and apple peels and orange rinds on the floor of the kitchen as the fruit is sliced and they clean up after they are finished. Keith is unaware of this event and the presence of fruit on the floor. Keith slips on a banana peel, falls awkwardly to the floor, and the television lands on top of him. The ambulance carries Keith to the hospital.

Keith is an invitee *vis a vis* the church and its property. He was volunteering for the church's and its members' benefit and the church probably owes to him the highest duty of care which it owes to anyone under premises liability law. Was the church negligent? That depends on whether or not twelve (12) strangers known as jurors believe that a reasonably prudent person would allow fruit peels to lay on the floor for hours in a room known to be accessed by people without prior knowledge of the danger, *i.e.* yes. Did Keith do anything to contribute to the accident? The defense attorney certainly will argue that he did, *e.g.* that Keith was not looking where he was going, should not have been carrying a television which obstructed his view, failed to follow procedure in taking the television without permission, and should not have taken a shortcut through an area known for slippery conditions. This situation describes a personal injury claim with defenses which, if resolved through a settlement, likely will involve two components: first, Keith signing a release prohibiting him from making any further claims related to the incident and, second, and the church's insurance company paying Keith some amount of money for his damages.

Karl Klutz, a minor and Keith's son, desires to participate in the church's annual skateboard and roller blade extreme sports demonstration, an outreach program developed by the youth minister, naturally. The program has been attracting many neighborhood children and youth and some have shown an interest in the church's youth group, staying past the demonstration for Bible study and fellowship. The program has been successful, but the church's insurance company has made some noise about cancelling the church's liability policy since Keith's accident. One of the deacons, an insurance defense attorney, suggests that, before allowing the demonstration to go forward, the church might want to consider having all of the participants sign a release. She reasons that, while the demonstration has been effective as an outreach tool, the liability to which the church is exposing itself and the risk of an accident are simply too great for the church to proceed without some protection. Thus, before an accident even occurs, Keith signs a release freeing the church from liability in the eventuality that Karl is injured as he grinds the handrail and falls headfirst into the holly.

There are many significant issues which must be considered when utilizing releases, especially releases which anticipate future circumstances. I shall not address those issues here, because they are addressed more appropriately in context in Chapter 1, Chapter 10, and Chapter 15. Suffice it to say that, for ministry reasons, I do not consider releases to be the panacea which some claim. I hope that you will consider the points made elsewhere in this book before asking parents and others to sign on the dotted line and will make a truly informed decision about whether or not to utilize releases. They have a place and I hope that you find comfort if and when you choose to use them.

CONTRACTUAL PROTECTION - SIGNATURES - HOW TO SIGN YOUR NAME

Perhaps the most important area of potential individual liability exists in executing a document for the church. The simple act of signing your name to one of the church's contracts may be a one way ticket to defending a lawsuit if a dispute regarding that contract erupts. Unless you demonstrate that you are signing your name in a representative capacity and indicate whom you represent, you may be found liable individually for the church's performance. Thus, when signing your name on the church's behalf, always ensure that you place a comma after your signature; you write in your corporate title, *e.g.* "John Doe, Trustee"; and the church's proper corporate name appears above or below your signature. It also is a good idea to place the date of your signature somewhere near the other wording. A proper example of a church's agent's signature appears immediately below.

John Doe, Trustee

First Church of Smalltown, Texas
By: John Doe
Its: Trustee
Date: December 31, 1999

A person may be individually liable if the document which he signs does not name the church represented or show that he signed the document in a representative capacity. A simple acronym to remember when signing any document on behalf of another entity is *PARCD*. It stands for principal, agent, representative capacity, and date. If you ensure that all four elements exist when you sign your name to a contract on the church's behalf, then you will have done well to protect yourself from individual liability. Although it is not required to note the date when you execute a document, it may become vital years later when a dispute arises.

If you are the church's treasurer or the one who signs the church's checks, you probably are cringing about now. Do you have to follow these rules for the hundreds of checks which your church writes every month? The short answer is probably not. If you sign a check in a representative capacity without indicating your capacity, you will not be liable if "the check is payable from an account of the represented person who is identified on the check."[116] This standard represents a change in the law, which prior to 1995 had provided contrary results from the same fact situation.[117] As no one really expects the treasurer to pay a bounced church check, the law reflects society's changing expectations. However, you should not rely on this statute to protect you when signing a "starter" check, as it usually will not have the church's name printed on it.

As to the "probably" in my earlier answer, my justification is fairly simple. There are no reported cases dealing with this new statute and contrary case law exists, even if those opinions rely on the former statute. Thus, I think that the safer strategy, until case law clearly supports the new statute, is to include an indication of representative capacity when signing a check. However, I recognize that there certainly is an argument that this is an overly cautious approach, in the face of the statute's plain language.

CONTRACTUAL PROTECTION - SIGNATURES - RELATED SIGNATURE ISSUES

On some related issues, the Texas Legislature has instructed the Secretary of State to accept documents for filing which bear original and facsimile signatures.[118] If your church has seen fit to have rubber stamps of signatures made, then the Secretary of State also will accept any document bearing a person's rubber-stamped signature. However, original signatures should be the rule for all other documents.

For those of you with incredibly illegible handwriting, take heart. The Texas Legislature adopted a loose standard for signatures which allows any mark which a person makes and intends to constitute his signature to pass scrutiny.[119] Even an illiterate person who only makes an "X" can sign his name under this test.[120]

Most importantly, though, when you sign your name on your church's behalf, ensure that the document's contents are true if you intend to deliver that document to the Secretary of State. The law provides that a "person commits an offense if he signs a document he knows is false in any material respect with intent that the document be delivered on behalf of a corporation to the Secretary of State for filing."[121] That statute goes on to provide that an offense committed under that article is a Class A misdemeanor or, in other words, a criminal offense. Although Paul tells us that he rejoiced in his imprisonment, I assure you that there is a world of difference in the attitude of a person jailed because of her faith, as expressed by Paul in Colossians 1:24, and a person jailed because she signed a fraudulent document.

STATUTORY PROTECTION - STATUTES OF LIMITATION

There are time limits within which a claim must be brought or it can be lost. Defendants occasionally assert the statute of limitations as a defense when they believe that a plaintiff has waited too long to bring a claim. If they are correct, then such a defense can bar a plaintiff's claim completely. While the following list is lengthy, it is not exhaustive. Other causes of action exist, although they are less common than those listed. Incidentally, some causes of action have notice periods during which a plaintiff must give notice to the potential defendant of her claims and/or file a complaint with a governmental entity prior to filing suit. Some claims, particularly those arising from contracts, even may have contractually altered limitations periods.[122]

Four Years	Breach of Contract
	Breach of Warranty
	Breach of Fiduciary Duty
	Fraud
Three Years	Sexual Exploitation
Two Years	Negligence
	Breach of the Duty of Good Faith and Fair Dealing
	Infliction of Emotional Distress
	Interference with Business Relations
	Interference with Contract
	Assault
	Battery
	False Imprisonment
	Invasion of Privacy
	Trespass to Chattels
	Conversion
	Wrongful Foreclosure
	Wrongful Termination
	Discrimination
	quantum meruit
One Year	Defamation
	Malicious Prosecution

The statutes of limitation have some limitations themselves. Most importantly, the limitations period cannot run while a plaintiff is under a disability. The law limits these disabilities to the following:

- being under eighteen years of age, also referred to as the age of majority
- incompetency
- in some cases, military service[123]

The law reasons that a person should have an adequate opportunity to recognize and to pursue a claim and that these disabilities unduly restrict a person from doing that. Thus, until these disabilities are no longer present, the statute of limitations does not begin to run.

A further restriction on statutes of limitation is that they will not begin to run until a plaintiff has had a reasonable opportunity to discover that a cause of action exists. Most of us do not need any encouragement to feel wronged. Occasionally, though, we do not realize that someone has done something to us, that we actually did not receive that for which we paid, or that we have been cheated. The law states that the applicable statute of limitation will not begin to run until the plaintiff discovers or reasonably should have discovered the wrong.[124] This usually is referred to as the discovery rule. It acts to extend the period during which a plaintiff can file suit.

STATUTORY PROTECTION - RECREATIONAL USE OF PROPERTY

Some would argue that Texans prize their land more than any other commodity. Some churches and schools are no exception and have acres of land surrounding their campuses. Inevitably, youth league baseball, softball, soccer, and football teams vie for the available space and routinely ask for a church's permission to use the land for practice. Despite extremely valid concerns over liability, the church may feel pressured into authorizing the use of the land so that it does not appear to be the grinch that stole baseball.

How have churches handled the liability issues in situations like this? Some churches simply have relied on youth sports leagues to have their own insurance policies in place, whether they do or not. Many have shrugged their figurative shoulders and granted permission for the premises' use with no further action or safeguards. Others have requested that the team and its members execute releases or that the league indemnify it for any accidents in consideration of the use of its property. That seems to be a fairly pragmatic course.

The Recreational Use Statute (the "RUS") is a little discussed statute that limits, but does not eliminate, a landowner's liability in situations like those described below. There are two key definitions for the statute's application. First, it defines "premises" as the following:

- land
- roads
- water

- watercourses
- private ways
- buildings, structures, machinery and equipment attached to or located on the land, road, water, watercourse, or private way.[125]

Next, it defines "recreation" as an activity like the following:

- hunting
- fishing
- swimming
- boating
- camping
- picnicking
- hiking
- pleasure driving
- nature study
- cave exploration
- water skiing
- other water sports
- any other activity associated with enjoying nature or the outdoors.[126]

The RUS then states its rule: "[i]f an owner, lessee, or occupant of real property . . . gives permission to another to enter the premises for recreation," then the owner, lessee, or occupant has not guaranteed that the premises are safe for the user's purposes, does not owe to the user a degree of care greater than that owed to a trespasser, and will not incur liability or responsibility for any property damage or personal injury caused by the user's conduct.[127]

Why in the world have I gone to such pains to discuss the RUS in such detail? There is one reason: it does not provide protection for what you might think of as the recreational use of your church's property. Would you think that a youth softball team, by practicing in a corner of your church's property, was making "recreational use" of that property and was "enjoying nature or the outdoors"? I would think so. However, at least one Texas court disagrees.

The *Torres* case contains this startling holding: "competitive team sports, such as softball, are not included in the definition of 'recreation'" in the RUS.[128] I understand, grudgingly, why the court came to the conclusion that it did. The reasoning is, unfortunately, legally sound. However, the case's holding discourages property owners from making their land available to youth sport leagues for practice facilities. That consequence seems to be far removed from a common sense understanding of the RUS' intent.

Apart from that major problem, there are other exceptions to the statute's limitation on liability. Comparable to the duty owed to all trespassers, an owner, lessee, or occupant "who has been grossly negligent, or has acted with malicious intent or in bad faith" remains liable for any property damage or personal injuries caused by his actions.[129] The statute also does not affect any claims by individuals younger than seventeen years of age based on an attractive nuisance theory, discussed in more detail in Chapter 4.[130] Further, the RUS' benefits are applicable only to the owner, lessee, or occupant who maintains liability insurance on the premises in specified amounts and either does not charge a fee for the use of his premises or charges a fee, but whose past year's income from those charges does not exceed twice the amount of the past year's *ad valorem* taxes.[131]

Why would a statute which purports to eliminate some forms of liability require you to have insurance, which arguably would not apply, in order for the statute to be effective? There are two possible reasons. First, the insurance industry maintains an army of lobbyists which persuades legislators to enact statutes which benefit the insurance industry, *i.e.* statutes which limit claims payable by insurance companies and which encourage the purchase of policies or the raising of premiums. The second reason is less obvious: the statute limits, but does not eliminate, liability. Some exposure always remains.

If an owner, lessee, or occupant has not purchased the statute's minimum requirements insurance policy ("$500,000 for each person and $1 million for each single occurrence of bodily injury or death and $100,000 for each single occurrence for injury to or destruction of property"), then the statute's protection is unavailable.[132] Second, even if the appropriate policy is in place, the statute does not limit liability under an attractive nuisance theory for minors under seventeen years of age. Thus, coverage needs to be in place for those claims. Finally, it is conceivable that a jury could find a church liable for violating the standard of care owed under the statute, that being the standard of care owed to a trespasser. A church even could be found liable for being "grossly negligent, or . . . [acting] with malicious intent or in bad faith."[133] The legislature also wanted to encourage the availability of coverage for this last category of claims. Most importantly, though, if a church maintains an appropriate insurance policy, then its financial exposure to recreational users usually will be limited to the coverage available in that policy, meaning that the church's assets will be protected even if an excess judgment is rendered.[134]

Thus, if your church wants to continue to allow softball teams to practice on its property, then I suggest that the church utilize insurance, releases, or other risk management tools in these situations. While the RUS is an extremely effective tool in decreasing exposure to claims, its focus is narrow and we should always keep that in mind. Further, it should not be relied upon to limit liability for claims by church members or the church's true invitees or licensees.[135] However, to the extent that the church can and should make itself and its land available in a variety of ways, this statute helps the church to extend its hand to the community without losing too many fingers.

STATUTORY PROTECTION - CHARITABLE IMMUNITY AND LIABILITY ACT

The Charitable Immunity and Liability Act's (the "CILA") purpose is to provide limited protection to charitable organizations and their employees, officers, directors, and volunteers from liability arising from their negligent actions. However, the CILA is extremely specific in its application and may exclude from its protection some situations which you might think would not be excluded. Thus, before relying on its coverage for your protection, make sure that you rely on an attorney's interpretation of that coverage for your specific situation.

Initially, the CILA covers two different types of groups: entities to which the IRS has granted tax-exempt status and other entities which meet certain tests. The statute distinguishes because there are some organizations which, for a variety of reasons, are truly charitable but which have not received tax-exempt status. The practical and legislative point of this distinction is that it is much easier to incorporate and to receive tax-exempt status from the IRS than it is to meet the behavioral guidelines for those entities which have not incorporated or received tax-exempt status. If your church belongs in the latter group, then all I can do is to state again what already has been stated in these materials: incorporate your church as soon as possible.

If you have received tax-exempt status, then your church will not need to prove any of the following in court:

- that it is organized and operated exclusively for an enumerated charitable purpose
- that it does not engage in any activities not strictly in furtherance of the charitable purpose
- that it does not engage directly or indirectly in any political process
- that it dedicates its assets to achieving the charitable purpose
- that it will not allow any of its assets, upon dissolution, to be distributed to any group, shareholder, or individual
- that it normally receives more than one-third of its support in any given year from private or public donations, gifts, contributions, or fees.[136]

If your church has not received tax-exempt status from the IRS, then it must prove each of these six elements in order to avail itself of the statute's protection. Essentially, the Texas Legislature is suggesting that you can do it the easy way or the hard way.

For the CILA's purposes, a volunteer is a person who renders "services for or on behalf of a charitable organization who does not receive compensation in excess of reimbursement for expenses" and may include a "director, officer, trustee, or direct service volunteer."[137] The statute also defines an employee as a person "who is in the paid service of a charitable organization" and includes an officer or director, but does not include contractors.[138] Finally, for reasons made clearer below, the statute defines good faith as "the honest, conscientious pursuit of activities and purposes that the organization is organized and operated to provide."[139]

The CILA protects direct service volunteers and volunteers serving as officers, directors, and trustees somewhat differently. First, it protects volunteers serving as officers, directors, and trustees from liability for their negligent acts if those acts are within the course and scope of their duties. Next, it protects direct service volunteers from liability for their negligent acts if they are "acting in good faith and in the course and scope of [their] . . . duties or functions within the organization."[140] Although direct service volunteers additionally must act in good faith to benefit from this law, if either type of volunteer acts outside the course and scope of their duties, then the statute's protection will not apply.

Consider the following scenario. Your church has a policy of screening and training volunteers for certain types of work. Laura, a direct service volunteer has been screened and trained to work in the nursery, but not in the kitchen. An emergency need arises during summer Bible school and, without anyone realizing it, Laura starts working in the kitchen preparing sandwiches, knowing that she has not received proper training. As her father always prepared her sandwiches, she does not realize that small, green dots on sandwich bread indicate that something is wrong. Some children become ill and claims are made. She may have been proceeding in good faith, but she also may be acting outside the course and scope of her duties and function with the church.

An important exception which applies to both volunteer categories rests in the "motor-driven equipment" claim.[141] In an insurance-driven decision, the Texas Legislature wanted to be certain that any insurance applicable to the operation or use of motor-driven equipment, *e.g.* a car, remains available to satisfy an injured person's claims. Such a solution satisfies your insurer's need for you to pay premiums, an individual's need to protect himself from the adverse consequences of an uncovered claim, and the injured person's need to receive compensation for his damages. In any case, though, this protection extends only to the volunteer and does not extend to liability which the organization may incur based on that volunteer's negligent acts.[142]

The CILA also offers limited protection to insured employees and organizations. Similar in concept to the protection offered to property owners for the recreational use of their premises discussed earlier in this chapter, the CILA requires employees and organizations to be insured prior to invoking its protection. Conveniently, this statute's minimum insurance policy is identical to the policy required by the RUS.[143] If the church does not have this policy in place, then the employee and organizational protections discussed immediately below will not apply. The volunteer protection discussed immediately above will apply, though, regardless of the existence of insurance coverage.[144] As long as an insured employee is acting in the course and scope of his employment with an organization and as long as that organization maintains the minimum insurance policy required, the liability of each will be limited to the minimum policy limits set forth above.[145]

Importantly, though, the CILA does not protect any person's or entity's conduct in the following situations:

- conduct which is intentional
- conduct which is willfully or wantonly negligent
- conduct done with conscious disregard for others' safety
- conduct concerning the duties owed by an officer, director, or trustee to the organization
- conduct concerning the treatment of hazardous waste
- conduct concerning an organization formed substantially for the protections afforded by the CILA
- conduct of most health care providers
- conduct of a governmental unit[146]

STATUTORY PROTECTION - EXEMPLARY DAMAGES

There have been volumes of articles about exemplary or punitive damages in Texas. However, for all of the hoopla, the Supreme Court of Texas in 1994 and the Texas Legislature in 1995 significantly curtailed plaintiffs' ability to win exemplary damage awards in Texas. The new statutes governing exemplary damages set forth significant hurdles for plaintiffs, such as proving their claims by clear and convincing evidence, not simply the preponderance of the evidence standard applicable to most civil claims.[147] The law also requires bifurcated trials on demand now, with the first part of a trial establishing liability for exemplary damages and the second part, if reached, determining the amount of exemplary damages.[148] Further, a plaintiff cannot collect pre-judgment interest on exemplary damages.[149] Limits on the amount of exemplary damages recoverable in certain cases also have been put in place.[150] Further, if two defendants are involved, then there is no joint and several liability as to any exemplary damages awarded.[151] Finally, the Texas Legislature has provided a definitive set of factors to be considered in making an award of exemplary damages. They are:

- the nature of the wrong
- the character of the conduct involved
- the degree of culpability of the wrongdoer
- the situation and sensibilities of the parties involved
- the extent to which such conduct offends a public sense of justice and propriety
- the defendant's net worth[152]

The law also limits an entity's potential liability for punitive damages for the criminal acts of a third party on or near its premises.[153] This relatively new statute was enacted 1995 in part as a response to growing concern from property owners regarding premises liability claims for inadequate security at their places of business. Frequent targets of such criminal activity were and remain apartment complexes, parking garages, shopping malls, automated teller machines, and other public places which provide criminals with easy access to people who are vulnerable and may have something worth stealing. People victimized in these situations sometimes accuse the property owners of not warning them of prior criminal activity at their places of business and of not providing a safe environment for them to transact their business. Thus, property owners, businesses, and their insurers reacted to these claims by lobbying the Texas Legislature to exempt them from punitive damages arising from these claims unless one of their employees was responsible for the criminal act, along with many of the other restrictions mentioned in the prior paragraph. Their efforts were rewarded.

STATUTORY PROTECTION - CONTRACTORS, SUBCONTRACTORS, AND THEIR EMPLOYEES

When a church hires a contractor to perform construction on its premises, a host of issues arises. The first scenario which may come to mind is what happens when the contractor's employee, a subcontractor's employee, or any other independent contractor has an accident on that church's premises. You can anticipate a claim being made against your church in these circumstances, regardless of how careful you have been.

One important factor in these cases has been to ensure that any construction company or worker who walks onto your property is covered by a worker's compensation insurance policy. Using a company, firm, or contractor which cannot provide a valid, effective certificate of worker's compensation insurance is the equivalent of placing your church in the insurer's shoes. Why? What are the odds of a company which cannot afford worker's compensation insurance coverage being able to pay a judgment? Further, even if that company can pay an injured worker's medical bills and other damages, that is no assurance that your church will escape targeting when the plaintiff's attorney looks to maximize his client's claim. If a company enters your property to do a job which has some profit built into it, then that company also should have the cost of its insurance built into its bid. Using uninsured contractors, even when their bids are the lowest, is like playing roulette with a personal injury claim.

The law provides a potential escape route from these types of claims, as long as the church meets the statute's requirements.[154] A "property owner is not liable for personal injury, death, or property damage to a contractor, subcontractor, or an employee of a contractor or subcontractor who constructs, renovates, repairs, or modifies an improvement to real property" based on a claim of providing an unsafe workplace.[155] This protection is unavailable, though, if the church "exercises or retains some control over the manner in which the work is performed, other than the right to order the work to start or stop or to inspect progress or receive reports" and "had actual knowledge of the danger or condition resulting in the personal injury, death, or property damage and failed to adequately warn."[156] Thus, one of the keys is to let the contractors do what you hired them to do. Do not put on your hard hat and try to play construction superintendent. Doing so will only make it look like you are controlling the project. Hire a contractor in whom you have confidence, tell that contractor what you want done, and let that contractor do the job. The second key is that, if you actually know about a dangerous condition on the property, then take care of it. Correct the condition or, if you cannot do that, then warn everyone about it. While not a cure for construction-related claims, this statute is helpful in managing risk when your church undertakes construction or repair projects.

STATUTORY PROTECTION - PROPORTIONATE RESPONSIBILITY

If an injured person has been more than fifty percent responsible for causing the damages which he suffered, then he may not recover anything against a defendant.[157] This sounds like a great deal. We can imagine a plaintiff being more than fifty percent responsible for causing his own accident. After all, each of us has done something careless which precipitated an accident in most cases. Thus, we can imagine that in almost any given situation a plaintiff should bear some responsibility for his own damages.

The difficulty rests in assessing that percentage without the aid of a jury, though. The plaintiff inevitably argues that he was not negligent in any way and that the defendant's negligence was the sole cause of his damages. Defendants may admit to generally being in the same area as the plaintiff at the time of the accident, but rarely admit to any negligence, blaming it all on the plaintiff. Consider how this might work in a hypothetical example.

I assess a client's slip and fall claim as being very solid, with the defendant bearing one hundred percent of the negligence. I cannot see how my client was in any way responsible, until I interview one of her co-workers. I discover that she has been involved and at fault in a few minor accidents on the job and that she married Keith Klutz, whom you know from our previous discussions. The defense attorney does not interview or depose her co-worker, so his knowledge is incomplete. Knowing that this testimony eventually may surface at trial provides us with a strong incentive to settle that case, even if it has not diminished the defense's valuation of the case, since the defense does not yet know of the damaging evidence. This type of testimony, even though it has nothing to do with the accident in question, could make it easier for a jury to find some fault in my client's conduct, thus decreasing or potentially eliminating any recovery.

Proportionate responsibility benefits defendants in two ways. First, it prevents a plaintiff from recovering anything if the defendant proves that the plaintiff has been more than fifty percent responsible for his own damages. Second, if a jury assigns any percentage of responsibility to the plaintiff, then the damages attributable to a defendant will be discounted by that percentage, as well as the percentage of responsibility borne by any co-defendants.[158] Defense attorneys use this statute to wear down plaintiffs and their attorneys by creating doubt as to the percentage of responsibility which a jury could assign to the plaintiff. Thus, if a claim is worth $100,000.00 when the plaintiff has not been negligent in any way, that same claim might be worth $60,000.00 or less if the plaintiff is forty percent responsible for his damages. This statute's protections are simply too important not to attempt this argument in all but those cases where the defendant and his attorney could be sanctioned for making a groundless argument.

Proportionate responsibility is only the beginning concept in the maze of determining responsibility and damages among plaintiffs and defendants. There are many more concepts, such as contribution among two or more defendants, joint and several liability, settlement credits, and punitive damages. I do not desire for more trees to die to support an analysis of these statutes when there is nothing specific that you can do to avoid their application in the first place. Further, the Texas Legislature has seen fit to amend these laws significantly at least twice in the past ten years. Given our legislative body's propensity to change these statutes, we may be discussing an entirely different method of determining responsibility and damages in the near future.

STATUTORY PROTECTION - INDEMNIFICATION

All nonprofit corporations have the right and in some situations the duty to indemnify their directors and other agents for certain liabilities.[159] In this litigious society, indemnification encourages reluctant people to serve. Without it, volunteers would be less likely to serve the church as decision makers based on the potential for personal liability for the church's obligations.

Generally speaking, a church voluntarily can indemnify its directors when those directors have conducted themselves in good faith and when they reasonably believed that their conduct was in the church's best interests.[160] This type of permissive indemnification is limited, however, if a director is found liable to the church or received a personal benefit from the conduct in question.[161] The statute also provides the mechanism for how a church should determine whether or not it desires to provide indemnification for a director.[162] Mandatory indemnification must be observed when a director is wholly successful in defending a claim against himself.[163]

This issue does not have to arise only after a claim is made. In fact, it is much easier to deal with before a claim is made. The statute allows a church to set forth its indemnification policy, subject to some restrictions, in its articles of incorporation or bylaws. Churches also can make decisions on this issues by board action, contract, or through any other method which does not contradict its articles, bylaws, or the statute.[164] Funding this obligation can be problematic, though, unless insurance policies are purchased beforehand or some type of self-insurance program has been instituted. The statute specifically approves these particular methods of funding indemnification obligations, among others.[165]

JUDICIAL PROTECTION - INTERNAL MATTERS

Generally, inquiries into whether or not a religious organization followed church policy and procedure violate the free exercise clause of the First Amendment of the United States Constitution.[166] Courts have noted that the ban on these inquiries extends to "matters of discipline, faith, internal organization, ecclesiastical rule, custom, or law."[167] Texas courts also must respect the federal Constitution and the protections afforded by the First Amendment and, for the most part, have avoided entangling themselves in ecclesiastical matters.[168] "[Q]uestions of church discipline and government are left to the church, limited only by the courts' supervision of property and civil rights."[169]

As discussed in Chapter 6, a church's compliance with its governing documents in a particular situation may or may not be a matter of church discipline and government. That situation and others may involve a member's or the church's civil rights or property rights. This is a determination which will depend largely on the facts of each case and the judicial temperament of the judge.[170] While we should guard our First Amendment rights zealously, property rights and civil rights are somewhat removed from the ecclesiastical issues found in *Patterson's* untouchables list and, to single out a specific case, *Dean's* issue of whether or not the church had properly or effectively fired its pastor.[171] I can easily envision a court injecting itself into a situation which the court finds to be non-ecclesiastical to determine whether or not a church's governing documents had been followed *vis a vis* civil rights and property rights. For example, the *Hawkins* case contains a persuasively written dissenting opinion which would have followed that exact path.

The more recent *Lacy* case upheld a congregant's request to inspect his church's financial records. The court noted that, through incorporating, the church had made itself subject to the law's requirements that non-profit corporations make their books and financial records available for inspection by its members. *Lacy* also notes that "courts have jurisdiction to review matters involving civil, contract, or property rights even though they may stem from a church controversy."[172] As an additional warning, if necessary, any person participating in an act which violates a church's governing documents may find himself the target of individual claims, as in the *Patterson* case. Finally, the analysis in any given case may depend on whether your church operates in a hierarchical or congregational setting.[173]

How are we so lucky that the courts, more or less, restrain themselves from meddling in our churches' purely internal affairs? Perhaps the answer is in the constant tension of the free exercise clause and the doctrine of separation of church and state. Perhaps, also, we find a two thousand year old answer, as related in Acts 18:12–16, in the wisdom shown by Gallio, the older brother of Seneca the philosopher and the governor of the senatorial province of Achaia in 52 A.D.

> While Gallio was proconsul of Achaia, the Jews made a united attack on Paul and brought him into court. "This man," they charged, "is persuading the people to worship God in ways contrary to the law." Just as Paul was about to speak, Gallio said to the Jews, "If you Jews were making a complaint about some misdemeanor or serious crime, it would be reasonable for me to listen to you. But since it involves questions about words and

names and your own law — settle the matter yourselves. I will not be a judge of such things." So he had them ejected from the court.

Gallio's decision encapsulates the free exercise clause. Although Christians continue to seek the power of courts in order to vindicate themselves in their misguided battles, those same courts have no business wading into church doctrine. When judges are asked to do so, they should limit themselves accordingly. We can do little more except to hope and to pray that Christians in litigation with each other today eventually understand that going to the law against their brothers and sisters has nothing to do with seeking the kingdom of God.

PART TWO

SUBSTANTIVE LEGAL ISSUES

CHAPTER 6

First Church, Inc.: Corporate

Texas Nonprofit Corporation Act

The Texas Nonprofit Corporation Act is a series of statutes designed to bestow the benefits of corporate status on nonprofit entities. In order to qualify as a nonprofit corporation, no part of a church's net income can be distributed to its members, directors, or officers as a return on investment. A church certainly may compensate its employees by paying reasonable wages and salaries, but it may not pay dividends, profits, or other types of returns on equity typically associated with business corporations.[174]

The Secretary of State accepts and approves a church's articles of incorporation. However, it is important to note that the piece of paper which the Secretary of State sends to you to confirm your church's corporate status does not confer tax-exempt status on your church. Other entities, such as the IRS, the Comptroller, and local taxing authorities, accept and approve various applications for exemption from specific taxes.

As you read in Chapter 1, the incorporation of an entity, even a nonprofit corporation, creates another person under Texas law. Any corporation has various statutory powers which it may exercise so long as it remains active with the Secretary of State, remains in good standing with the Comptroller, and does not violate its articles of incorporation and bylaws in so doing. Among these powers are the following:

- to have a perpetual period of duration
- to sue third parties and to defend itself in courts

- to buy, to sell, and to hold real, personal, and intangible property
- to lend money to officers and employees under certain conditions
- to own stock or to hold equity positions in other companies, partnerships, and other business entities
- to contract with third parties
- to make investments and to borrow money
- to take all necessary corporate action, including dissolution, and to appoint employees, officers, directors, and other agents to carry out corporate purposes[175]

The law allows nonprofit corporations to organize themselves like traditional corporations, with directors and officers, or to organize themselves in other ways. For example, churches may circumvent traditional corporate structure by opting to operate under a congregational system.[176] That does not mean that the members are shareholders or should be treated as such, though, as nonprofit corporations' members cannot have any equity interest in the corporation or its assets.[177] The nonprofit statutes also direct nonprofit corporations' governance on a host of other issues, including articles of incorporation, bylaws, financial dealings, registered agents, quorums, and standards of conduct for directors, some of which are discussed below.

One of the primary advantages of incorporating is that of limited liability for the church's congregants, employees, directors, staff members, and trustees. In other words, the individuals comprising the church should not be held liable for its debts, whether under a tort or contract theory, absent other successful theories of liability. The concept of limited liability can be negated, though, and the same congregants, employees, directors, staff members, and trustees can be held individually liable in a variety of circumstances. For example, a director (or another similarly situated decision-maker) is personally liable for improper distributions of the church's assets if he voted for or assented to the distribution of those assets.[178] A church's decision makers also may be personally liable for breaking state and federal securities laws in connection with the issuance of bonds and other securities. This may become a concern for those churches which use bond programs as financing tools.

On the tort side, those who own and / or are employed by business corporations generally are immune from individual liability, unless the plaintiff convinces the judge or jury to disregard the corporate entity, erasing the protection of limited liability. Similar reasoning applies to nonprofit corporations. Further, if a church member personally participates in tortious conduct, such as leaving a banana peel on the floor the moment before someone slips on it, then that member probably will be sued and held individually liable for his negligent act. Another example is when the member is driving to or from a church function and is involved in an automobile accident. Whether or not the member was in the course and scope of any church duties is the question which will determine whether or not the church is successfully sued, in addition to the claims which will be made against the person driving. Aiding us in the defense of these claims is the Charitable Immunities & Liability Act, which acts to limit individual liability in the face of claims against the church. These and other claims, the exposure which can arise from them, and defenses to them are discussed in more detail in Chapters 4 and 5.

What else can be done to avoid such liability? One of the best avoidance techniques is to be prepared for these situations before they arise. Educate yourself about your church's business and various aspects of the activities in which it is involved. If you are a director, officer, or trustee, then be familiar with your legal duties. Analyze the decisions which you will be asked to make and study the facts upon which you will base your decision. If appropriate, retain attorneys, accountants, or other professionals or experts who can give sound advice upon which you may rely. Second, ensure that your church and its assets are insured. Insurance policies are relatively inexpensive when compared to the dollar amounts involved in the potential claims against churches. Insurance simply adds another layer of protection for the church and its members in certain situations. These considerations are discussed in more detail in Chapters 5 and 10.

OTHER TEXAS CORPORATE LAWS

Cases interpreting the Texas Business Corporation Act have developed their analysis of those statutes in much more detail than cases interpreting the Texas Nonprofit Corporation Act. To cover any statutory gaps, the Texas Legislature has decreed that any provisions of the Texas Business Corporation Act which are not inconsistent with the Texas Nonprofit Corporation Act will apply to nonprofit corporations.[179] Thus, if an answer to a specific situation does not appear in the Texas Nonprofit Corporation Act or in the cases interpreting it, then an applicable provision may be found in the Texas Business Corporation Act.

GOVERNING DOCUMENTS - ARTICLES OF INCORPORATION

There are several distinctions between articles of incorporation for a business corporation and a nonprofit corporation. These differences and other requirements are addressed below in topical form.

Incorporators - An incorporator is the individual who signs the articles of incorporation. Only one incorporator is required, although there may be more than one.[180] This could be useful, perhaps, for ceremonial purposes in connection with a church's charter members memorializing their commitment to a new church.

Choice of Name - A nonprofit corporation's name cannot be the same as or deceptively similar to the name of another corporation.[181] The "same" test is self-explanatory. The deceptively similar test is whether, even if there is an apparent difference, "the difference is such that the names are likely to be confused."[182] If either of these tests is not passed, then the Secretary of State will not approve the filing of a church's articles. Under a third standard, though, a church may file articles bearing a similar name if it obtains the written, unconditional consent of the entity whose name is similar. The similar test can be stated as follows: "[having] similarities which may tend to be misleading as to the identity or affiliation of the entity, but not to the extent that the names are the same or deceptively similar."[183] Normally, if the distinguishing factor is geographic in nature, then the Secretary of State will require a letter of consent, even if corporate names are similar or if the first two words are identical to another corporation's name.[184] However, that rule would be impractical if applied to churches, as any new "First Church of Smalltown, Texas" would be required to obtain a letter of consent from every other "First Church" in Texas. Thankfully, the Secretary of State will not consider church names to be similar "if there is some sufficient basis for distinguishing the name from an existing entity name."[185] Thus, all "First Churches" can breathe easily.

Purpose - State law and federal law require a nonprofit corporation to state its purpose or purposes in their articles. State law requires a nonprofit corporation to identify itself as such in its articles of incorporation. Included among a litany of descriptive state nonprofit purposes are the following:

- charitable
- benevolent
- religious
- patriotic
- civic
- missionary
- educational
- scientific
- social
- fraternal
- athletic

- aesthetic
- agricultural
- horticultural
- trade or professional organizations.

The IRS has a similar list, that being the following:

- charitable
- religious
- educational
- scientific
- literary
- amateur sports
- cruelty prevention

As you can see, the state list appears to be more expansive than the federal list. However, the federal list deals only with those organizations which can qualify for tax-exempt status as Internal Revenue Code § 501(c)(3) organizations.

The second and third purpose clauses usually found in a nonprofit corporation's articles, although not required by Texas law, consist of broad, general statements prohibiting distributions of net earnings to the corporation's members, directors, trustees, officers, *et cetera* and directing that the corporation's assets, upon dissolution, will be distributed for an exempt purpose, as defined in Internal Revenue Code § 501(c)(3). The second clause is a paper defense against unscrupulous people who would use charity to their own advantage in operating a nonprofit corporation. It is not a perfect safeguard, but it does assist somewhat by making those who operate nonprofit corporations initially state the nature of their purpose. This potentially opens the door for civil and criminal fraud charges if that clause is not observed. The third clause, similarly, guards against those who would use a nonprofit corporation to accumulate wealth and distribute it to themselves upon the corporation's dissolution. These two clauses attempt to ensure that the proper people and organizations benefit from the corporation's activities.

Directors - A business corporation only needs one director. A nonprofit corporation generally needs three directors.[186] While a nonprofit corporation's articles do not have to use the word "directors," the actual words used to designate the offices of director (*e.g.* manager, administrator, fiduciary, or trustee) should clearly state that the persons named in the articles have management control of the entity.[187] The role of directors in the business corporation may differ some from their nonprofit corporation role, though. In a business corporation, directors exercise the company's powers in conjunction with the company's other directors, manage the company's business and affairs, and make most significant decisions affecting the company, all subject to that company's Bylaws. A church may place decision-making power in the church body or congregation or expressly limit the directors' authority in some manner. If that occurs, then that church essentially operates without directors, but usually will appoint trustees to carry out any legal duties for the church. If a church operates under a congregational system, then it should specifically state that fact in its articles.[188] The duties of directors and other individuals holding similar offices are discussed in more detail later in this Chapter.

Registered Agent and Registered Office - This topic also is addressed in much more detail later in this Chapter. Suffice it to say that the articles must name a registered agent (which can be a corporation and must be a resident of Texas), and must identify the church's registered office. While the registered agent's business office and the church's registered office are identical, the church may maintain a different principal place of business.[189]

Duration - The articles must set forth the intended duration of the entity. While there are methods for dissolving corporations prior to the end of their intended durations, the Secretary of State demands to know the period which the incorporator intends for this entity to last. Business corporations and nonprofit corporations can state that their duration is perpetual, for a certain period of time, or until a certain date. Most churches choose a perpetual duration. If a church's articles of incorporation set forth either a certain period of duration or a certain date upon which the church's charter will expire and it desires for that period to be perpetual, then it may need to amend its articles of incorporation, depending on its date of incorporation.[190]

GOVERNING DOCUMENTS - BYLAWS

A church's bylaws tell it how to govern its own activities. A good analogy is that the articles of incorporation are simply the printing on the outside of any product's packaging. They tell you what the name of the product is, who made it, where and when it was made, how big it is, and how long it lasts. The bylaws are the instructions telling us how to assemble the contents. The bylaws tell us how it runs, what its power source is, when it needs to be recharged, what parts fit where, what its intended purpose is, what not to use it for, and what to do when it breaks.

As the bylaws need to be flexible in order to adapt to changing needs within a church, one of the more important issues of the bylaws is their relative susceptibility to amendment. If they are easily amended, then they can adapt to your needs. This is somewhat more preferable to bylaws which, for want of a quorum or supermajority affirmative vote, cannot be amended when they need to be amended, thus allowing the tail to wag the dog.

Some of the topics which should be addressed in a thorough set of bylaws are as follows:

- membership - admission, maintaining a roll, discipline, and termination
- organizational structures - men's groups, women's groups, mission groups, polity issues, *et cetera*
- officers and staff - selection, vacancies, tenure, duties, authority, compensation, and dismissal
- committees - member selection, vacancies, tenure, duties, authority, and dismissal
- formal meetings - procedures, notices, agendas, quorums, voting requirements, action taken, and minutes
- special observances - rites, sacraments, ceremonies, ordination, and participation
- finances and administration - designated funds, financial records, indemnification, trustees, legal/accounting/banking issues, *et cetera*
- amendments

Governing Documents - Constitution

You may have heard of the term "conflict of laws." As you would suspect, this occurs when one law conflicts with another law. When this happens, there is a hierarchy which determines just which law should be the determining law. What you might not expect is that your church's articles of incorporation and bylaws also can be considered to be laws in this sense. The reasoning behind this assumption is that they are the "laws" that control the details of how your church is to be governed. The hierarchy is as follows:

- The United States Constitution controls federal laws.
- Federal laws control state constitutions.
- State constitutions control state laws.
- State laws control articles of incorporation.
- Articles of incorporation control bylaws.

If a conflict between any two laws occurs, then the law which controls will prevail. In an ironic case of role reversal, though, a church's constitution has little, if any, legal significance, and should not address legal issues. If it does, then those issues probably would be addressed more properly by the bylaws. Conversely, articles of incorporation have very little theological significance. Thus, each has its place. Some churches have adopted constitutions as a means to expound upon the church's mission and theological beliefs, sometimes inserting a statement of faith. That is their place and they should be used for such purposes.

9.01 REPORT AND CHARTER FORFEITURE

Every nonprofit corporation is required to file a report (the "9.01 Report") with the Secretary of State every four years subsequent to its incorporation date.[191] The report relates basic information about the organization, directors' names, addresses, *et cetera*. It is the Secretary of State's way of making his nonprofit children call home to let him know where they are.

The Secretary of State and the Comptroller receive little information on nonprofit corporations in comparison to the volumes of information which they receive on profit entities. Business corporations, limited liability companies, *et cetera* are required to file annual franchise tax returns; to submit periodic sales and use tax reports and payments; and to make other disclosures which allow these offices to track them more effectively. Nonprofit corporations, on the other hand, are generally tax-exempt in most respects. Do not allow the more lax record-keeping requirements to catch your church asleep, though. The progressive penalties for failing to file the 9.01 Report in a timely manner include the following:

- a church forfeiting its right to conduct affairs in the corporate form
- a church forfeiting its charter
- a church being dissolved as a corporation

These penalties carry with them two important consequences which cannot be over-emphasized.[192] One of these is that the church's officers and directors are individually liable for each debt or liability created or incurred during the forfeiture period.[193] That statement alone should grab your attention. If you sign a $3,000,000.00 construction contract on your church's behalf the day after your charter was forfeited because someone forgot to file the 9.01 Report, then the construction company, the lender, the subcontractors, the materials suppliers, and their relatives may look to you for payment if the church cannot meet its obligations. Further, what if a worker falls during the project and is hurt? While we would like to rely on Tex. Civ. Prac. & Rem. Code Ann. § 95.001 *et seq.* to limit everyone's liability in that situation, I believe that the provisions of that statute and Tex. Tax Code Ann. § 171.255(a) *et seq.* are in direct conflict. The latter says that the church's officers and directors will be liable during a forfeiture period for any liabilities incurred. The former says that the church will not be liable unless it exercised control over the project or knew of a danger and failed to warn of that danger. A smart plaintiff's attorney might like to make you into a test case. You do not want to "make new law," as attorneys say, on this point.

An additional consequence is found in the Texas Tax Code.[194] This section states that, during the pendency of any forfeiture period, an organization which has not paid a tax otherwise due is prohibited from prosecuting or defending any claims in a court of law. Thus, if the church is in litigation and its charter is forfeited, then it may not be able to press its claims or to defend itself until the 9.01 Report is filed, the $5.00 fee is paid, and the Secretary of State reinstates the church's charter.

Before I file any case involving a corporate defendant, I contact the Secretary of State and find out as much information as I can about that corporation. If I find that the corporation incurred a liability during a forfeiture period, then the officers and directors are included individually in that suit. A few mouse clicks on the Secretary of State's web site can reveal much more about a corporation than it wants known, including the following:

- date of incorporation
- charter number
- current status (good standing or forfeited)
- directors' names and addresses
- incorporator's name and address
- registered agent's name and address
- changes in corporate name
- principal place of business
- assumed names
- date on which good standing status terminates
- charter forfeiture periods

If the church's charter has been forfeited, you can bet that a smart plaintiff's attorney will wait until the absolutely most opportune time to bring that to the court's attention, perhaps the day of a hearing on a motion for summary judgment. While this may seem unfair, it is the law and it is every attorney's duty to use the law to better his client's interests, which may not necessarily coincide with our own sense of justice. While the application of the Texas Tax Code's provisions to an organization exempt from franchise tax payment is uncertain, the church should never place itself in the position of potentially being unable to defend itself.[195] Failing to file the 9.01 Report does exactly that.

The Secretary of State's official position is that it will mail a copy of the form to each nonprofit corporation at the appropriate time. Do not rely on that representation. Calendar the due date and ensure that the 9.01 Report is filed in a timely manner or, better yet, assign the task to the church's attorney. If the church promptly files the 9.01 Report and pays the $5.00 filing fee on a timely basis, then all is well. If the church is delinquent in filing the 9.01 Report, then its charter is forfeited. If the church fails to file the 9.01 Report within one hundred twenty days after its charter has been forfeited, then the Secretary of State will dissolve the corporation. However, if the church files the 9.01 Report within this one hundred twenty day period, then it may request that the Secretary of State reinstate its charter, but it must pay an additional filing fee to accomplish this. Do not go down this road.

REGISTERED AGENTS

A registered agent is a church's point of contact when the government attempts to communicate with it. Unless otherwise directed, the Secretary of State, the Comptroller, the IRS, and other governmental agencies will forward correspondence to your organization's registered agent at his registered address. Further, if a church is sued, then the person serving the court's citation and a copy of the petition or complaint, usually a deputy constable, may serve it on that church's registered agent and will expect him to be at the church's registered address. Although we rarely desire to receive correspondence from the government or news of a suit, learning about these things in a timely manner is much better than learning about them when it is too late to do anything about them.

How many of us lose at least some pieces of mail when we move? How many of us are certain that we will be doing the same thing one year from now that we are doing today? Perhaps some are, but there are no guaranties in life. Two of the most important qualities that a registered agent can have are the ability to stay in the same place and the ability to continue functioning as your registered agent. If he moves or changes churches, then your church should notify the Secretary of State and all other agencies who have been forwarding correspondence to the old address of the change in address or change in the identity of the registered agent. In fact, your church's failure to do so could have dire results.

If someone sues your church, then the law requires the plaintiff to serve the church with citation (a document issued by the court clerk and providing basic information about the filing of the suit and the necessity of responding) and a copy of the petition by serving its registered agent, president, or any vice-president. The customary practice has evolved into serving the registered agent.[196] If the agent's name or the address contained in the Secretary of State's records is not current, then that probably will not invalidate service at the old address. The law presumes that your church has been served if the plaintiff follows the correct procedure, even if your church never receives actual service. In other words, your organization has left itself wide open to being sued without ever hearing about it and a default judgment is as likely a result as there is.

The fault bullet can be aimed at a variety of people in such a situation. The registered agent position is a much neglected position to which very few pay attention because it rarely is an issue. Everyone always thinks that someone else is paying attention to it, if they think about it at all. However, you should think about your church's registered agent as someone who is vitally important to your church. If you give this position the proper attention which it deserves, then it will serve you well.

There typically is a lapse in the registered agent position when the registered agent moves. He forgets about his duties as a registered agent, forgets that he even is a registered agent, and/or forgets to notify anyone about the new registered address. He may continue being a member of the organization, but the letters from the Secretary of State, the Comptroller, and the IRS go undelivered, perhaps even being returned to those agencies for round filing. Those agencies assume that the church does not like them or, even worse, is ignoring them. The consequences of ignoring a governmental agency with the authority to regulate, to judge, or to tax your church are adverse, to say the least.

Another typical scenario is when the registered agent ceases to be a member of your organization, whether or not he moves. While his resignation or removal either may be amicable or bitter, a member who is no longer affiliated with an organization is much less likely to tend to that organization's business than he once was. Thus, he may not care to notify the organization when he receives correspondence related to it. If hard feelings accompanied his departure, then he consciously may decide to hide important information from that organization. Your church is responsible for his actions or inaction as long as it retains his name on its records.

Since only your church can ensure that its registered agent and registered address are current, the law charges it with responsibility for ensuring that this information is current. If your church shirks that responsibility, then the law expects it to be accountable for that neglect and to suffer the consequences, whether those consequences are a default judgment or penalties for filing something four years too late.

STANDARD OF CONDUCT FOR DIRECTORS,
STAFF MEMBERS, AND TRUSTEES

If a church chooses to operate with trustees, then that church's trustees have various statutory and common law duties and obligations which the law imposes upon them in connection with their relationship to the corporation. If a church chooses to operate under a congregational system, then it probably will not call these people directors, but may have some similarly functioning office or offices to which the standards discussed below may apply. Depending upon the level of authority and duties, a congregational system's trustees and staff members could be held to the same standard as a nonprofit corporation's directors, although there is little, if any, case law either to support or to reject this view.

There is some statutory authority to support this view, though. Different statutes treat all of these offices similarly for the purpose of discussing the duties which they owe to a corporation.[197] The law seems to include the functions of the traditional office of trustee within its definition of director and recent statutory changes seem to treat corporate officers comparably with directors.[198] As such, I believe that it is wise to conduct yourself under the following standards of care if you are a director, staff member, officer, or trustee or if you hold a similar office, regardless of the title.

As corporate agents, a church's directors owe to that church their "uncorrupted business judgment for the sole benefit of the corporation."[199] A fiduciary's business judgment has been analyzed as having three distinct facets:

- the duty of obedience - to obey any and all laws governing corporations and their executives
- the duty of care - to manage the corporation's business as a reasonably prudent person in that position would manage it
- the duty of loyalty - not to usurp corporate opportunities or otherwise to act against the corporation's best interests[200]

Put more succinctly, a corporation's fiduciaries have a duty to exercise that degree of care which a person of ordinary prudence would exercise under the same or similar circumstances.[201]

These duties collectively are known as the business judgment rule. While we normally do not think of churches as businesses, the law sometimes treats a church as just another corporation. Thus, we need to begin looking at our churches from that perspective, as businesses whose directors exercise judgment. The Fifth Circuit Court of Appeals approved jury instructions which stated the business judgment rule as follows:

> A director . . . shall not be liable for claims against him if, in the discharge of his duties, he exercised ordinary care and acted in good faith and honestly exercised his best business judgment within the limits of the actual authority of his position. . . . A director . . . shall not be held liable for an honest mistake of judgment if he acted with due care, in good faith, and in furtherance of a rational business purpose.[202]

Another court enforced the business judgment rule when it stated that, although the rule's origin "appeared anachronistic or at least counter-intuitive to some notions of director liability . . . [it] remains a viable part of Texas jurisprudence."[203] The same court also noted that the business judgment rule acts to encourage individuals to serve as corporate directors by limiting their liability against "acts and omissions that in hindsight proved to be wrong, as long as the directors were not personally interested in the transaction or did not act fraudulently or contrary to their lawful authority."[204]

The Texas Nonprofit Corporation Act also sets forth standards of conduct for directors of nonprofit corporations.[205] That statute states that a director should discharge his duties "in good faith, with ordinary care, and in a manner the director reasonably believes to be in the best interest of the corporation." That statute's commentary states that it expects directors

> to exercise their judgment with due regard to the nature, operations, finances, and objectives of their organization. The "ordinarily prudent person" concept is used in various contexts. In the context of nonprofit corporations it applies to directors that balance potential risks and rewards in exercising their duties as directors. It is intended to protect directors who innovate and take informed risks to carry out the corporate goals and objectives. The directors need not be right, but they must act with common sense and informed judgment. . . . [The] requirement that the director act in a manner the director reasonably believes is in the best interests of the corporation is both objective and subjective. It is objective in that the director must reasonably believe the action is in the best interests of the corporation. It is subjective in that the director must in fact believe the action is in the best interests of the corporation. As with the good faith requirement, a court is likely to look to objective facts to determine whether a director's state of mind appears unreasonable and whether the director really believed that the action was in the best interests of the corporation.[206]

Thus, the church's directors, staff members, and trustees should remember these guidelines when making decisions for the church. If their conduct is later found not to conform to these standards, then they may be individually liable for any damage which their actions caused.

LOANING MONEY TO DIRECTORS, STAFF MEMBERS, AND TRUSTEES

Loaning money to any church employee, officer, staff member, director, trustee, *et cetera* usually carries negative consequences. Although the issue of loaning money to employees is discussed in more detail earlier in this chapter and later in Chapter 8, loaning money to directors carries some special considerations beyond those accompanying loaning money to employees.

Just who is a director in a church setting? Given the variety of organizational structures used by Texas churches, that is a difficult question to answer precisely. However, unless your church's governing documents set forth a definitive answer, I believe that it is much safer to assume that any officer, director, trustee, or staff member should consider himself to be in the position of director for the purpose of this issue. As discussed immediately above, directors owe certain duties to their churches. Among these duties is the duty of loyalty, which basically means that you are to act in the church's best interests and that you are not to take undue advantage of your authority for your personal benefit. Directing your church to loan money to you or accepting a loan, even if it is initiated by another, may be in your best interests, but it may not be in your church's best interests. Thus, you probably violate that duty when you accept a loan. I know that situations arise in which a church wants to help out a staff member with a loan and the church is the only available (or most convenient) account from which to dip, but, our good intentions aside, these arrangements usually are not for the best.

Despite the many situations in which a loan is made, appreciated, and promptly repaid, the Texas Legislature has seen fit to make this potentially grey situation very black and white. "No loans shall be made by a corporation to its directors."[207] If your church violates this statute, then all of the church's directors who voted for or assented to the loan are personally liable for the debt until it is repaid.[208] As mentioned before, this liability could extend to trustees, staff members, and other similarly situated personnel.

QUORUMS

What do quorums have to do with corporate and church issues? As with registered agents, we sometimes overlook them because they usually don't squeal for attention when they are ignored. However, ensuring that a quorum is present can mean the difference between a court rescinding your church's business or personnel decision and a court leaving your church alone. We should struggle at least as diligently to establish a quorum as we should struggle to stay out of the courtroom.

When a church incorporates, it asks the state to recognize a legally separate entity. It files articles, drafts and approves bylaws and a constitution, and begins its corporate life. It takes action through the will of its members, but only through set procedures. The simple way to establish a quorum is to define it in the articles of incorporation or the bylaws as those members present at the meeting.[209] However, many churches' governing documents do not have such a provision. In those cases, after proper notice of a meeting has been given to all of those who are entitled to attend it and to vote on matters properly put before the membership, a quorum must be established. The quorum is not just a head count of those present.

When properly done, it is a two part process. First, you must determine the identity and number of members on your roll who are entitled to attend that meeting and to vote on its issues. Then you must determine how many of those people are there. The fact that other, ineligible people may be attending should be largely inconsequential. The key is to determine the larger number (eligible members) and the smaller number (present eligible members). Depending on the number or percentage of people required for a quorum either by statute (ten percent) or the articles or bylaws (smaller and larger percentages are allowed), some simple division should reveal whether or not a quorum is present.[210]

If a quorum is present, then you should proceed with the meeting in accordance with the church's procedures. If, however, a quorum is not present, then you should adjourn the meeting, again in accordance with the church's procedures, and begin the notification process of a subsequent meeting, urging eligible members to attend. The consequences of not following this path could lead to the following:

- actions that later are determined to be void
- personal liability for the individuals acting on the decisions improperly reached during that meeting
- corporate liability for failing to follow appropriate procedures

Imagine the situation in which a staff member is disciplined and/or dismissed at a meeting in which a quorum is not present. The almost certain result is that everyone involved will have an attorney in a very short time.

DISSOLUTION

Just as any business corporation can be dissolved, any nonprofit corporation, such as a church, also can be dissolved. While it may seem distasteful or inappropriate at first to consider dissolving a church, it may be the best option under the right circumstances. To begin with, dissolving a church does not necessarily equate with admitting defeat. A church could have a dwindling membership for reasons beyond its control and its members may see a better use for its assets. In these situations, the church's members could decide to dissolve the church, to distribute its assets to another church, school, *et cetera*, and to move their respective memberships to other churches. There may be a need for a congregation to wrap up its church's affairs for financial reasons and it may be the responsible thing to do. Also, some churches have merged in the past, leaving an unnecessary "person" on record with the Secretary of State. In short, there are many valid reasons for a church to dissolve. Conversely, it may be a very inappropriate response to difficult circumstances.

When a church dissolves, its assets should not be transferred to its members, ministers, or employees under any circumstances.[211] While some may expect to receive a windfall on their "investment" in a church upon its dissolution, the law is very clear: the assets of a nonprofit corporation may not be distributed to its members, ministers, or employees upon dissolution. Doing so subjects the recipient, the church, and the individual(s) responsible for the distribution to potential civil liability for the amount of the assets received and potential criminal prosecution for tax fraud.[212]

Where can the assets go, if not to those who put in the blood, sweat, and tears? This answer, also, is very clear: the assets of a nonprofit corporation should be distributed to another nonprofit corporation with a similar purpose upon dissolution. The donee's selection usually is made in the church's governing documents. However, even if the church's governing documents name the donee, that designation may be changed in the same manner as the church would make any other change to those governing documents. For example, if your church's bylaws, approved in 1975, dictate that its assets be donated to the Southern Baptist Convention upon its dissolution, then your church should replace that donee if it desires for another church, school, convention, or association to receive its assets. It simply needs to amend the bylaws, identifying the new donee in the process. If your church's governing documents do not specify a donee, then your church may designate a donee.

The process of dissolving can be an emotional one, as people make incredible financial, spiritual, and physical investments in churches. It is important (especially, perhaps, for attorneys) to remember this aspect of an otherwise straightforward corporate transaction. To begin the process, the church must follow the instructions in its governing documents for dissolution. If those governing documents are silent or do not impose stricter standards than those contained in the corporate statutes, then the law instructs us that a two-thirds affirmative majority vote, after establishing an appropriate quorum, is necessary to proceed with dissolution.[213] After this vote has been recorded, then it is appropriate for the church to instruct an attorney to draft articles of dissolution, to be filed with the Secretary of State, and to draft a statement withdrawing any assumed names under which the church or any of its missions or ministries have been operating, to be filed with the Secretary of State and appropriate county clerk.

There are a myriad of practical issues connected with the dissolution of a church. I have listed some of these below.

- satisfying all outstanding debts
- selling or otherwise transferring all real property and improvements
- selling or otherwise disposing of all personal property which the church does not intend for the donee to receive (*e.g.* another church may have a better use for a children's library than the university which will receive the lion's share of the church's assets) and accounting for the proceeds from any sale
- terminating and fulfilling all obligations remaining under all leases
- disconnecting and / or transferring utility services
- safekeeping the church's records
- responding to membership or information requests from other churches
- terminating the employment of clergy and staff
- fulfilling all financial obligations owed to clergy and staff
- fulfilling all financial, filing, and reporting obligations owed to governmental agencies, *e.g.* the IRS and the Secretary of State
- communicating relevant information to a denomination or other umbrella organization

As you can see, dissolution is not merely the simple throwing in of a towel. It should be a carefully measured, prayerful decision reached by a consensus of a church's members. Further, while it is a fairly straightforward process, violating any of the rules along the way may have very serious consequences for the violators. Thus, as in almost all corporate matters, an attorney should be consulted throughout the process.

UNINCORPORATED ASSOCIATIONS

A few years ago, it was not very safe to be operating a nonprofit organization without doing business as a corporation. It still may not be as safe to do so as we would like for it to be, but the enactment of the Texas Uniform Unincorporated Association Act in 1995 made great strides in at least setting forth the rules under which such associations could operate.[214]

Many churches, especially smaller churches, missions, and other cooperative ventures, essentially do business without taking into account the legal issues relevant to how they are doing business. Needless to say, incorporation is rarely on the front burner, even assuming that the money exists to contemplate doing so. When something goes awry, as it inevitably does, issues such as who is liable, who can sue, who should be sued, *et cetera* raise their ugly heads and it is only then that the people involved give first consideration to these issues.

The Texas Legislature has seen fit to deem nonprofit associations to be legal entities which are separate and apart from their members.[215] This is very analogous to how corporations and their members are treated. However, the association should not need to file articles of incorporation or, presumably, its 9.01 report. The association should draft and ratify some form of formal bylaws at a minimum, though, in order to give some structure to its organization and decision-making processes. Tax issues are a different story, though, as is qualifying for exemption as a tax-exempt organization. In every case (as these associations have such a wide variety of purposes, membership, and contribution sources), individual advice from a tax attorney or certified public accountant is appropriate.

Just as there are many differences in how nonprofit associations are treated *vis a vis* nonprofit corporations, there also are many similarities. A nonprofit association should file a statement with the Secretary of State regarding its appointment of an agent to receive service of process.[216] Although not referred to in the statute as a registered agent, this person appears to fulfill the same function as that corporate office.

The statute also treats the potential liability of the organization and its members in much the same way that corporate law treats those subjects. The association may be sued for contracts and torts in its own name.[217] Its members are not proper defendants in such suits on the bases that they either are or are considered to be members of the association or to participate in the management of the association's affairs. As with corporations, though, members will remain liable for any tortious conduct in which they participate individually.

Like corporations, an association can hold real property and personal property in its name.[218] Similarly, an association can borrow money, grant liens, and transfer such property, just like a corporation. Further, there is no current need to place legal title to property in a trustee's name to hold it for the benefit of the group. This was standard practice for years and placed trustees in the likely, yet undesirable, position of being named as an individual defendant when a third party sued the group.

The statute also authorizes an association to file a certificate of authority with the appropriate county clerk when it deals with real property. This filing is analogous to that of a corporate resolution, which usually is not filed, but is required to satisfy lenders and others that a corporation is acting on its own authority and initiative after having followed proper corporate procedures.[219]

Another similarity to corporations is that third parties and members alike can sue associations.[220] In years past, it was very difficult for an individual to sue an unincorporated group of which he was a member. You may not necessarily consider this to be an advancement in the law, but it does reflect the prevailing legal thinking, after the abolition of charitable immunity, that incorporated and unincorporated entities alike should answer for any damages for which they are legally responsible, whether in tort or contract.

Curiously, the statute may not prohibit the distribution of an unincorporated association's property to a natural person upon the dissolution or dormancy of an association.[221] That is at extreme odds with IRS provisions and with state law governing nonprofit corporations. The statute does prohibit that result if an association has gained classification as an IRC § 501(c)(3) association or is established for religious, educational, or charitable purposes, but it is strange that this exception exists in the first place.[222] Regardless of legislative intent, I certainly would advise against the distribution of an association's assets to a natural person upon its dissolution or dormancy.

I do not want to leave a false impression about this statute and its protection of individual members from liability, though. It is a relatively new statute which protects individuals who may not have received that same protection under common law prior to its enactment. Given the right circumstances, this statute could be challenged on any number of grounds and could be ruled, for example, inapplicable, unconstitutional, or too ambiguous to be enforced. I do not believe that this is a likely result. However, until the statute is challenged and upheld on a regular basis, anyone invoking its protection should expect this type of challenge.

CHAPTER 7

Rendering Unto Caesar: Taxes

With the exception of encouraging your church to seek a taxpayer identification number and tax-exempt status, I do not even attempt to address many of the federal tax issues that affect churches, staff members, and employees. There are two reasons why I do not do so. First and foremost is that I simply do not have the expertise and experience in this area to feel remotely comfortable in writing about it. Next, there already exists a number of authors who have produced and continue to produce excellent texts, bulletins, newsletters, and web sites dealing with these issues. A good place to start for official information is the IRS' web site and its *Tax Guide for Churches and Religious Organizations*, although information found there certainly will contain the IRS' views, not those of an independent attorney or accountant specializing in tax issues affecting churches. I hope that you will turn to that source and others for further guidance in this area.

FORM SS-4

Upon commencing a church's operations, someone should have applied for and received a new employer identification number from the IRS. This number functions in much the same way as your personal social security number. It is the way that the IRS keeps track of the church. Any payments of taxes, reports, or filings which are directed to the IRS should bear this number and the church's legal, corporate name for proper reference. The IRS' Form SS-4 should be used to obtain the employer identification number.

Most churches already have taken care of this issue, but it is particularly important for beginning missions and start-up churches to obtain an employer identification number separate from that of their sponsoring churches or, in some cases, charter members. Any confusion arising out of a mission or satellite church using a sponsoring church's employer identification number could be costly to remedy or, worse, could lead to an allegation that the two entities are really only one, if a claim is made against one of the entities. The person completing the form must be an officer or director of the church and should not be your church's attorney. If you are the person completing the application, then you should be prepared to give your social security number and any other personal information requested. The IRS' response to the application can be almost immediate by using its web site and / or telephone number.

The importance of obtaining an employer identification number is understood immediately when your church attempts to open an account at a financial institution. Without that number, a bank, credit union, savings and loan association, brokerage, or other institution should reject your application, leaving your church without the ability to write checks. As most other forms of paying business debts pale in comparison to the ease and accustomed usage of checks, this reason alone should provide you with enough incentive to obtain an employer identification number.

GAINING FEDERAL TAX EXEMPT STATUS

Gaining tax exempt status for your church, whether incorporated or unincorporated, should be a priority if that status has not been attained already. Some churches can rely on the IRS' policy of implicitly recognizing churches as tax exempt, without even applying with the IRS.

> If your organization is a subordinate one controlled by a central organization (for example, a church, the Boy Scouts, or a fraternal organization), you should check with the central organization to see if it has been issued a group exemption letter that covers your organization. If it has, you do not have to file a separate application unless your organization no longer wants to be included in the group exemption letter.[223]

There are many situations in which a church may want to apply, though. IRC § 501©)(3) is the appropriate statute upon which to rely. Under that statute, an organization organized for charitable, religious, or educational purposes, among others, may qualify for tax exempt status, meaning that contributions which it receives from donors will be tax-deductible and that certain favorable presumptions will apply under state law. If your church determines that it should seek formal approval for its tax-exempt status, then it should file Form 1023, a somewhat involved, confusing, and technical form. Thus, professional assistance should be sought in its completion and with any revisions or amendments requested by the IRS.

If you file Form 1023, then an incorporated church must include with its application a conformed copy of its articles of incorporation. These articles must meet certain criteria concerning the organization of your church and the dedication and distribution of its assets. Under the organizational test, the articles must limit your church's purpose to one of the purposes recognized by IRC § 501(c)(3), *e.g.* religious purposes. Further, the articles must demonstrate that the contributions, income, and other assets which your church receives must be permanently dedicated to a tax exempt purpose. The logical result of this requirement is that your church's assets must be distributed, upon your church's dissolution, to a similarly tax exempt organization with a tax exempt purpose. Many churches' articles name the organization to which their assets should be distributed in the event of dissolution and I would advise any church considering this issue to name two or more sequential distributees in the event that the first or even second distributee named cannot lawfully accept your church's assets upon dissolution. This topic is discussed in more detail in Chapter 6.

LOSING FEDERAL TAX EXEMPT STATUS

The loss of tax exempt status can be challenging to a church at best. While there may be situations in which a church is convicted that its voice should be heard, despite any legal restrictions to the contrary, that church should proceed with full knowledge of the potential consequences of its actions. The following consequences can be expected.

- net income becomes subject to federal income taxation
- net income potentially becomes subject to state corporate franchise taxation
- members' contributions are no longer tax-deductible
- inability to establish or to maintain 403(b) tax-sheltered annuities
- loss of real and personal property and parsonage tax exemption for *ad valorem* taxation purposes
- loss of sales and use tax exemption
- loss of unemployment tax exemption
- loss of ADA compliance exemption
- loss of religious purposes employment discrimination exemption

- loss of Church Audit Procedures Act protection
- adverse impact on zoning classifications
- adverse impact on mailing rates
- adverse impact on housing allowances
- adverse impact on ministers' social security treatment

TEXAS SALES AND USE TAX

In one way or another, sales and use tax ("sales tax") affects every commercial transaction. You pay sales tax if you purchase something, collect sales tax if you sell something, or seek a legal way to avoid it. In any case, you must deal with it. The Comptroller administers the collection of sales tax. Local governmental entities add various sales taxes, all of which are collected by the Comptroller and refunded accordingly to the appropriate entity.[224] As you would suspect, these tax rates are subject to review, *i.e.* predictable periodic increases.[225]

The church should avoid paying sales tax in connection with its commercial transactions. The law provides that a taxable transaction is exempt from sales tax if an organization exists for religious purposes.[226] Alternatively, a taxable transaction may be exempt if an organization has qualified for an exemption under Internal Revenue Code § 501(c)(3).[227] In either case, the exemption is unavailable if the church uses it in a transaction with an improper purpose or beneficiary.

Since being exempt from sales tax sounds like such a good deal, it makes sense that the church should elect to use its exemption. The Comptroller's procedures require that the church request exempt status in writing.[228] That request should include the following:

- a description of the activities conducted by the church
- a copy of the church's articles of incorporation, bylaws, constitution, and other governing documents
- a copy of the IRS' letter granting tax exempt status under Internal Revenue Code § 501©)(3)

The Comptroller may require further information if he deems it to be needed to determine whether or not an exemption is warranted. Upon receipt of the Comptroller's written approval of exempt status, a church may buy, lease, or rent otherwise taxable items without paying sales tax. Unlike the issuance of an account number by the Comptroller to collect sales tax, the Comptroller will not issue any type of number or authorization code accompanying its approval of tax exempt status. The next step is for the church to furnish to each vendor with whom it deals a form entitled *Texas Sales and Use Tax Exemption Certification*. This is a specific form which is available from the Comptroller. It may be reproduced and given to as many vendors as is necessary for the church to continue benefitting from tax exempt status.

Having addressed how to avoid paying sales tax, we must look at how to avoid collecting sales tax. In recent years, it has become popular for churches to hold fund-raising events and to offer user fee items as part of its ministry. For example, many churches offer dinner on Sunday or Wednesday evening prior to services. They usually charge an amount for the meals which covers the cost of the food and preparation of the food, but not sales tax. The law provides that food products "served, prepared, or sold ready for immediate consumption in or by restaurants, lunch counters, cafeterias, vending machines, hotels, or like places of business" are not exempt from sales tax.[229] At first glance, that is bad news. However, the law also provides for an exemption for food products, even if prepared for immediate consumption, if they are "sold by a church or at a function of a church."[230] Further, the law provides that the sale of food products also may be exempt if they are sold in situations in which the sale is made by a church member under 19 years old, the sale is part of a fund-raising activity, and the net proceeds from the sale are received by the church for its exclusive use.[231]

Other fund-raising activities held by the church also may be exempt from sales tax if those events come within the definition of "occasional sale."[232] For the church's purpose, "occasional sale" means that the church may not engage in more than two fund-raising events in any twelve month period. Any one day fund-raising event may not exceed a consecutive twenty-four hour period or it will be considered to be two consecutive one day fund-raising events.[233] In that case, the church could not hold another fund-raising event for twelve months. This rule obviously prohibits weekly garage sales and puts new meaning into the definition of the word "occasional."

Texas Franchise Tax

Any corporation formed under the laws of the State of Texas, unless exempt, is subject to the state's franchise tax.[234] The franchise tax is a corporate tax which is determined by analyzing a corporation's net taxable capital and net taxable earned surplus.[235] Historically, Texas has recognized several exemptions for charitable organizations. Churches, conventions, associations, and affiliated schools should qualify under at least one of the exempt categories.

The law provides franchise tax exemptions for non-profit corporations organized for the purpose of "religious worship" and for educational purposes, respectively.[236] It states that "a nonprofit corporation exempted from the federal income tax under Section 501(c)(3)" also is exempted from the franchise tax.[237] A church may apply for the exemption in reliance on either section. Umbrella organizations, like conventions or associations, should apply under Tex. Tax Code Ann. § 171.063, as they probably cannot meet the "religious worship" requirement under Tex. Tax Code Ann. § 171.058. The Comptroller requires that any entity seeking "exemption as a religious organization must be an organized group of people regularly meeting for the primary purpose of holding, conducting, and sponsoring religious worship services according to the rites of their sect."[238] Thus, in the Comptroller's eyes, associations and conventions may not be organized for religious purposes.

Any religiously affiliated, non-profit schools which seek an exemption as an educational organization should not rely on Tex. Tax Code Ann. § 171.058. A nonprofit school is eligible for an exemption from franchise taxes if

> its activities are devoted solely to systematic instruction, particularly in the accepted arts, sciences, and vocations, and [it] has a regularly scheduled curriculum, using the commonly accepted methods of teaching, faculty of qualified instructors, and an enrolled student body or students in attendance at a place where the educational activities are regularly conducted.[239]

Instead, these entities should rely on Tex. Tax Code Ann. § 171.061 as educational organizations or on Tex. Tax Code Ann. § 171.063, but not on Tex. Tax Code Ann. § 171.058.

The filing procedure is similar to the application for a sales tax exemption.[240] The organization must forward the following to the Comptroller:

- a detailed description of the organization's past activities and future plans, as those activities and plans relate to the purposes clause contained in the articles of incorporation
- a copy of the organization's articles of incorporation
- a copy of the IRS' letter granting tax exempt status under Internal Revenue Code § 501©)(3), if relevant to the application
- an indication of the particular Texas Tax Code provision relied on for exempt status

The Comptroller may require further information if she deems it necessary to determine whether or not an exemption is warranted. After the Comptroller receives your application and sufficient supporting documentation, then she will forward a written notice to your organization granting the application.

An organization's application for exempt status does not need to be filed concurrently with its articles of incorporation or any other corporate filing. There is no advantage in delaying its filing, though. The law provides that the church should file its application with the Comptroller "within fifteen months after the last day of the calendar month in which the corporation's charter is dated."[241] As I read the statute, an organization incorporated between January 1 and 31, 2000, should file its application with the Comptroller on or before April 30, 2001. If filed on a timely basis, then the exemption will relate back to the date of incorporation. If not filed on a timely basis, then the organization may have to pay franchise tax. Try being the only church in your association to have that honor.

TEXAS REAL PROPERTY AND TANGIBLE PERSONAL PROPERTY TAXATION

Most of us who own houses or commercial real estate are familiar with the concept of *ad valorem* taxation. Various governmental entities assess taxes against our real property and its improvements to fund the government's operations. Those of us who own businesses are also familiar with the taxation of tangible personal property, meaning that these same entities assess taxes against our tangible personal property that is used in business operations or otherwise for the production of income.

The Texas Constitution provides that the Texas Legislature can exempt certain categories of property owned by religious institutions from taxation.[242] These categories are as follows:

- real property which is used primarily as a regular place of religious worship and which is reasonably necessary for engaging in religious worship
- tangible personal property which is reasonably necessary for engaging in religious worship at that institution's place of worship
- real property which is reasonably necessary for use as a residence for that institution's clergymen (limited to one acre per residence)
- tangible personal property which is reasonably necessary for use of the residence(s)
- improvements either under active construction or other physical preparation that are intended to be used primarily as a regular place of religious worship and which are reasonably necessary for engaging in religious worship and the land on which the improvements are located or are to be located, but only for a two year period.[243]

What exactly is a religious organization for the purpose of this law? It does not have to be a corporation.[244] However, it must be "organized and operated primarily for the purpose of engaging in religious worship or promoting . . . spiritual development or well-being," regardless of what form it takes.[245] If it meets that test, then it also must limit its payments to employees to reasonable compensation and must abide by its governing documents' provisions restricting the use and eventual distribution of its assets, as discussed in more detail in Chapter 6, in order to qualify for the exemption.[246]

While the statute requires that the property in question be used primarily for the purpose of engaging in religious worship, it does not require that it be used exclusively for that purpose. Thus, many of the disputes involving applications for tax exempt status have revolved around property which the church either leased to third parties for commercial purposes or used for purposes ancillary to religious worship, such as parking lots, recreational areas, buildings, and other grounds associated with other places of religious worship.

First, your church must own the property which it desires to claim as exempt. Property leased by your church from a third party will not entitle the third party to an exemption in the hope of lowering any subsequent rental payments.[247] Second, simply furthering religious work does not qualify as engaging in religious worship.[248] Thus, those properties owned by religious institutions which are not used primarily as a regular place of religious worship and which are not reasonably necessary for engaging in religious worship may not receive the exemption. Examples of such properties are publishing houses, bookstores, associational or denominational buildings, campgrounds, recreational facilities, administrative offices, *et cetera*. Further, keep in mind that most ambiguities or close calls in these situations generally will not go in the church's favor. As one court noted,

> [a]ll statutes for the exemption of property from taxation are to be strictly construed against the exemption and in favor of the state and taxation. An exemption cannot be raised by implication, but the intention to relieve from the burden of taxation must appear affirmatively. If there by (sic) an ambiguity as to what is exempt, it must operate against the owners of the property and in favor of the public, and all reasonable doubts as to the proper interpretation of a statute providing for exemptions from taxation must be resolved in favor of the right to tax.[249]

The trial results in many of these cases rest squarely on how juries interpret the requirement that property be used primarily as a regular place of religious worship or be reasonably necessary for engaging in religious worship. In one case, a jury held that sixty-four acres described by the owner as a "religious retreat," were exempt as a place of religious worship.[250] While that case may give hope to other similarly situated properties and institutions, the role of persuading a jury that a particular place is used primarily as a place of religious worship cannot be underestimated.

Some cases involve an ancillary issue, that being whether or not a church can receive compensation for the use of otherwise exempt property and still maintain that exemption. Some cases have supported that proposition. However, others did not find their facts persuasive. The law states that use of real property for

> occasional secular purposes other than religious worship does not result in loss of the exemption if the primary use of the property is for religious worship and all income from the other use is devoted exclusively to the maintenance and development of the property as a place of religious worship.[251]

Some taxing entities do not seem to appreciate churches receiving compensation for the use of otherwise exempt church property and have expressed that dislike by occasionally denying exempt status to church-owned parking lots. That is not to say that there is a wholesale conspiracy to tax church parking and I am not commenting on whether or not the following two rulings are correct. However, it is quite apparent that some taxing entities, jurors, and courts do not see exemptions as being appropriate when church parking lots are rented out for income.

In the *University Christian Church* case, the church owned some parking lots.[252] It reserved the exclusive use of all parking spaces for its members on Sundays, reserved some of the spaces for its members during weekdays, and rented the remainder to a company which, in turn, supervised commercial parking during the week. The government argued that the primary use requirement be applied to the parking lots in isolation. After jury findings against the church and a lower appellate court reversal favoring the church, the supreme court asked the lower appellate court to reconsider whether or not the primary use of the lots was for religious worship. Based on the jury's finding against the church, the lower appellate court reversed itself and ruled in favor of the taxing authority.[253]

The *First Baptist Church of San Antonio* case involves more parking lots.[254] As in *University Christian Church*, the church allowed a company to rent the majority of those lots for commercial parking during the weekdays. Again, the supreme court focused on whether or not there was evidence to support a finding that the lots were used primarily for religious purposes. This time the supreme court found in favor of the church.

In the earlier appellate case, the San Antonio appellate court reversed the jury's finding, which was in accord with the eventual supreme court ruling. The opinion stated that

[t]he question therefore is whether (1) access to the lots for a majority of the week plus (2) the fact that the actual use by the church is for religious purposes constitutes some evidence that the property is used primarily for religious purposes. We hold that this evidence is legally insufficient because under the statute and *University Christian Church* the inquiry is the actual use of the property, not the church's primary reason for owning it or the amount of theoretical access the church enjoys.[255]

The lengthy appellate process eventually upheld the exemption, but only after unrecoverable attorney's fees of well over $100,000.00.[256]

From the church's perspective, I understand the following arguments:

- that these arrangements benefit the church by providing income from an asset that is not being utilized to its fullest extent
- that it is good stewardship to treat our assets in such a manner
- that church parking lots are absolutely necessary in a society which relies on the automobile as its primary means of transportation
- that church parking lots are ancillary to our buildings' primary function as places of religious worship and should be included with those buildings in our applications for exempt status
- that church parking lots are reasonably necessary for engaging in religious worship.

These and other arguments were made during the course of these cases by very good lawyers representing the churches. However, the law's and the supreme court's repeated focus has been on whether or not the primary use of these lots is for religious worship. The statute provides an allowable use, while maintaining exempt status, for "occasional secular purposes." It seems to me that if the Texas Legislature had intended to exempt anything more than occasional, then it would have done so through explicit words. However, it chose to use the word occasional and I can see why some courts and jurors have interpreted regular weekday use as constituting something more than occasional.

If Profitable Parking Company fills up that lot five days a week and First Church fills it up on one day and uses some spaces on Wednesday nights, what is that lot's primary purpose? Fortunately, the supreme court acknowledged in *First Baptist Church of San Antonio* that simply looking at the math involved is not purely determinative; it is a relevant and persuasive factor, nonetheless. Churches can argue and have argued that, but for the church's parking needs, the lot would not exist and the church's attendance would be minuscule. However, we simply do not receive a jury of our peers and we need to face that fact. As such, our reasons for conducting our affairs in a certain manner may not be appreciated. Our actions are judged by a jury comprised of a cross-section of the community. Some of them are not sympathetic to the church for personal reasons and others may begrudge charitable organizations' tax-exempt status. In short, we should not count on a sympathetic jury just because a church's benevolent name appears on the docket sheet. In acknowledging that fact, perhaps we should begin factoring in the cost of taxes on our parking lots when we start renting them out. It still is a stewardship argument. The only problem is that the cost of parking our cars arguably has increased under the *University Christian Church* and *First Baptist Church of San Antonio* cases.

To address a final exemption issue, Texas requires all religious organizations which desire for their personal property to be exempt from taxation to file a written application requesting that exemption.[257] A church may apply for the exemption far after the imposition of a tax liability, but should do so as soon as possible.

> The chief appraiser shall accept and approve or deny an application for a religious organization exemption under Section 11.20 after the filing deadline provided by Section 11.43 if the application is filed not later than December 31 of the fifth year after the year in which the taxes for which the exemption is claimed were imposed.[258]

Thus, as long as churches stay within the parameters of the law, both personal property and real property should be exempt from taxation.

CHAPTER 8

Hiring, Firing, and Other Forms of Quicksand: Employment

EMPLOYMENT AT WILL DOCTRINE - THE RULE

The employment at will doctrine means that either an employer or an employee can terminate an employment relationship at any time, either for cause or without cause. This concept has been Texas law for many decades, although courts, the Texas Legislature, and Congress have created some exceptions to it and may enlarge the scope of those exceptions in the future. These exceptions are at the root of many disputes between employers and employees.

When an at will employee quits, the employer usually can do absolutely nothing about it, except to search for a new employee who is less likely to quit. When an employer fires an at will employee, though, the converse is not true. An employee may decide to contest his termination and/or to seek damages for what I shall refer to simply as being fired for a "bad reason." The specter of an employee successfully challenging his termination by seeking reinstatement and/or damages from your church and your church's desire to treat employees fairly, in the first place, certainly should be sufficient reasons to take this area of the law seriously.

Preeminent among any lesson which you may draw from this chapter is that you should guard your rights under the employment at will doctrine. Ensure that the pastor, personnel committee members, staff members, and others with hiring authority do not make statements to potential or existing employees assuring them that they can work at the church until they retire, for as long as they like, for as long as they perform well, *et cetera*. Also ensure that your employee handbook preserves your church's rights under this doctrine. Promises or even statements that are perceived or can be interpreted as promises can alter the at will nature of an employment relationship, thus unnecessarily tilting the scales of justice in the employee's favor.

EMPLOYMENT AT WILL DOCTRINE - THE EXCEPTIONS

When an employer fires an employee, the employee may allege that the employer fired him for a bad reason. What are the good and bad reasons? For a start, Texas common law states that an employer may not take adverse employment action against an employee based on that employee's refusal to perform an act which might subject the employee to criminal prosecution.[259] In this situation, Texas courts have determined that the public good served by barring action against the employee outweighs the public good of enforcing the employment at will doctrine.

Firing an employee is not the only way that an employer can run afoul of a statute or create a wrongful discharge claim. Taking any action adverse to the employee's interests and based on a bad reason can give rise to an employment claim. Such actions can include, but are not limited to, the following:

- refusing to consider an applicant
- firing an employee
- demoting an employee
- harassing an employee
- creating or tolerating a hostile work environment
- refusing to promote an employee
- refusing to increase an employee's pay
- lowering an employee's pay
- rescheduling an employee's hours
- reassigning an employee's duties

Many in the industry refer to these actions collectively as tangible or "adverse employment actions."

Almost all laws creating a protected classification for employees or for employee conduct prohibit not only firing a person protected by that classification, but also taking adverse employment action against that person. The point is that employers should never take any adverse employment action in reaction to an employee exercising his rights.

This advice is true whether an employer makes a hasty, poorly-reasoned decision to fire an employee immediately or engages in a sophisticated, yet equally poorly-reasoned scheme to force an employee to resign.

Any adverse employment action short of termination may give rise to a constructive discharge claim. This means, broadly, that the employer, while not technically having fired the employee, made the employee's work environment or the continued performance of the employee's duties much more difficult or impossible for a reasonable person to tolerate. Thus, the employer which makes life difficult for an employee may find the tables quickly turned by being found to have taken an unjustified adverse employment action and, thus, to have constructively discharged the employee.

Prohibited Employer Conduct

Legal arguments exist contending that Texas does not recognize wrongful discharge claims, only claims for exceptions to the employment at will doctrine or for statutory violations. Such arguments exalt form over substance, though, because many employees are claiming exactly that, wrongful discharge. Whether or not a given court recognizes the legal distinction, an employee claiming that her employer fired her for a bad reason also may make a claim for one, some, or all of the following:

- reinstatement
- past wages
- future wages
- attorney's fees and court costs
- punitive damages

In addition to the employment at will doctrine's exceptions, there are several situations in which adverse employment actions are prohibited by statute. Some of these statutes may not apply to your church, depending on the number of employees. Regardless of how big or small your church is, though, it still is a good idea to observe these statutes' requirements. Some of these statutes even contain penal provisions, potentially leading to fines and / or imprisonment for the offending employer. If your church responds to an employee engaging in any of the activities listed below by taking adverse employment action, then it may be faced with an employment claim and, depending on the statute, possible criminal prosecution.

- serving in Texas' armed forces[260]

- attending a political meeting or convention[261]
- voting[262]
- serving on a jury[263]
- obeying a subpoena[264]
- participating or not participating in a union[265]
- filing a worker's compensation claim, hiring an attorney to do so, or testifying in such a claim[266]
- belonging to or having a particular race, color, disability, religion, national origin, age, or gender[267]

While there are exceptions for refusing to hire people with certain characteristics, referred to as *bona fide* occupational qualifications ("BFOQ"s) and discussed in more detail below, termination based on discriminatory reasons or otherwise protected conduct generally will lead your church straight to the courthouse. There are, of course right ways and wrong ways to go about the business of dealing with employees, distinctions which you should study as you attempt to remain ignorant of the courthouse's location.

HIRING

Hire employees very carefully. Spending more time in initially considering applicants pays dividends in hiring employees best suited for the job. The old saying, an ounce of prevention is worth a pound of cure, applies here. Spending the ounce of prevention by ensuring that the best applicant is hired often will save you the expense of the cure, *i.e.* terminating him. This process includes, without limitation, the following:

- defining the education, training, and experience required for the job
- creating a job description or refining an existing job description
- soliciting applications in a non-discriminatory manner
- considering as many qualified applicants as possible and practical
- conducting a thorough interview or even series of interviews with each applicant
- verifying applicants' references
- verifying all information reported in each applicant's employment application
- performing thorough background checks
- making an offer of employment to the applicant best suited for the job based on legally permissible reasons

Hiring - Interviewing

When interviewing applicants the interviewer always should work from a structured interview format, *i.e.* using the same patterned set of interview questions for each applicant. While the questions usually will differ in some respects based on the particular position for which the interview is being conducted, you will reduce the likelihood that any one candidate will bring a discrimination claim against your church if you have asked all applicants and have based your hiring decision on the same set of proper questions.

The interviewer also should ask only objective questions that directly relate to the applicant's ability to perform the position's essential requirements. This is one area in which the importance of a good job description arises. If the interviewer can point to an aspect of a valid job description as directly reflecting on an interview question, then there can be little argument that the question is discriminatory. The converse of that is true, also. If a question will not assist you in determining whether or not a particular applicant is the one best qualified for the position, then avoid asking that question.

The interviewer should use a form on which to take notes during the interview. If a claim is ever made, this improves upon the torn sheet of paper and scribbled notes image usually presented in court. It also assists the interviewer in structuring the flow of the interview and in ensuring that a patterned set of questions is asked. However, the interviewer should avoid asking any questions which could elicit a response revealing a disability or other protected trait. In other words, ask questions which focus on whether or not the applicant can meet the job's primary requirements, not questions which reveal whether or not the applicant has any characteristics protected by an applicable statute. An example of this type of question is whether or not the applicant has had any back problems, family members prone to being ill, prior drug use, workers' compensation claims, *et cetera*. The law looks at such questions as being irrelevant to proper inquiry. The focus of permissible questions should be on whether or not the applicant can meet the job requirements now. The questions asked and the notes taken should focus strictly on his current ability to do the job. Speculation about factors which might affect the applicant's ability to do the job in the future also should be avoided.

We should be concerned with the structure and contents of interviews because rejected applicants and terminated employees can bring claims against potential and former employers based on discrimination. Government agencies, such as the Equal Employment Opportunity Commission (the "EEOC") investigate and may prosecute complaints made against employers. They even may send their investigators in the guise of applicants to verify that an employer is not violating applicants' rights. Following a patterned set of interview questions, avoiding potentially troublesome areas, and adhering to relevant, legally permissible questions which are focused on the job's requirements protects the employer and provides a good start to defending a claim of discrimination. As such, the following topics should be completely avoided in any interview, unless you can justify them as BFOQs:

- race and color - Do not inquire into an applicant's or an applicant's spouse's race or color or ask an applicant how he would feel about working with someone from a certain race or color. If an applicant raises the race issue or any other suspect classification, either decline to discuss it as an improper subject or ignore it and proceed to another question. He may be asking an innocent question or may be testing you for a reaction. These characteristics may never be used as BFOQs.

- citizenship, national origin, and place of birth - While you can ask if the applicant is a United States citizen or if he is authorized to work in the United States, you should not discuss an applicant's cultural background in any manner. Like race and color, these characteristics should not be used as BFOQs.

- religious preference - You certainly may inquire of an applicant's religious faith, beliefs, and experience if these issues impact on the job's requirements. Otherwise, you should not ask an applicant about the origin of his name or where he was born, as the answer to either question could indicate a certain religious preference.

- age - In addition to Texas law, the federal Age Discrimination in Employment Act and Older Workers Protection Act protect applicants and employees from discrimination based on their age. Thus, while you can discuss educational and experiential components of an applicant's background as extensively as you desire, do not ask his age.

- gender, including pregnancy, marital status, and dependents - Yes, you will have to obtain these details for insurance purposes if the applicant becomes an employee, but you should not inquire about these issues prior to establishing an employment relationship. These questions should be asked, except for the pregnancy issue, after the person has been hired. Do not inquire about pregnancy, though, even after you have hired an applicant. As with the race issue, do not ask an applicant how he would feel about working with someone from another gender and do not consider how existing employees would feel about working with a potential employee of another gender.

- disability, prescription drug use, past alcoholism or other drug abuse, mental illness, worker's compensation claims, and medical claims - In addition to Texas law, the Americans with Disabilities Act protects applicants with disabilities from discrimination based on their disability and, in some cases, requires an employer to make a reasonable accommodation for a disabled applicant or employee. It does not, however, apply to churches. Thus, if you are acting for an entity that is not a church, you can discuss the job's requirements and inquire as to whether or not an applicant can perform those requirements, but you should not ask any questions which could elicit a response revealing a disability.
- sexual preferences - The law regarding whether or not sexual preference constitutes a protected class is under a state of constant review. Thus, simply avoid it until clearer guidelines are in place. Of course, the BFOQ standard may apply to an appropriate position.
- prior arrests - You usually can ask if an applicant has been convicted of a felony or crime involving moral turpitude. The EEOC takes the position, however, that any question regarding these issues should have direct relevance to the job's requirements, as the answer might tend to categorize an applicant as a member of a protected classification, which might have a more frequent affirmative response to some of these questions. In other words, why ask an applicant for a landscaping position if he has been convicted of embezzlement? That question, however, might be appropriate for an applicant who would have access to the church's financial assets. If you ask this type of question, you should ask for details about any convictions or obtain those details through a criminal records search. Avoid asking about arrests, indictments, acquittals, dismissals, and civil suits, though, for the same reasons discussed immediately above.

Having read what is prohibited, you might assume that you can no longer ask any questions in an interview. Take heart, though. Behind BFOQs is a recognition that certain positions require certain attributes and allow employers to discriminate against suspect classes (except on the basis of national origin, race, or color) in very limited cases where it is essential to the employer's operations. State law defines a BFOQ as a qualification which is "reasonably related to the satisfactory performance of the duties of the job" and for which a "factual basis exists for the belief that no person of an excluded group would be able to satisfactorily perform the duties of the job with safety or efficiency."[268] The law on this issue is very clear. If a church desires to exclude certain applicants from consideration based on a position's BFOQs, then it may do so.

HIRING - BACKGROUND CHECKS

In past years, employers may have thought that they were going above and beyond the call of duty by actually calling an applicant's references. There usually was little, if any, effort that went into objective verification of the reference's statements. A new day has dawned and churches are now faced with the daunting prospect of verifying all of the following very carefully:

- employees' and volunteers' references
- past employment history by requesting written confirmation from prior employers
- academic records by requesting transcripts from schools
- a variety of other information by searching public records, such as credit reports, driving records, and criminal records, among others.

Public records can reveal a wealth of information about most individuals. Public records can verify any professional licenses claimed to be held by an applicant. They can reveal whether someone who has volunteered to drive the youth on trips has a valid driver's license or is driving with a revoked license because of several driving while intoxicated convictions. If your applicant will have access to the church's money or accounts, public records can reveal if the applicant has judgment liens or tax liens filed against him, indicating a possible lack of responsibility with money. They also can reveal if he has filed for bankruptcy, which would certainly be good to know before the church entrusts him with its money. Inquiries with credit reporting agencies also can reveal valuable information about applicants for these positions. If a woman has a poor credit record, then it is indicative of poor money management habits and raises serious questions about allowing her to have access to the church's financial accounts and records. Finally, criminal records searches, while imperfect in predicting future behavior, can prove invaluable in eliminating candidates with troubled pasts.

If you have decided to run background checks, then your application for employment and volunteer positions should contain a statement, to be signed by the applicant, authorizing you to run these checks. That not only is good advice, but is the law in some situations. For instance, the Fair Credit Reporting Act requires that any person desiring to obtain a credit report on a person obtain that person's written consent prior to doing so. However, if you ask for permission, decide not to run the search, and the search would have revealed information which would have changed your decision, then you will look fairly foolish for being bright enough to consider asking about something, but not diligent enough to actually confirm it. Thus, if you decide not to run these checks, then do not ask for permission to do so on the application. If a problem arises later which could have been discovered by running a check, then a smart plaintiff's lawyer will argue that you were aware of potential risks and could have discovered the problem, but chose not to do so. How will you explain that seeming inconsistency after the employment application has been admitted into evidence? The dialogue in the cross-examination scene from the televised movie about the serial rapist your church hired might go something like this: "Pastor Smith, was it that you were too lazy or just too cheap to run a background check?"[269]

Very few employers are required to run a background check on all potential employees or volunteers, but, your church may be required to run specific background checks if it employs certain health care or child care workers.[270] The absence of a general statutory requirement does not mean, though, that a reasonably prudent man would not do so under similar circumstances. This is the argument which will be made over and over to juries. The fact pattern is rather consistent. You hire someone whose past conduct would disqualify them from being hired for a particular position. You either do not conduct checks at all or do not conduct sufficient checks to discover an alarming fact about that person's past. The employee's subsequent actions, whether or not intentional, give rise to a claim. The injured plaintiff may or may not have what the law terms a "special relationship" with the church. If a special relationship, *e.g.* between the church and a student or another particularly vulnerable individual, exists, then the church probably will be held to a higher level of conduct in conducting background checks. Since the plaintiff's attorney knows that the employee has no assets with which to satisfy a judgment, the church puts on its defendant hat.[271]

Theories in the cases above essentially state that the employer was negligent in hiring or retaining the employee or entrusting the employee with certain responsibilities. If the employer had done a thorough check, then it would have discovered facts which would have disqualified the employee from employment. If that had happened, then the employee would not have been in a position to injure the plaintiff. It is a persuasive argument and is addressed in further detail in Chapter 4. Thus, the decision regarding whether or not to run background checks is a very serious one. I understand that they are costly, especially in the context of researching volunteers' backgrounds, but it can be much more costly to risk proceeding without them.

Before anyone becomes too upset about the law's intrusion into the manner in which churches select staff members, employees, and volunteers, let us consider whether or not the Word deals with this issue. Paul instructs churches in I Timothy 5:22 that they should "not be hasty in the laying on of hands and do not share in the sins of others." *The Living Bible* interprets the same verse similarly. "Never be in a hurry about choosing a pastor; you may overlook his sins and it will look as if you approve of them."[272] Paul similarly cautions us to "[r]emember that some men, even pastors, lead sinful lives and everyone knows it. In such situations you can do something about it."[273] Perhaps the most illuminating translation is from *The New American Standard Bible,* that we should "not lay hands upon any one too hastily and thus share responsibility for the sins of others."[274]

What do plaintiffs claim in many situations? The obvious answer is that the church should share responsibility for what that church's employee did, even if what that employee did was so outside the realm of rational thinking that the church could never have foreseen or condoned it. Paul is telling us to be careful, thorough, and patient, lest we share responsibility for the sins of others. The old ways of checking out an applicant by asking around or calling his former pastor or seminary professor, while valuable, simply are inadequate in our society. The time has come to accept that your church needs to conduct background checks in order to protect your church's assets, ministries, and members. It should be the standard to which your church should conform.

HIRING - REFERENCES - REQUESTING

You should review, confirm, and document responses from every reference listed on an employment application by a prospective employee. Many applicants rely on an assumption, perhaps well-grounded, that not many employers actually check references. How would you feel years later, after a child abuse incident occurs, if you discover that one of the references listed by an applicant would have revealed to you an allegation that the applicant already had abused a child? The law requires employers in certain situations to warn a prospective employer of an incident of abuse. If you had checked that reference, then your church never would have hired the applicant. If your church had never hired the applicant, then, most importantly, the abuse never would have occurred. If the abuse had never occurred, then you would not be in a courtroom.

Part of every employment application which I draft for clients contains a clause authorizing my clients to verify an applicant's references. That form should authorize the person or entity listed as a reference to provide as much relevant information as you desire to obtain about the applicant and should release the person or entity listed from liability for providing such information. This form is very much like the form discussed below. Such an authorization and release should provide some comfort regarding potential liability, but you should keep in mind that there are very few, if any, instances in which a reference has a legally enforceable obligation to cooperate with your request.

Hiring - References - Providing

Many attorneys advise their employer clients not to give references under any circumstances or to limit the content of a reference to confirmation of dates worked and job title. I advise all of my employer clients to obtain, as a condition of employment, a signed authorization from the employee which authorizes the employer to release information to those who may ask for a reference in the future. The authorization also should release the employer from any liability for providing such a reference.

This does not mean that I encourage my clients to talk freely about a former or present employee to a prospective employer. It simply is an acknowledgement that there may be some instances in which my client wants to provide a reference as a standard practice, to assist the former or present employee in securing subsequent employment, or to inform the prospective employer about some fact of which he should be aware. In those instances, I want my clients to have that signed authorization, releasing them from liability for giving a reference, in hand. That does not mean that the employer will not be sued if he gives out information viewed by the employee as derogatory. It also does not mean that, if sued, these authorizations and releases will be enforced by the courts, as they are largely untested in this arena.[275]

Employers with such forms should not consider themselves to be bulletproof in light of their perceived freedom to discuss former or current employees. If an employer gives a false or misleading reference, then it probably will not be protected by a written authorization or by any statutory protection, discussed below. One statute in particular prohibits the practice of blacklisting, meaning "to place on a book or list or publish the name of an employee . . . intending to prevent the employee from engaging in or securing employment of any kind with any other person . . . ."[276] A violation of that statute is a criminal offense.[277] I trust that no church would ever engage in such a practice, but I am sure that it has been considered from time to time by others.

A new statute should prove to be very helpful regarding this issue. It states that an employer will not be liable for "giving, on application from a discharged employee or other person desiring to employ the employee, a written truthful statement of the reason for the [employee's] discharge . . . . The written statement may not be used as the cause for a civil or criminal action for libel against the person who furnished the statement."[278] This action, "a written truthful statement," is the only action that a church should take if it decides to give a reference for a discharged employee.

For employers who want to give a truthful, objective reference, even if damaging to the former employee, there are at least two Texas cases which are helpful.[279] In each of these cases, the Houston appellate courts held that a qualified privilege inures to the benefit of an employer who makes a defamatory statement while giving a reference, unless that statement was made with malice. In this situation, you should assume that malice means that the employer made the statement with actual knowledge of its falsity or with reckless disregard for the truth. The problem with reliance on these cases is that a qualified privilege is an affirmative defense, meaning that the burden of proof and the inevitable higher cost of litigation on this issue will rest with the employer.

Whatever your church's policy is regarding references, it should be consistent. If your church's policy is not to give any references, then you should not make an exception for a favored son, as that could be interpreted as a negative comment *vis a vis* another former employee seeking a reference. With that in mind, the best means to avoid trouble when asked for a reference usually is to decline to do so.[280] However, there are some situations in which a church has a moral or legal obligation to provide a reference for a former or current employee.

If you intend to give a reference for a discharged employee, then do not give an oral reference. It should be your church's policy to receive all requests for references and to forward all responsive information in writing. This reduces the potential damage of a "your personnel director said that so and so was a . . ." claim. If everything is in writing, then there are no "he said / she said" arguments. Second, discuss only facts which can be substantiated by two or more persons. Keep your opinions to yourself and disclose only facts which can be proven objectively.

If your church's policy is to provide references, then each request for a reference which you receive should be treated with care. A decision should be made as to what information to forward only after reviewing the employee's personnel file, speaking with that employee's supervisor(s), and considering the context of the requested reference. In complicated situations or when you are considering giving a negative reference, you should consult with your attorney.

HIRING - EMPLOYEE HANDBOOK

I simply do not want to know how many churches function without an employee handbook or function with one borrowed, cut, and pasted from the local school district. I fear the answer. An employee handbook should be a unique document drafted specifically to address your church's employee-related issues. It should take into account your church's size, history, denominational affiliation, polity, number of employees, experience with former employees, and projections for church and staff growth. It should address your church's concern for its employees and their welfare as well as its expectations for their performance and conduct. It should be reviewed and revised periodically and each employee should have a current copy at all times. It should be written clearly, concisely, and on a level which is understandable to every employee and adult church member.

Most churches avoid dealing with employee handbooks for any or all of the following reasons:

- They usually are lengthy documents replete with legalese.
- There usually is disagreement regarding their provisions because every personnel committee member brings different experiences, perspectives, and agendas to the table.
- They remind the church of the difficulties involved in dealing with employees when there are problems.
- They cost money.

We tend to think that churches should be exempt from personnel problems and, therefore, have little, if any, need for personnel policies. That simply is not the case. The public, of which unsympathetic juries are comprised, expects profit and non-profit organizations to have those policies in place and to follow them.

Ensure that your church has an employee handbook in place and that each employee receives a copy of it. Require employees to sign a statement acknowledging their receipt of the handbook. Most importantly, your church should actually observe what it says. If your church does not observe it, then why should the employees think that it applies to them, also? Also, if you do not observe its provisions, then why should a jury enforce them, after you have terminated an employee for violating a rule that other employees regularly ignore?

As stated earlier, ensure that any employment contracts and the employee handbook set forth and specifically retain the employment at will doctrine, explicitly telling employees that there are no guarantees of continued employment or of employment for a certain period. Requiring employees to sign a statement acknowledging the employment at will doctrine also adds another layer of protection. Disclaimers or notices like this should be conspicuous, *i.e.* in bold print, italicized print, and / or a relatively larger typeset.

Every employee handbook should be different. There are different choices for churches to make in almost every area of employee relations based on their unique circumstances. Churches essentially have the opportunity to set forth, clearly and intelligibly, all of the rules by which they expect their employees to abide in these documents. It is hard work to create one, but a well-drafted employee handbook should pay dividends by achieving the following:

- creating a more harmonious working environment
- minimizing conflict by establishing consistent expectations
- setting forth rules by which the employer and employees should abide
- providing a ready structure for the resolution of misunderstandings, disputes, and complaints

The following topics may be proper for inclusion in these handbooks.

- Office Hours
- On the Job Injuries
- Time Clocks
- Medical Emergencies
- Computation / Payment of Wages
- Flexible Hours
- Absenteeism and Tardiness
- First Aid Training
- Holidays
- Employees' Bill of Rights
- Personal Leave
- Complaints
- Leaves of Absence
- Disciplinary Actions
- Maximum Absence Policy
- Employment at Will Statement
- Alternative Dispute Resolution
- Communications Monitoring Policy
- Confidential Information Policy
- Employee Relationships
- Workplace Violence Policy
- Right to Amend
- Employee Privacy Policy
- Computer Use Policy
- Retaliation Policy
- Internet Access Policy
- Overtime
- Performance Evaluations
- Compensatory Time
- Personnel Files

- Lunches
- Drug Testing
- Breaks
- Personal Information
- Loans
- Job Descriptions
- Expenses
- Personal Use of Office Equipment
- Vacation
- Severance Pay
- Sabbaticals
- Dress Code
- Group Health / Dental Insurance
- Personal Use of Church Vehicles
- COBRA Rights
- Alcohol and Tobacco Use
- Life Insurance
- Disability Insurance
- Equal Employment Opportunity
- Safety Rules
- Worker's Compensation Insurance
- Safety Equipment and Location
- Professional Liability Insurance
- Weapons
- Sexual Harassment, Intimidation, and Discrimination
- Nepotism
- Labor Law Postings
- Solicitation and Distribution of Outside Information
- Part Time Employees
- Driving on Church Business

HIRING - JOB DESCRIPTIONS

A good job description does more than simply name the position and to whom the employee reports. It informs an applicant of what the church expects from him in the performance of his duties and holds an employee accountable for those duties. Both employer and employee can review the job description periodically to assess whether or not the description reflects the job that the employee is performing. The church should revise it to conform to the employee's actual duties and its changing needs. In developing comprehensive descriptions for all employee positions, it also can assist the church in determining who does what, what needs are being met, and what needs are not being met. Finally, if disciplinary action becomes warranted, a written job description created before a problem arises can assist an employer by providing a standard against which to measure misconduct or poor performance.

Specifically, a good job description at a minimum will identify the following:

- the position by title
- the days and hours required during standard workweeks
- whether or not overtime will be required
- the job location and environment
- the position's essential functions
- the position's other duties and responsibilities
- the educational requirements
- the general and specific experience required
- the physical demands
- any special skills needed
- any special licenses or certificates required
- the supervisor
- any employees to be supervised

Good job descriptions do not simply write themselves, though. The process of creating job descriptions should include the following steps:

- identifying the tasks to be performed by the employee (interaction with people, objects, machinery, data, *et cetera*)
- identifying the knowledge, skills, and abilities needed for the position
- listing and prioritizing experiential, educational, and professional qualifications needed for the position
- consulting with those familiar with the position's responsibilities
- reviewing comparable job descriptions used by other churches

Developing good descriptions for each position will assist your church in understanding who does what from an employment perspective and in holding employees accountable for the performance of their assigned duties. They also are vital in responding to requests for temporary or permanent accommodations due to disabilities or injuries and they assist in determining whether or not a disabled or injured employee is ready to return to work and / or to resume his normal duties.

HIRING - EMPLOYMENT CONTRACTS

There is no legal requirement for any employee's relationship with an employer to be governed by a written employment contract. There may be practical benefits to doing so for key positions, though. Further, employment at will status can be maintained in a written contract. Considering whether or not the parties can benefit from a written employment contract hinges on whether or not the parties can do the following:

- know how they can benefit from a written contract
- know which issues should be included in that contract
- agree on the precise terms to be included in that contract
- ensure that the finished product reflects their agreement

Employment contracts in a church setting may be difficult as a practical matter, though. Some denominations exercise quite a bit of control over the clergy, assigning them to a church for a set or even flexible number of years and then re-assigning them whenever a change is felt to be needed. These denominations' control over church assignments effectively obviates the need for any written contractual arrangements between the local church and its staff members.

Other denominations and certainly independent churches, in contrast, call staff members without consulting with or receiving guidance from any denominational hierarchy. Their staff members usually serve a church as long as they and their church remain in agreement that they should continue to serve. Thus, many churches and their staff members operate on a true at will basis, *i.e.* either can terminate the relationship at any time with or without cause.

Further, there has developed a certain protocol in some denominations concerning the filling of vacant staff positions. For example, First Church Neartown, whose pastor recently announced his retirement, may feel the need to scout First Church Fartown's pastor by sending a "pulpit committee" or "search committee" to First Church Fartown's services. While pulpit committee members in years past may have sat conspicuously together on the back row, thus tipping off First Church Fartown to their presence and providing an incentive for First Church Fartown to raise its pastor's salary, contemporary pulpit committees utilize far more discreet strategies to accomplish their goals. Thus,

First Church Fartown, very suddenly and surprisingly, may lose its pastor after he responds to a call issued by First Church Neartown. The predictable result is that First Church Fartown then sends a pulpit committee to First Church Aroundtown and the process repeats itself.

I intend neither to condone nor to criticize any church's conduct in the prior example. It simply is a recognized practice and, because it is fairly common, I usually do not recommend that any traditional staff positions be subject to written employment contracts. The manner in which many Texas churches traditionally have operated simply does not lend itself to binding either the church or a staff member to employment for a certain term. That is not to say that other positions, *e.g.* teachers or administrators in a school operated by a church or faculty and staff at any of Texas' church-affiliated universities, are subject to the same comment. I certainly do not mean to say, either, that the terms of employment may be vague and left to the parties' respective imaginations. It simply is a reflection of my observation that formal employment contracts for fixed periods of time are incongruous with the *de facto* relationships among many Texas churches and their staff members.

HIRING - PERSONNEL FILES

Every employer should maintain a personnel file on every employee. Certain documents, discussed below, should be kept on file and should be available immediately for review by the employer and certain government agencies. Access to these files should be restricted carefully. Many churches do not keep personnel files or, if they do, then these files are too easily accessible to too many people. Such access could lead to, among other claims, an invasion of privacy claim. Many employees, especially in a church setting, feel comfortable walking into any office and opening whatever drawer they need to obtain whatever they are seeking. These employees usually do not have improper motives and such openness has a place in a church setting. However, there needs to be a more businesslike attitude regarding privacy, especially as it affects sensitive and confidential employee records. At a minimum, these records need to be kept in a locked cabinet or need to be in a staff member's office where the door or cabinet drawer can be locked when that staff member is away.

An employee's personnel file may include the following:

- completed employment application
- resume, if received
- search committee notes, if applicable

- copies of advertisements soliciting applications, if applicable
- completed employment interview form
- completed employee reference checks
- completed employee background checks
- job description
- completed W-4 form
- signed acknowledgement demonstrating receipt of the employee handbook
- an employee number, for tracking and payroll purposes
- completed periodic employee performance evaluations
- completed and approved/rejected leave request forms
- completed employee disciplinary forms, if applicable
- insurance applications, beneficiary designations, and other miscellaneous insurance information (but no medical information)
- hours worked/payroll reports
- upon termination, exit interview form (this may be difficult to obtain, depending on the circumstances)
- upon termination, COBRA notification letter and returned election form
- upon termination, a checklist noting the employee's forwarding address and telephone number; his new employer's address and telephone number; and the return of all keys, credit cards, and other property issued to the employee
- completed I-9 form, along with copies of supporting documentation, although this document probably should be retained in a separate file

Your church may want to restrict its employees' access to their own personnel files. Many businesses allow employees to review their entire files, but only in the presence of the personnel director or a supervisor. Some businesses even restrict their employees' ability to obtain copies of their personnel files to those documents which have been signed by the employee. This even has been interpreted as strictly as not allowing an employee to have a copy of the entire document when he signed only the last page. Such a requirement goes far beyond any real or perceived need on the employer's part and in many cases may raise an employee's suspicion to the point where he or she files a suit just to see what is in the file. As the file's contents will normally be discoverable in litigation, it begs the question as to what purpose is served in being so highly restrictive. Nonetheless, your church should have a policy setting forth under what conditions an employee may review his personnel file and, afterward, what documents may be copied and retained by the employee.

REQUIRED NOTICES

We all have wandered through various businesses and other churches noticing posters announcing this or that legal right. Sometimes we even have wondered if we are required to display a certain poster that we absolutely know is not to be found in our church. Private businesses have developed two sets of posters which are designed to meet the requirements of the notices described below, excluding the sales and use tax certificate. While you may thrill to the challenge of obtaining each poster directly from the governmental source, the convenience of obtaining all of these posters from one source can hardly be matched. I recommend posting both the English and Spanish versions, along with posters reflecting the other languages spoken by your church's employees. It is better to spend the extra few dollars than to have an employee misunderstand his rights and subsequently blame you for the misunderstanding.

- Texas Unemployment Compensation Act and Texas Payday Act Poster - One poster announces employees' basic rights under each of these acts. All Texas employers must display this poster in a prominent place accessible to employees.
- Texas Workers' Compensation Act Posters - This poster announces whether or not an employer carries workers' compensation insurance and directs employees as to how to report workplace safety violations. All Texas employers must display this poster and deliver handouts to its employees announcing their decision regarding whether or not to carry workers' compensation insurance.
- Equal Employment Opportunity Poster - This poster announces that discriminating against persons in employment decisions is illegal when those decisions are based on race, national origin, gender, religious preference, citizenship, and age. All Texas employers must display this poster in a prominent place accessible to employees.
- Fair Labor Standards Act Poster - This poster announces various rights which employees have in connection with minimum wage and overtime laws. All Texas employers must display this poster in a prominent place accessible to employees.
- Polygraph Protection Act Poster - This poster announces various rights which employees have in connection with polygraph tests. All Texas employers must display this poster in a prominent place accessible to employees.
- Family and Medical Leave Act Poster - This poster announces various rights which employees have in connection with leaves of absence from employment for medical or family-related reasons. Texas employers with over fifty employees within a

seventy-five mile radius must display this poster in a prominent place accessible to employees.

- OSHA Poster - This poster announces various duties which employers have under the Occupational Safety and Health Act.
- Texas Sales and Use Tax Certificate - Your church probably is exempt from obtaining such a certificate. See Chapter 7 for more details about this issue. However, almost all other Texas businesses, including non-profit entities who have not received or have lost their exempt status, must display this certificate at their respective places of business.

PERFORMANCE REVIEWS

Conduct periodic performance reviews. If an employee is doing a good job, then tell him so. Conversely, admonish poor performance honestly and tell an employee to straighten up if he needs that warning. Also, do not give good reviews to someone who does not deserve them. If a discharged employee later files a claim and you need to justify your decision to terminate him, then you will need all of the credibility that you can muster. Admitting that you were less than honest in evaluating that employee, even if you thought that you were doing so to give that an employee a break or the benefit of the doubt, will come back to haunt you. Similarly, do not fire an employee without warning after allowing him to work at an unacceptable level for years. That is unfair to the employee, who may have had no idea that his performance was poor or that he needed to improve it. Instead, work harder with him to assist him in raising his performance to an acceptable level.

LOANING MONEY TO EMPLOYEES

First, I advise all of my business clients not to loan money to any of their employees. For a variety of reasons, absent extraordinary circumstances, an employee seeking a loan from his employer is shooting a flare in the air. One of my clients who was in the regular habit of loaning money to his employees began referring to any employee loan as the "kiss of death," because he coincidentally, yet inevitably, fired the employee for misconduct shortly after making each loan. He lost the money almost every time. I would like to think that it is possible for a good employee to borrow money from an employer, to repay that loan, and for it not to affect their relationship, but that result has not occurred frequently. It simply puts an unnecessary and inappropriate strain on the relationship.

It also creates cumbersome compliance procedures for the employer if the loan is to be repaid through payroll deductions. In these cases, the Texas Payday Law requires that the employee execute a written authorization for the employer to withhold the repayment from the employee's paycheck.[281] Further, if interest is to be charged, then the rate and terms of repayment need to be in writing and executed by the employee. Most employers either do not realize this or do not bother with it, thinking that no employee could be so ungrateful as to raise these issues when the employer has been so gracious. A disgruntled employee probably will raise any issue as a defense to repaying the loan, though, especially if she has been fired.

Another difficult issue is whether or not the TNPCA's absolute ban on loans to directors applies to certain employees. Analyzing whether or not a particular employee is an officer or director of a non-profit corporation, when most church leaders are not called "directors," is an inexact science, at best. While this topic is addressed more specifically in Chapter 6, I believe that it is best to assume that any clergy member is a director for the purpose of receiving a loan from your church. Thus, your church should not make loans to its staff members.

In any of these situations, if the loan is not repaid, then the likelihood of your church ever recovering that money is extremely low. The reason is that it is extremely difficult and potentially expensive to collect personal debts of this nature in Texas. Bankruptcy is always an option for a person in financial difficulties and unsecured personal obligations are the debts most likely to be discharged in bankruptcy. In fact, the phrase "throwing good money after bad" may have been coined by an employer trying to collect a loan from a former employee. Once again, this is a stewardship argument. Is it a wise use of the church's assets to loan its money to an employee when that loan carries so many potentially negative consequences?

Supervisors

If an employee manages or supervises another employee, then he should have some type of management training. The employee in charge of human relations responsibilities at your church cannot be in every place at once. Those who supervise and manage must be able to do so effectively, being familiar with general employment policies and being able to apply those policies consistently. Supervisors should be trained in when and how to document various occurrences and in dealing with minor disciplinary issues. They also should receive periodic reviews and, perhaps, even specific training in appropriate employment law and human relations topics.

Further, while all managers and supervisors should be generally knowledgeable about employment law issues, your church should designate one person to be responsible for or at least involved in all termination decisions. This person should be knowledgeable about employment law issues and should be in charge of receiving any claims which a terminated employee may make after termination. Having responsibility for this function spread over a number of different people only increases the possibility of mistakes being made and minimizes the advantage of utilizing a person's expertise in this area.

GRIEVANCE / COMPLAINT REPORTING

Have an effective grievance / complaint system in place. This accomplishes several goals. First, it provides an avenue for your church to hear about, hopefully, small problems before they become big problems. Second, it is an outlet for employees to vent. Employees often feel frustrated by the seeming brick wall into which they must continually run. Simply voicing frustrations without fear of retribution is valuable for morale and knowing that some good might actually come of it is even better. Finally, if a claim arises and your church has a grievance system in place, yet it never knew about a certain problem before being dragged into court, you garner more sympathy for your defense. If the plaintiff hid his problem while your church had in place a system which could have averted the problem from arising or at least could have resolved it while it was manageable or before more damage was done, then your church has placed itself in a stronger (albeit assailable still) position to defend the claim.

DISCIPLINE AND TERMINATION OF EMPLOYEES

Firing and disciplining employees are never easy experiences for employers. There usually is far too much anguish involved in these decisions and there may be hard feelings, especially on the employee's part. I have yet to hear even one of my clients report that a discharged employee understood and agreed with the bases for the decision. Employees may take these decisions poorly, but there are right and wrong ways to go about this process in order to preserve the employee's dignity and to protect your church from a claim.

First, make considered, rational, and reasoned decisions. Firing or disciplining an employee in the heat of the moment is never good for keeping other employees' morale up or your blood pressure down. If necessary, walk away and live to fire another day.

Consult with your attorney, other staff members, and any oversight or personnel committees that may have valuable advice. Obtain as many perspectives on employee disciplinary issues as you can and, in most circumstances, investigate allegations before you confront the accused. In doing so, you may obviate the need for a confrontation by discovering that the allegation is unfounded or simply based on a misunderstanding. If the allegation is serious, then consider suspending the employee, with or without pay, prior to reaching a termination decision. If your investigation clears the employee, then simply remove the suspension and reinstate back pay, if necessary. In doing so, you have avoided terminating the employee, hopefully decreasing his motivation to make a claim against your church. If the investigation substantiates the allegation, then take further disciplinary action, if necessary, in addition to the suspension.

Know the employee handbook and enforce its provisions consistently. As discussed earlier, the handbook should set forth a system of progressive discipline. The number and progression of oral or written warnings will depend on the severity, frequency, purposefulness, and consequences of any employee's misconduct. The system should include verbal warnings for first or minor offenses and written warnings for serious or repeated offenses, reserving termination as a last resort. Of primary importance, though, is not to allow progressive discipline to handcuff your church when misconduct is so severe that it warrants immediate termination. Thus, your church's handbook should specifically reserve the right to terminate an employee immediately without prior notice or disciplinary action if any specific incident warrants termination. In order of increasing consequences, this system should include the following actions:

- verbal warning
- written warning
- written warning including a statement that your job is in jeopardy
- suspension with or without pay
- termination

While you may not equate the handbook with a written contract and while employers generally reserve the right to amend those handbooks unilaterally, the Fifth Circuit Court of Appeals has held that handbooks' provisions govern the parties' conduct while those provisions are in effect and that those handbooks' provisions are contractual in nature, even if they mandate employment at will relationships.[282] Thus, follow the handbook, especially in regard to documenting disciplinary actions and periodic performance reviews. Doing so should leave an employee with little, if any, room to argue that he did not anticipate being fired.

Respect an employee's right to disagree with action taken by your church. While an initial explanation of the church's position and the reasons behind any adverse employment action taken should be provided, both orally and in writing, the employee should retain the right to disagree without being browbeaten into submission. Cries of ""Confess!" justifiably died (or at least should have done so) with the Spanish Inquisition.

When your church takes disciplinary action against an employee, it should request that the employee sign a form acknowledging that he either agrees or disagrees with the facts stated on the form and the action taken by the church. Doing so in the former case provides evidence of the reasonableness of the church's actions and in the latter case documents the areas of conflict. If the employee refuses to sign the form, then the supervisor should note on the form that he was given an opportunity to sign the form, but declined.

When you have resolved to give only one more chance to an employee, then ensure that you communicate this fact to the employee. In most cases, I believe that employers make this resolution and then keep it to themselves. What good does keeping this resolution to yourself do, though? Write the words "your job is in jeopardy" on the written warning. This not only should communicate to the employee the seriousness of the situation, but also should communicate your reasonableness to a potential juror, in that you gave the employee fair warning of the potential consequences of his behavior. Another practical idea is that, if your church decides that it is necessary to discipline an employee, then two supervisors should be present during the meeting in which the discipline is discussed with the employee. Doing so provides the benefit of an added witness to what is said and done in that meeting.

When you are considering disciplining an employee, remember to respect that employee's right to engage in conduct which is protected by law. Are you disciplining him for being a member of a protected class, for engaging in protected conduct, or for conduct that you can support as misconduct? Remember all of the protected areas of conduct from earlier in this chapter. Taking adverse employment action against an employee because he is a member of a protected class of because he participated in a protected activity could have very adverse consequences for your church and even the individuals participating in that action.

Some types of employee behavior that could constitute misconduct are listed below:

- excessive tardiness
- excessive absenteeism
- failing to report an absence or tardiness pursuant to the church's policy

- failing to provide substantiation of illness, funeral leave, jury duty, military duty, or other situations affecting attendance
- insubordination
- using the church's property for personal business or gain
- failing to report an incident of personal injury or property damage
- theft, concealment, impairment, or destruction of church property
- assaulting, battering, threatening, discriminating against, harassing, or intimidating another employee or church member
- dishonesty regarding any aspect of employment
- commission of an illegal act associated with the church's affairs
- unjustifiably interfering with the performance of other employees' duties
- failing to notify a supervisor promptly of problems
- creating or contributing toward the creation of unsafe work conditions
- horseplay, sleeping, throwing things, loitering, loafing, *et cetera*
- being on the church's premises under the influence of illegal drugs or unapproved legal drugs
- tampering with or falsifying employment-related or church-related documents
- failure to follow stated instructions, rules, regulations, provisions, directives, orders, assignments, policies, or procedures, whether or not contained in the employee handbook

You also should document everything that could affect an employee's status. If it is important enough to impact on an employment decision (whether hiring, firing, promotion, demotion, raise, fringe benefits, *et cetera*), then it is important enough to document. While it increases the administrative workload, it also increases your credibility when it comes down to your word against a terminated employee's word on a particular issue.

If you decide that an employee should be terminated, then make every effort to preserve his dignity. The employee may make this impossible by his response, but "[c]ourtesy, common sense, and discretion will go a long way in preventing embarrassment and avoiding emotional distress."[283] Your good conduct, in turn, may make a valuable difference in whether or not that employee makes a claim against your church. Finally, if a terminated employee makes a claim against the church, then turn the matter over to an attorney immediately. We can no longer afford to rely on the church's good name as a rebuttal to every charge.

CHAPTER 9

Sticks and Stones, Bricks and Loans: Real Property

PURCHASING AND SELLING REAL PROPERTY

The purchase or sale of real property, more commonly called real estate, is a major step in almost any church's financial life. Such a decision brings with it a host of considerations. This chapter will attempt to highlight some of the more prominent issues which deserve consideration prior to your church making any decision in regard to real property.

The complexity of real property transactions seems to have increased exponentially over the past several years. With buyers and sellers voicing concerns regarding tax, consumer, insurance, and environmental rights, among others, it has become customary for a variety of people to become involved in each transaction. Licensed real estate brokers and agents, environmental consultants, engineers, surveyors, inspectors, insurance agents, attorneys, and title company examiners and closers are but a few of the people whose names commonly appear in a standard transaction file. Despite this trend, it is interesting to note that there is absolutely no law which mandates that any of these people be involved. If people knowledgeable about the real estate industry are not involved, though, then legal difficulties usually arise before and, especially, after the deal is done due to various, predictable errors which occur when a buyer and a seller try to circumvent the complex, confusing, and frustrating process of buying and selling real estate by themselves.

When considering purchasing a piece of property and in addition to being in prayer, your church should be asking itself the following questions.

- Will existing improvements meet your church's current needs?
- If improvements exist, is the lot size sufficient to allow for future construction?
- If no improvements exist, is the lot size sufficient to allow for current and future construction?
- Is there adequate parking and, if so, does it provide enough space for current and future members?
- Is access to the property from surrounding neighborhoods easy or difficult?
- Do the improvements provide enough storage space?
- Will your church be forced to rent or to build additional storage space for its personal property?
- Are there aspects of the property which may grow burdensome over time, *e.g.* mowing excess acreage, inefficient or outdated mechanical equipment which will lead to higher utility bills, or recreational equipment requiring fencing?
- Is the neighborhood in which the property is located likely to change significantly in the future?
- If so, how will these changes affect your church?
- Will zoning or deed restrictions prohibit any use that you have planned for the property?
- Are there any aspects of the property or the surrounding neighborhood which your church may consider to be incompatible with its mission and ministries?
- Is the degree and nature of any rehabilitation which your church will have to do to the improvements acceptable?
- Is the purchase price within your church's budget?
- Is the price of any needed improvements within your church's budget?
- Do current interest rates make monthly mortgage payments within your church's budget?
- Has your church accurately researched and estimated liability, hazard, flood, and windstorm insurance premiums and closing costs?
- If your church owns the property from which it will move, can it afford two monthly mortgage payments if the existing property does not sell quickly?
- If your church owns the property from which it will move, will there be continuing maintenance and utility responsibilities on the property to be vacated and, if so, what is the cost of those responsibilities?

- If your church leases the property from which it will move, can it afford the payments through the remaining term of the lease while also making a mortgage payment?
- If your church leases the property from which it will move, will there be continuing maintenance and utility responsibilities on the leased property until the lease expires and, if so, what is the cost of those responsibilities?
- Is your church being realistic about how much it will cost to move (movers, temporary storage charges, utility transfers and deposits, *et cetera*), in addition to the closing costs?
- Has your church assessed potential membership gain and loss resulting from the move?
- Has your church assessed the probabilities of the property's increase or decrease in value subsequent to the purchase?
- Has your church assessed the difficulty involved in any potential resale of the property?
- Has your church assessed any potential environmental hazards which the property may harbor?

PURCHASING AND SELLING REAL PROPERTY - BROKERS

The Texas Real Estate License Act governs who may represent buyers and sellers in transactions and dictates how and when a license may be obtained from the Texas Real Estate Commission ("TREC").[284] The brokerage and the property owner begin their relationship by executing a contract, usually referred to as a listing agreement, which sets forth the terms of the brokerage's representation. If your church desires to sell its property, then the brokerage attempts to sell the property for your church by advertising it and by soliciting offers for its purchase. If your church desires to purchase property, then it may request a specific broker to seek out many potential properties or it may choose to deal directly with the brokerage or broker which lists a particular property for sale.

Brokerages cooperate with each other in the sale of real property. Most brokerages subscribe to a service which maintains all sales listings and includes pertinent information on individual properties. In this manner, almost every piece of property listed in a given area is at the fingertips of other participating brokerages at the speed of the personal computer. When a prospective buyer approaches a broker for the purpose of making an offer on a property or seeking that broker's assistance in viewing various properties, that broker is sometimes referred to as the "co-op broker" or "selling broker." The selling broker receives permission from the brokerage which listed the property, sometimes referred to as the "listing broker," to show the property to the prospective buyer.

Confusion can result when your church believes that a selling broker represents its interests. Unless your church specifically contracts with a broker or agent to represent it, any broker or agent involved in the transaction represents only the seller's interests. Thus, if your church is in the middle of a negotiation and informs the selling broker that what it has offered is not the highest price that it will pay, consider that information already to have been conveyed to the seller. In order to avoid this confusion, brokers and agents are now required to provide written disclosure to potential buyers of the nature of their representation and the beneficiary of their duty of loyalty, which usually is the seller.[285]

Selling brokers and listing brokers play important roles in these transactions. They assist the seller and buyer in negotiating the sale of the property, in arranging any desired inspections, and in counseling the parties through the closing process. They remain in close contact with the seller and buyer to ensure that the transaction closes and are usually paid only if a sale closes and funds, with a percentage of the purchase price being shared among the participating brokerages, brokers, and agents. Their fees are listed on the closing statement and should be determined by the percentage stated in the listing agreement, which usually is six percent. While that percentage is standard, it is not mandated by statute and is negotiable.

PURCHASING AND SELLING REAL PROPERTY - INSPECTIONS

If the property which your church is buying is residential and consists of "not more than one dwelling," then, in conjunction with the inspections and contemporaneously with or shortly after the execution of the earnest money contract, the seller should deliver a written, signed disclosure of the property's condition to you.[286] Review both of these documents carefully. If the inspector's report or the seller's disclosure reveals any problems with the property, then you should evaluate your decision to purchase the property in light of the significance of those problems. Further, if the seller fails to deliver the disclosure to you along with the execution of the earnest money contract, then you have seven days after the actual date of delivery to terminate the contract.[287] There is a property condition disclosure form for commercial property, also, but its use is optional, as contrasted with the mandatory residential form.

If your church is in the seller's role, then review any disclosure form carefully to ensure that all of the information is correct. A knowing failure to disclose a problem could raise the specter of fraud or a deceptive trade practice claim against your church and any individuals who signed the disclosure form or participated in completing it. Remember that the disclosure form applies only to residential, "one dwelling" properties, though, and that this scenario usually will arise in the context of a parsonage or other dwelling for a staff member. However, some churches have purchased residential property for non-residential purposes, such as the following:

- administrative offices for church staff
- counseling centers
- youth activities
- support groups
- educational space
- in contemplation of demolition of the improvements for future expansion

Regardless of whether the property your church purchases is considered residential or commercial, new or old, your church should hire an inspector to check out, among others, the following areas of concern:

- heating, ventilation, and air conditioning systems
- electrical system
- plumbing system
- gas system
- structural system
- termites
- roof
- foundation
- insulation
- appliances
- lead paint (especially if the building will be occupied by children)
- radon gas

Prior to sending an inspector to any building, all utilities should be turned on. Detecting leaks, electrical shorts, *et cetera* in a building with no utilities turns an easy process into an impossible one for an inspector. To become familiar with the inspection process, read any of the many topical books, in addition to retaining qualified inspectors. Some properties, such as those formerly used in manufacturing or in transporting liquids or chemicals, also should receive an environmental inspection before you sign on the dotted line. This type of inspection only should be undertaken by an environmental engineer, consultant, or inspector who specializes in this type of issue.

PURCHASING AND SELLING REAL PROPERTY - FINANCING

There are many financing sources. That is the good news. The bad news is that they all take time to investigate and many charge an application fee. Thus, even asking for a loan may be an expensive process, placing your church in the somewhat ironic situation of having to pay someone for the privilege of admitting that you do not have enough money to purchase something. Denominations, related institutions, private mortgage companies, financial institutions, assumable mortgages, and even owner financing are some of the more common financing sources from which your church may be able to secure financing. Different lenders, however, offer different loan programs. You should review these different programs and their individual requirements very carefully, selecting the program which fits your church's needs best. Your church also might want to consider raising the money internally prior to the purchase or construction as an option. Such programs are commonly known as "building campaigns" and there are a number of companies, many of which view themselves as a ministry, which specialize in assisting churches in this process.

All lenders require a written loan application and supporting documentation, which they will review closely. Upon submitting your application, you may receive a copy of a booklet entitled *Settlement Costs*, which also discusses some of the issues addressed in this chapter. Your lender will review your church's credit history and scrutinize recent financial records to verify that your church has the financial resources and sufficient forecasted income to make the monthly payments. Your church also may be required to submit financial statements, explanations of any derogatory credit references, copies of existing leases or other documentation of real estate interests, and copies of other documents which may have an impact on its financial status. In some cases, certain members of your congregation even may be asked to guarantee the loan personally. By definition, lenders are in business to make money from their loans and they want to minimize the risk of your church defaulting. Thus, they will be very thorough, even picky, in analyzing your church's finances.

PURCHASING AND SELLING REAL PROPERTY - FINANCING - APPRAISALS

If your church is seeking third party financing, then the lender will require that the property be appraised by an independent appraiser. The lender requires an appraisal because it wants to ensure that the property is worth more than the loan amount which your church has requested. Why should this matter if your church intends to pay for the property exactly as it has promised? It matters because your church's lender probably has had the experience of not being paid exactly as promised and knows that it may have to foreclose its lien on the property if your church defaults in repaying the loan. That means that the lender will sell the property, even against your church's wishes, to recoup the balance owed on the loan. As properties used by churches have a very limited number of uses and buyers, demand is traditionally low and no lender wants to take a bath, regardless of your church's baptismal method, if your church defaults on the loan. Thus, an appraisal is a very important part of the financing process, especially for the lender.

The goal of the appraisal is to render an opinion on the property's fair market value. Fair market value, in turn, is the price a property would be sold for if the following conditions exist:

- if payment is made in cash or cash equivalent
- if the property is marketed for a reasonable length of time
- if the buyer and seller are reasonably informed as to the property's uses, characteristics, and condition
- if neither the buyer nor the seller is under unusual pressure to buy or to sell
- if the seller can convey marketable title.

There are many approaches to appraising real estate. The most common three are the market, cost, and income approaches. To deal with the last first, the income approach usually is used when appraising income-producing properties, such as apartment complexes, strip centers, shopping malls, and office buildings. Thus, it really is not very useful in appraising properties used by churches.

The market approach involves reviewing recent sales data for similar properties and comparing those properties to the subject property. Differences among the properties are noted (one may be larger, another may have been sold by a distressed seller, yet another may be in notably better condition) and adjustments are made for these differences. This description is, necessarily, a very cursory way of describing what is in practice a very detailed and sophisticated process.

The cost approach estimates the value of the land as if it were vacant, adding the estimated cost of constructing improvements similar to those existing and then subtracting an amount for depreciation on the improvements. These seemingly simple three steps have a great deal of room for variation, though. Estimating the value of vacant land is problematic, although appraisers certainly have methods to deal with this problem. Further, estimating construction costs is not exactly a precise science, either. Added to that are the many different methods for determining a building's depreciation. With so many variables, the cost approach may or may not approach the degree of definiteness desired by a lender.

PURCHASING AND SELLING REAL PROPERTY - FINANCING - ASSUMPTIONS

Assumption transactions provide a convenient way to convey property in many cases. Essentially, the buyer assumes the indebtedness owed on the property and, depending on the purchase price, pays an additional amount to the seller for its equity. The buyer agrees to pay the existing loan, originally taken out by the seller, according to the loan's terms, without having to search for new financing. Some of these loans are conditionally assumable, in that the lender has the right to accept or to reject the prospective buyer as the new owner, usually based on the lender's financial criteria. Lenders do not have that right in other assumable loans and must accept the new owner as the one obligated to repay the loan. In either case, the documentation originally executed between the seller and the lender will govern the parties' rights.

Similarly, simply because a loan can be assumed does not mean that the original borrower is necessarily released from his obligation to repay the loan when the buyer assumes it. Again, the loan documentation determines the parties' rights. If the seller remains liable on the loan, then it is critical for the seller to be able to monitor the buyer's repayment of the loan and performance under the note and deed of trust, perhaps through notices of default from the lender, and to be able to cure any default which the buyer commits. If the buyer defaults and the seller does not cure the default, then the lender may foreclose its lien on the property and sue the seller and the buyer for the balance owed on the note. This could lead to an unbearable financial loss with few, if any, viable alternatives, instead of the profitable sale which the seller thought that it had arranged years before. Thus, in an assumption transaction it is imperative for the seller to obtain a release from the lender if the seller's intention is to rid itself of its liabilities under the note and deed of trust and to sever its financial ties. If it does not do so, then it may remain liable for the original indebtedness for years, perhaps even after the buyer conveys the property to a subsequent assuming buyer.

PURCHASING AND SELLING REAL PROPERTY - DOCUMENTATION

The first substantive step in acquiring real property in Texas usually is the preparation, offer, and acceptance of an earnest money contract. As is apparent from the document's name, contract law bears heavily on this document and others involved in the process.

The process of offer and acceptance in real estate transactions is a game of "chicken." The buyer offers to buy the property through forwarding a partially executed earnest money contract to the seller, along with a check for earnest money. The seller and buyer usually will exchange a series of counteroffers, gradually working toward an agreeable price, knowing that either one of them can walk away from this process at any point if the other's response is unacceptable. Eventually, they either reach an impasse or agreement. In addition to price, other issues usually addressed in the earnest money contract are as follows:

- closing deadlines
- the amount of earnest money
- purchase price details
- financing conditions
- payment of transaction expenses
- inspections
- repairs
- title insurance
- surveys
- taxes
- tax and insurance prorations
- casualty loss
- condemnation
- property condition disclosures and representations
- default remedies
- contract assignability
- broker's fees

Aside from the disclosure regarding the broker's representation, the earnest money contract probably is the first document which any buyer signs. As a buyer, it demonstrates your intention and binds you to carry through with the purchase of a certain piece of property. Brokers, sellers, and others may refer to this contract as a real estate sales contract or purchase and sale agreement, as well as many other variations on those names. It is, nonetheless, a legally binding contract and your church should not sign it under any circumstances without having an attorney review it. It sets forth the rules governing the transaction and has far-reaching ramifications, many or most of which you may not be aware when you sign it. You should insist as a buyer on including clauses which allow you to terminate the contract and to receive the earnest money if:

- you cannot secure favorable financing within a certain period, if applicable
- the inspections which you require or your lender requires yield unsatisfactory results
- you cannot sell existing property within a certain time period, if applicable
- the title commitment reveals title defects which cannot be cured within a reasonable time by the seller
- the survey reveals problems which cannot be cured within a reasonable time by the seller
- the seller fails to produce certain documents for your review and approval, such as the seller's utility bills, prior inspection reports, building plans, maintenance and repair records, and building and appliance warranties
- you determine that purchasing the property simply is not feasible for you, to be accompanied by the payment of separate consideration to avoid the contract being declared an unenforceable option contract

These clauses are sometimes referred to as "escape clauses" and allow buyers to terminate the contract without a significant loss in time and money.

A word of caution is in order here, though. Simply having the right to have the earnest money refunded does not mean that the check is in the mail. A title insurance company will require that the seller and the buyer sign a release instructing it as to how the earnest money should be refunded before it will issue a check. A seller may become angry when a buyer terminates a contract and may refuse to release the earnest money. That seller may feel that the buyer terminated the contract without cause and, therefore, should not receive a refund of the earnest money. Likewise, a buyer who terminates a contract without cause may not desire for the seller to receive the earnest money as liquidated damages, even though the earnest money contract specifically calls for that result. In either case, the amount of any eventual recovery may not justify paying an attorney to sue the other party.

Naturally, the seller will want to limit the escape clauses' scope and the buyer will want them as broadly worded as possible. However, these clauses are subject to negotiation, just like every part of the contract, and you should expect some give and take as a part of that process. As a corollary to that comment, do not let a broker or seller tell you that you have to do something, you cannot do something else, or you have to pay this or that cost. Unless there is an applicable law mandating that one party perform some act, virtually every aspect of a real estate transaction is negotiable. While some standard practices as to which party bears what cost may be followed, you should not let anyone, except your attorney, tell you that you, as a buyer, must do something. If a person cannot produce a copy of the law telling you that you must do it, then it is subject to negotiation.

The most heavily negotiated item in real estate transactions is the price. That is crucial to any deal. However, a variety of other issues play a very important role in whether or not you should commit to and, after you have committed, whether or not you should consummate a certain transaction. These issues include the following:

- the closing date
- the possession date, if that differs from the closing date
- who bears which closing costs
- how much or if the seller must pay for repairs you require or your lender requires before it approves your loan
- whether the seller will warrant the condition of the building or certain features, such as appliances
- what personal property belonging to the seller remains with the building after closing
- what mineral rights, if any, the seller or prior sellers have retained
- the possibility and potential consequences of a tax rollback
- the resolution of title commitment exceptions
- the resolution of survey discrepancies

At closing, the seller conveys the property to the buyer in a deed. There are several types of deeds, with general warranty deeds and special warranty deeds predominating. The title company, which not only issues the title policy, but also closes the transaction, collects the buyer's money and withholds enough money from the purchase price to satisfy any indebtedness owed by the seller arising from transaction expenses, existing financing, taxes, or other outstanding liens. It then tenders the balance, if any, to the seller. If the buyer finances any part of the purchase price, then the buyer probably will be required to execute a promissory note and deed of trust for the lender's benefit. The promissory note evidences the buyer's promise to repay the money which the lender (which can be the seller as well as a third party like a bank, credit union, or mortgage company) has loaned for the purchase of the property. The deed of trust obligates the buyer to maintain the property, to pay the taxes, to insure the property, and to do anything else which the lender requires in order to make the lender as comfortable as possible with the soundness of the collateral securing its loan. The deed of trust also contains provisions which allow the lender to foreclose its lien on the property if the buyer does not comply with any of the deed of trust's or promissory note's provisions, usually occasioned by the buyer failing to make the loan payments on a timely basis.

In the past, closings consisted of the buyer signing a promissory note and a deed of trust, with the seller signing a deed. Those still are the three most important documents. However, because experience is a hard teacher and because sellers, buyers, title companies, brokers, lenders, lawyers, appraisers, surveyors, and all of the people involved in real estate want to minimize their risk as much as possible in these situations, closings now usually take at least one hour, consisting mostly of the buyer and seller signing all kinds of different documents. Among these documents are the following:

- promissory note - The buyer promises to pay the lender a certain amount of principal and interest at specified dates and a specified interest rate for a specified length of time.
- deed of trust - The buyer grants a lien on the property for the lender's benefit. If the buyer does not abide by the deed of trust or pay the promissory note, then the lender can foreclose on this lien, becoming the new owner or selling the property to another person or entity. If this happens, then you will lose title to and possession of the property, along with the money which you have invested, and perhaps be sued for any deficiency remaining on the note after application of the proceeds from the foreclosure sale.
- deed - The seller executes this document to demonstrate that legal title has passed to the buyer.
- owner's / lender's title insurance policies - These are contracts of indemnity protecting you and your lender against defects in the title to your property. When the seller sells the property *via* a general warranty deed, he is warranting that he has conveyed legal title to you and that no one, except those shown on the preliminary title commitment, has a claim on the property. The title policy will exclude certain defects which it finds prior to closing from its coverage, such as purchase money liens, judgment liens, tax liens, mineral interests, and easements.
- settlement statement - Also called a HUD-1 statement, this document lists all of the costs which are assessed and paid at closing, to whom those costs are paid, and by whom those costs are paid.
- good faith estimate of closing costs - While not a closing document, it is just that, an estimate, and does not reflect the final figure. Your lender prepares it in conjunction with the submission of your loan application and you should receive it shortly after submitting your loan application.
- various notices from your lender - These notices will tell you where to send your payment, when your payments are due, what and when late charges apply, that

your loan may be sold to a third party, *et cetera*.

- federal truth-in-lending disclosure statement - This document explains what your interest rate will be, how much your monthly principal and interest payment will be, how much in interest you will pay over the life of your loan, whether or not your loan is assumable, whether or not your loan contains a prepayment penalty, and the amount and application of late charges.

- tax affidavits and tax information requests - These documents allow your lender to rely upon and to verify the information which you supplied on your loan application. They sometimes are used to do so after you have defaulted. If you supplied false information on the application, serious, perhaps even criminal, consequences could follow. Always be truthful when submitting financial information, even if it means that you fail to qualify for a loan.

- survey - This document is a drawing which shows where all improvements, encroachments, and easements sit on your property. It should contain a legally sufficient property description and outline buildings as they are situated on the property. It should note the dimensions of all buildings, parking lots, driveways, garages, outbuildings, sidewalks, and other improvements. It also should note any easements affecting the property, as well as improvements built by surrounding property owners which may encroach on your church's property line. Finally, it should note building setback lines and determine whether or not any buildings comply with those restrictions.

- escrow account notices - These notices will tell you how much your monthly escrow payments will be and which obligations those payments satisfy.

- disclosure regarding legal representation - This document will tell you that any lawyer, except the church's lawyer, who is involved in the transaction represents not your church, but his client, and, as such, is not looking out for your church's best interests.

- various affidavits - Your church may attest to such things in these documents as its incorporation, its intention to use the property in compliance with deed restrictions or zoning regulations, the correctness of any information supplied to its lender on the loan application, *et cetera*.

- corporate resolutions - Your church and its officers will attest to the fact that the church desires to acquire or to sell the property, that the church followed its own procedures properly in deciding to acquire or to sell the property, and that the person at closing is authorized to execute closing documents on your church's behalf.

- various title company forms - Your church and its officers will sign forms acknowledging that you have received certain documents, forms acknowledging that the title company has not made any representations or warranties or given any legal advice to you, forms acknowledging the truthfulness of information which you have provided, and other forms limiting the scope of the title company's liability.

This by no means is a complete list. Each title company and each transaction will have different procedures and forms. Suffice it to say that your hand may be cramped when you finish closing.

PURCHASING AND SELLING REAL PROPERTY - TITLE INSURANCE COMPANIES

Once your church has closed the transaction through which it is purchasing property, all concerns about the property are over. Right? Wrong! Imagine your church's horror when it discovers that neither the seller nor the title company disclosed an easement through the middle of the parking lot in favor of the monthly motorcycle rally? That is an extreme example, but it demonstrates how much we have come to rely on title insurance companies to tell us what defects in title exist that affect property. An easement is an example of a defect in title in that it detracts from the owner's ability to use the property as he wishes.

What does a title insurance company do? Essentially, it does three things. First, it researches the status of title to a property. After it receives a properly executed earnest money contract and the earnest money, it issues a preliminary title commitment containing, among other information, the buyer's and seller's identity, a legally sufficient description of the property, and any defects in title. The foremost defect in title is a lien, which may be granted in a deed of trust. These liens affect the property in that the lienholder generally may foreclose the lien and sell the property against the owner's wishes if the owner defaults in the repayment of the debt underlying the lien. Any amounts received at foreclosure are then applied to the debt, a process which may or may not relieve the owner of responsibility for satisfying any remaining balance *vis a vis* the debt. Further, these liens are not extinguished by an owner's covert sale of the property and remain valid even though ownership changes hands.

One or more purchase money liens may be found on many, if not most, properties in our state. Other examples of liens include the following:

- judgment liens - filed by a person who receives a judgment from a court against one who owns real property

- tax liens - filed by governmental agencies who have a right to collect unpaid taxes attributable to the property or its owner
- mechanic's and materialmen's liens - filed by those who have supplied materials or furnished labor in connection with the construction of improvements on the property.

An easement, a right held by a third party to use another person's property, is another example of a defect in title. Utility companies commonly hold easements to perform work on their wires, cables, support poles, pipes, *et cetera*. Community associations, governmental entities, and even adjoining landowners are some of the other typical easement holders who may need to use part of your church's property for some purpose. Another example of a defect in title is an encroachment. An encroachment usually occurs when an improvement constructed by an adjoining landowner goes just a bit beyond the property line and sits on your church's property. Further, building setback lines, in place through municipal ordinance, zoning, or deed restrictions, prohibit property owners from constructing any improvements within a given number of feet from the property's boundaries.

When the title insurance company has researched these issues and is certain that it has noted all that it can find in the county real property records, it will issue a preliminary title commitment, setting forth exactly how any defects in title affect a property. If the commitment lists defects, then your church essentially has two options. First, your church can ignore those defects and proceed with closing. Depending upon the type of defect, though, that may not be in your church's best interests. If defects exist, then your church may object to a defect, unless that defect is disclosed and agreed to in the earnest money contract, and demand that the seller cure the defect before closing occurs. If the seller cures the defect, then the transaction can proceed. If the seller refuses to cure the defect, though, then your church can resort to the first option, proceeding with closing with knowledge of the defect, or terminate the contract. To complicate matters, if your church is financing the purchase of the property with a third party lender, then it is likely that the lender will require that any defects in title be cured as a condition precedent to its obligation to fund the loan.

If the parties can work their way through all of these issues, then the title insurance company will organize all of the documents which the parties and / or lenders may require and will prepare a settlement statement setting forth all of the closing costs. The title insurance company will make the arrangements necessary to secure the execution of all of these documents, receive the buyer's and lender's payments toward the purchase price, pay all third parties entitled to receive payments from the closing, secure the release of any liens, and, if any money remains, give the seller a check for the balance. This is a time consuming and somewhat complicated service which title insurance companies provide in addition to the issuance of the title insurance policy.

Finally, at closing or shortly thereafter, the title insurance company will issue a title insurance policy for the buyer's and, perhaps, the lender's benefit. The policy insures that the buyer has acquired marketable title to the property, with the exception of any defects in title listed in the commitment and the policy. Importantly, a title insurance policy does not insure that the buyer has done or will be able to do any of the following:

- made a good deal when buying the property
- sell the property for the original purchase price
- sell the property at all
- use the property as intended
- find the property to be in the represented condition once the buyer takes possession

A title insurance policy simply insures that the title is *marketable* or, in other words, able to be conveyed to a third party. If any defects in title exist at the time of closing which are not noted in the commitment and the policy, then the title insurance company will be obligated to indemnify the buyer against any damages sustained as a result of the defect in an amount not to exceed the policy's coverage limits. Conversely, if those defects arise after the closing occurs, then the title insurance company will bear no responsibility for them at all.

PURCHASING AND SELLING REAL PROPERTY - CLOSING COSTS

You may think of the greatest expense in closing a real estate transaction as your down payment. That may not be true. Closing costs usually range from four to six percent of the purchase price and are a very significant and surprisingly high component of buying real estate. Sellers, like buyers, want to minimize the amount of closing costs. The seller is trying to close this deal as inexpensively as the buyer and may need the money from closing for another deal. Historically, most closing costs, excluding brokers' commissions and title insurance premiums, are borne by the buyer and may include charges for such services and products as:

- appraisal fees
- loan origination fees
- lender's attorney's fees

- loan buydown fees
- surveyor's fees
- courier/messenger fees
- inspection fees
- title examination fees
- administrative fees
- tax certificate fees
- insurance premiums
- warranty premiums
- community association fees
- taxes
- bank wiring fees
- recording fees
- notary public fees
- credit report fees
- private mortgage insurance premiums

These charges will be listed on a document called "Settlement Statement" and should be available to you to review before closing, just as a document called "Good Faith Estimate of Closing Costs" should be available to you shortly after submitting your loan application. As an aside, inspection fees should be paid outside of closing and independently of whether or not you close the sale. Do you really want to trust a building's integrity to an inspector who has a vested interest in the sale closing? You should refuse to work with any inspector who offers his services contingent upon a closing.

LEASING REAL PROPERTY

It may seem somewhat less complicated to lease a piece of property than to buy it, but that may be deceiving. The landlord must decide with what portions of the property he is willing to part, for how long, and for how much. Further, the continuing viability of any lease is dependent upon both the landlord and the tenant performing each and every obligation of the lease throughout its entire term. Conversely, in a sale, the closing should be the end of all issues.

Among the issues with which your church should be concerned when it leases property as a landlord or tenant are as follows:

- the lease term, *i.e.* how long the lease will last

- options to renew the lease or to purchase the property
- description of the property
- limitations on access to portions of the property
- identity of the landlord and tenant
- amount of and payment schedule for rent
- restrictions on the use of the property
- responsibility for utility charges, taxes, insurance, maintenance, and repairs
- indemnification clause for the landlord's benefit
- landlord's right to inspect the property
- security deposit terms
- existence and applicability of any implied or express warranties
- condemnation or destruction of the property
- eminent domain
- construction of improvements on the property
- assigning the lease or subleasing the property
- default
- remedies for default, including liens
- holdover situations

There may be more issues that should be included in a lease depending on the given situation. Further, the law regarding leases can vary, depending on whether the lease involved is a residential or commercial lease. That line may become blurred if your church leases a house for an institutional purpose. Add to these complexities the fact that many leases vary some statute's requirements by containing agreements designed to counteract the statute's requirements and you have the recipe for a very confusing situation. This should be enough to convince you that leasing can be very complicated.

LEASING REAL PROPERTY - *AD VALOREM* TAXES

One problematic issue in leasing real property which is exempt from *ad valorem* taxation is that a church may lose the exemption on the portion of property which it leases to a third party. If you will review the exemption requirements in Chapter 7, you will remember that the government focuses on the use of the property. If your church owns the property and leases it to a third party whose use of the property is primarily for religious purposes, then your church may be able to retain the exemption. This issue remains undecided, though, and I have not been able to locate a case resolving this scenario. However, if you lease that same property to a third party whose use of the property is not primarily for religious purposes, then you should deduct the added expense of paying *ad valorem* taxes from the gross amount which you envision receiving from the lease. Such a use of the property probably will not allow your church to retain the exemption from *ad valorem* taxes.

LEASING REAL PROPERTY - SECURITY DEPOSITS

Many people believe that a security deposit is simply an advance payment of the last month's rent under a lease. That is simply not the case.[288] Unless contractually agreed, a tenant is never justified in telling the landlord to take his last month's rent or any month's rent out of the security deposit. In fact, a tenant who pursues this course may be liable to a landlord for treble damages and attorney's fees and expenses.[289]

The security deposit is a deposit required by the landlord, usually equal to one month's rent, but which may be more or less, to assure the landlord that any amounts not paid under the lease or any damage done to the leased premises will be paid. Obviously, more damage could be done to any property than is represented by the average security deposit, but it usually is economically untenable to request any higher amount. Needing monthly income, landlords are not about to drive themselves out of a lease by demanding an excessive security deposit, thereby forcing a prospective tenant to seek another property.

Under most leases, a landlord may deduct amounts from the security deposit for, among other items, delinquent rental payments and any amounts necessary to repair damage to the leased premises for which the tenant is liable. If the landlord makes these deductions, then it is the tenant's responsibility to replenish the security deposit to the point at which it equals the original security deposit amount. Further, the landlord has no responsibility to maintain the security deposit in an interest bearing account or to credit the tenant with any interest earned on the security deposit during the term of the lease, even if the landlord is earning interest from the security deposit. It is very rare for interest from a security deposit to be credited to a tenant, except in some sophisticated commercial leases.

If a tenant pays his rent on time, abides by the lease's terms, leaves the property in good condition (normal wear and tear excepted), and leaves his forwarding address with the landlord at the expiration of the lease, then there is no reason that he should not receive a full refund of the security deposit within thirty days after the expiration of the lease. Unless the landlord has legally justifiable deductions which he may take from the security deposit, he has an obligation to forward the full amount of the security deposit to the tenant within this time frame.[290] A landlord's failure to do so may result in liability for the amount of the security deposit, attorney's fees and expenses, and other damages for acting in bad faith.[291]

LEASING REAL PROPERTY - LANDLORD'S DEFAULT

Most of us think that a landlord's job description consists of cashing checks every month. That is not the sum total of a landlord's job, though. Depending on the nature of the building and the language contained in your lease, the landlord may have various responsibilities to repair the leased premises, to ensure that they are habitable or suitable for your intended purpose, and to provide certain security-related equipment, *e.g.* front door peepholes, deadbolts, locks on windows, and smoke detectors.

Additionally, during periods between leases, the landlord must clean the leased premises and make any needed repairs or improvements to attract new tenants. A landlord also may need to protect your enjoyment of the leased premises from others, such as tenants or other landowners occupying nearby property. A landlord must pay *ad valorem* taxes on the property and, if a mortgage exists, must continue making mortgage payments on a timely basis. A landlord's failure to pay the government and the lender will subject the property to foreclosure, which probably will terminate the lease and will make everyone's life a little more complicated. Further, if the leased premises are damaged or destroyed by fire, storm, flood, *et cetera*, then your lease will speak to any responsibilities which the landlord has regarding repairing or replacing the leased premises and your obligation, if any, to continue paying rent while the leased premises cannot be used. If the leased premises are damaged or destroyed to the extent that you cannot continue using them, albeit temporarily, then the insurance which the landlord hopefully has in place should assist in quickly restoring the leased premises to a usable condition.

What can a tenant do if the landlord defaults in performing these obligations? The short answer is not nearly as much as the landlord can do to a tenant if the roles are reversed. Aside from an obligation to refund the security deposit, a landlord's primary obligation under most leases is to make repairs to the leased premises. Each lease differs in what a landlord must do and there are different statutory standards governing residential and commercial property, which may or may not be modified or replaced by the lease's terms, so a careful review of the lease and the appropriate statutes is always the first step in evaluating a landlord's responsibilities.

If a landlord has a duty to make repairs, then that duty usually will not arise unless the tenant notifies the landlord of the problem in writing. A landlord usually will have a reasonable amount of time in which to make any needed repair, but if he fails to do so, then a tenant's only recourse usually is to notify a landlord of the problem again and, as always, in writing. If a landlord fails to make the needed repair after a second notice, then a tenant can make the needed repair and withhold the amount actually paid from the next month's rent under certain circumstances. Doing so correctly is a difficult task, though, and it is rarely done properly, resulting in a tenant breaching the lease by not paying the appropriate amount of rent. My advice to tenants usually is to keep paying rent and to keep writing letters to the landlord until the problem is corrected. It usually does not hurt for those letters to contain various statements of what the tenant intends to do and to inform the landlord that the tenant knows his rights.

LEASING REAL PROPERTY - TENANT'S DEFAULT

When a tenant defaults, it usually is in the timely payment of the monthly rent. Most leases provide for the payment of rent on the first day of a month, with payment being accepted through the fifth or so day without a late fee. There are many other ways to breach a lease, though, including the following:

- failing to maintain the leased premises in good condition
- failing to maintain minimum insurance amounts agreed to in the lease
- failing to indemnify the landlord for any claims made against the landlord as a result of the tenant's use of the leased premises
- using the leased premises for a purpose prohibited by the lease
- creating or sustaining a nuisance which presents a danger to the public or which threatens surrounding landowners' and tenants' quiet enjoyment of their property
- holding over after the lease's expiration
- failing to replenish the amount of the security deposit if the landlord makes any deductions
- failing to allow the landlord to inspect or to make repairs to the leased premises
- making improvements to the leased premises without the landlord's prior, written approval

- assigning the lease or subletting the leased premises without the landlord's prior, written approval

What are a landlord's options? In regard to late payments, a landlord typically will enforce a late fee, that being either a stated amount or a percentage of the monthly rent. However, depending on the circumstances, a tenant's default entitles a landlord to resort to any one or more of an array of remedies, including the following:

- ignoring the default
- charging the tenant with the cost of repairing any damage done to the leased premises by the tenant or the tenant's guests
- changing the locks, in some cases
- terminating the utility service, in some cases
- terminating the lease and taking possession of the leased premises, charging the tenant with the amount of rent due through the date of termination
- terminating the lease and taking possession of the leased premises, reletting the leased premises to a third party, and charging the difference in rental received over the tenant's original term to the tenant
- without terminating the lease, taking possession of the leased premises and continuing to charge all accruing rent to the tenant
- taking possession of the tenant's personal property through exercise of either a statutory or contractual lien
- charging the tenant with a reletting fee
- charging the tenant with a termination fee
- charging the tenant with the costs of cleaning the leased premises and preparing the leased premises for a subsequent tenant
- suing the tenant for eviction, if the tenant will not vacate the leased premises
- suing the tenant for amounts due under the lease, including attorney's fees and expenses

LEASING REAL PROPERTY - ASSIGNMENT AND SUBLETTING

There is no inherent right enabling a tenant to assign a lease or to sublet the leased premises to a third party. Indeed, most leases specifically prohibit assignment and subletting without specific, written approval from the landlord. Thus, even if your church desires to move and finds a tenant to fulfill the remaining lease term, do not assume that all is well. A landlord is justified in reviewing the prospective tenant's financial records, rental history, *et cetera* and in making his decision to accept or to reject a proposed subtenant on his own criteria. A landlord may demand an increased rental amount, an increased security deposit, or other consideration for accepting the proposed subtenant. Further, a landlord may not necessarily relieve your church of liability on the lease even if it accepts the new tenant. If being released from liability on the lease is a major consideration for your church, then be prepared in all but the most favorable of circumstances either to pay for that privilege or to be disappointed.

PREMISES LIABILITY

Two words to remember as a property owner and tenant are premises liability. We look at this personal injury concept in greater depth in Chapter 4, Chapter 5, and Chapter 11. Simply put, you owe a duty of reasonable care to your invitees. When you know or should know of a condition on your property which poses an unreasonable risk of harm to invitees, then you must take whatever action is reasonably prudent under the circumstances to eliminate or to reduce the unreasonable risk. The duty which you owe to a licensee is similar: you must avoid injuring him willfully, wantonly, or through gross negligence, in addition to warning him of any dangers of which he is not aware, but you are.

If someone on your property is a trespasser, then you must avoid wantonly or willfully injuring that person. I assume that this latter duty will seldom be an issue for churches. Trespasser injury cases usually involve a property owner taking unduly extreme measures to protect his property, such as setting animal traps or trip-wire guns specifically to deter trespassers. Thus, aside from the obvious advice to avoid those measures, the trespasser duty should not be a huge concern for the church.

The former two duties are big concerns, however, and have given rise to significant claims against churches. The best advice is to keep your eyes open for potential claims. Your church should have a set procedure for inspecting and visibly marking any suspect facilities or equipment as needing further inspection, repair, and/or replacement. There also should be a set procedure for notifying those responsible for tending to an item so that a clear path of accountability is established. Marking pieces of equipment or property, such as a defective handrail, a slippery floor, or a faulty electrical outlet, provides a visible reminder to church staff to do something about a problem and a visible warning to invitees and licensees to avoid a potentially dangerous situation. Noting and correcting problems before accidents occur is the key to avoiding premises liability claims.

ZONING AND DEED RESTRICTIONS

Deed restrictions, also referred to as restrictive covenants, affect a significant number of buildings in planned communities. These restrictions usually deal with matters like the following:

- how the association governs itself
- how assessments are levied
- specific rules governing driveways, building setback lines, antennae, fences, signs, *et cetera* within the community
- architectural control committees' authority over subsequent improvements
- easements and other restrictions on the use of your property
- the types of buildings and activities which may occur within the affected community

Zoning regulations have a similar effect. One significant difference, though, is that the enforcement of zoning regulations falls to a municipal government, which usually has a separate department staffed by one or more employees who are familiar with the zoning regulations by chapter and verse. Enforcement by an association, which usually has no employees and may be staffed by people who were unfortunate enough to have been absent at the annual meeting, may or may not be as strict as a municipality's enforcement.

Regardless of whether or not the restrictions placed on your church's property derive from deed restrictions or zoning regulations, though, the net effect is that violating applicable rules can subject your church to monetary fines or damages in addition to responsibility for remedying the violation. In other words, a violation could result in any of the following adverse consequences:

- your church paying the association or government a fine, perhaps even based on a fixed daily amount for the number of days the violation exists
- your church paying the association's or the government's attorney's fees
- your church complying with the existing restriction or regulation
- your church paying its own attorney's fees

At the end of the day, that may be a very high price to pay to be in exactly the same position from which you started before the violation began.

Who would sue a church over a deed restriction? The answer is that there are many people just waiting for a chance to do exactly that. Further, this is not simply a case of how times have changed. Consider the case in which the plaintiffs alleged that, if the local church had its way, the plaintiffs

> will be greatly annoyed and harassed by a large number of automobiles and motor ve-
> hicles assembling in streets and alleys adjoining said property, by continuous noises
> caused by starting and stopping such vehicles, and the congestion of traffic along the
> streets in the vicinity of the proposed church building, and by the noises and confusion
> caused by those holding services and public meetings in the church, by loud singing,
> loud preaching, and the playing of various instruments of music; and that by reason of
> such annoyances plaintiffs and their families will be disturbed in their rest and sleep,
> also that the market value of the plaintiffs' property will be greatly depreciated - all to
> the irreparable injury of the plaintiffs.[292]

Those allegations, made over seventy-five years ago in an age when suing churches was not so popular, can be made by any homeowners' association or any resident in that association if a church runs afoul of the deed restrictions. In its opinion, the *Waggoner* court acknowledged that a

> church building is as lawful as any other structure. It is not only lawful, but essential to
> our Christian civilization, and will be given the same protection of the law as is afforded
> the residence / for the family, or the place for exercising the pursuit of one's lawful
> business. It is not, however, above the law. Like any other edifice or structure, however
> lawful in purpose and use ordinarily, it may become unlawful. The place of its location,
> and the time and manner of its use, may be such, under the circumstances, as to consti-
> tute that interference with the rights of others as to become in law a nuisance.[293]

It is indeed a complicated, fallen world and deed restrictions and zoning ordinances are just two more examples of the traps and snares which await an unsuspecting church.

COMPLIANCE WITH GOVERNING DOCUMENTS

When I purchase a piece of real property individually, I simply execute various pieces of paper documenting the transaction. No one usually questions whether or not I am legally allowed to enter into a contract (as I definitely appear to be more than seventeen years of age); have the mental capacity to do so (if I look like I have my wits about me on that particular day); or have asked for permission to do so from my parents or guardian.

All of these issues affect whether or not I have the capacity and authority to do what I am doing. We almost always assume that individuals possess those qualities. Organizations are different, though, in that they act through their agents. To protect your organization from the actions of members who might act without authority, you should require that every transaction pass muster under your governing documents.

Your church's articles of incorporation, bylaws, and/or constitution probably will speak to the method by which your church makes significant business decisions. I refer to these as the church's governing documents. In the normal course of business, a church's membership may be notified of any interest in buying or selling a piece of property. The governing documents may require that a meeting or meetings take place, at which the membership can freely discuss the merits of the proposed action, if any required quorum of the membership is present. The governing documents also may provide that a vote or votes should be taken on the decision, which may or may not be held at the same time of the meeting(s).

Some types of decisions may require a supermajority of the membership's vote in order to take action. A supermajority is any percentage higher than a simple majority, usually set at sixty, sixty-seven, or even seventy-five percent. Normal business decisions usually do not require a supermajority vote, though. The other requirement in terms of voting is to ensure that a quorum of voters is present, either in person or by proxy, to hold the vote. Quorums are set at widely varying percentages and, as with almost all such issues, your church's governing documents will control whether or not a quorum has been reached. Quorums and governing documents are discussed in more detail in Chapter 6.

Following the governing documents is important because any action taken not in accordance with a church's governing documents may be set aside later. Regardless of your church's constituency, it seems that there always is someone against a proposition which everyone favors or *vice versa*. Anyone who still carries a torch on an issue may decide to challenge the decision as being improper at a later date if the church does not tend to details in the first place. I am not suggesting that conscientious opposition should be stifled at any level, only that there are procedures which should be observed and that you should do everything which you can to ensure the propriety and finality of a decision properly put to your church. Whether or not such a claim would succeed is questionable. However, as stated before, it always is better to avoid, rather than to engage in, an unnecessary battle. For more specific information on judicial challenges to a church's internal actions, please review Chapter 5.

MAINTENANCE

If your church has owned real property and buildings in the past, then you should know all about the responsibilities inherent in maintaining such a property. If this is your church's first building, then get ready to start paying people to perform maintenance on the buildings or get ready to start doing it yourself, realizing that older buildings generally require more maintenance than newer ones. In addition, everything eventually breaks the day after the warranty expires, so just realize that ownership can be an expensive proposition, even apart from the purchase price. Among the more common chores around church buildings that you may be able to tend to as a church body are the following:

- mowing, edging, weeding, planting, raking, and landscaping
- preparing pipes and landscaping for winter freezes
- changing air conditioner filters
- painting the buildings
- cleaning the buildings' exterior
- repairing or replacing appliances that break
- repairing leaks
- repairing door locks and deadbolts
- replacing broken windows and screens
- hurricane preparation (*e.g.* boarding and taping windows, tying down loose items)
- repairing damage by vandals, storms, and accidents
- replacing fence posts, pickets, and gates
- changing batteries on smoke detectors and other alarms

The foregoing maintenance issues can be tended to by almost anyone associated with your church. In larger churches, an entire staff of janitorial employees may be needed or the task even may be contracted out to an independent company. In new churches, the budget might not support janitorial service and the task may fall to the members.

Several problems can arise if your church's members are responsible for maintenance issues. First, someone in the church may not believe that the person assigned to maintenance for that month or week did a good job. Being volunteers, the typical response might be "Fine, you do it!" That scenario certainly will lead to hard feelings, regardless of whether or not they are expressed. Second, what if an injury occurs while someone is tending to a maintenance issue? Should that person be considered an employee covered by the church's worker's compensation policy? Does the church even have a worker's compensation policy? If not, could that person sue the church directly because the church was somehow negligent in connection with that particular maintenance assignment? Finally, the likelihood that volunteers will ever perform any job as reliably, safely, and professionally as someone who does that type of work for a living are slim and none.

More extensive maintenance, usually requiring professional help outside the abilities of any janitorial service, includes at least some of the following:

- replacing the roof
- repairing foundation problems
- treating for termites
- removing intrusive trees because of potential or actual root damage
- repairing and replacing plumbing or electrical wiring
- removing and replacing flooded carpet and drywall
- replacing and servicing hvac equipment

People have written hundreds of books about the process of maintaining and making repairs to real property and about the other issues raised in this chapter. This obviously represents an extremely condensed effort toward simply raising your awareness about the existence of these issues. I have intended to suggest that buying or leasing real property may not be as simply done or as cheaply done as it was in the past. Hopefully you have come to that conclusion as well.

CHAPTER 10

Do You Feel Lucky?: Insurance

GENERAL CONSIDERATIONS

Approximately 2,100 insurance companies are registered to do business in Texas. Some are big; some are small. Some have good reputations; some have bad reputations. Further complicating the picture is that there are many different types of policies. The complexity of those policies, with varying deductibles, premiums, exclusions, and coverage amounts, along with the disparate nature of many companies, makes an apples to apples comparison of those companies and policies very difficult. Thus, you should evaluate all potential insurers and analyze all potential policies carefully to ensure that you understand your contractual rights and what to expect from your insurer.

Parties, including insurers and insureds, enter into contracts because they think that they can better themselves in some way by doing so. That is the very essence and purpose of doing business. The usual scenario is that one party pays money while the other party renders a service or provides goods or materials. Each party performs its obligations under this contract and, hopefully, all goes well. An insurance policy is an example of a contract.

Insurers issue policies to earn money through their receipt of premiums. Insureds purchase policies to exchange the risk of a smaller, certain loss, the monthly premium, for a potentially larger, uncertain loss. If a loss occurs and the insured has been paying the premium and complying with other policy obligations, then the insured should file a claim and the insurer should pay benefits pursuant to the policy's provisions. If an insured fails to pay a premium, then the policy and its coverage usually will be cancelled. If an insured fails to comply with any of its other obligations, then coverage may be denied and the insured may bear the loss. However, if an insured has complied with all of its obligations and an insurer fails to pay a claim, then we have an unexpected and undeserved financial hardship for the insured and, many times, a law suit must be filed to move the insurer off of dead center.

Insurance companies are formed, like other businesses, with one purpose and can stay in business only by adhering to that purpose: they must receive more money in premiums than they pay in claims, overhead, and other expenses. Predictably, these economic factors drive insurance companies to take those actions which increase accounts receivable and decrease accounts payable. If you doubt this observation, then analyze each and every action which your insurance company's lobbyists or trade representatives took before the Texas Legislature or United States Congress in the last session. Insurance companies and other businesses act in their own best interests and will continue to do so until we no longer have to concern ourselves with insurance. Your interests may coincide with your insurer's interests, but they also may diverge occasionally. In the latter situation, conflicts may arise which require more than casual attention to your rights.

Because agents represent insurers, not you, the same concerns can apply to agents as well. However, the relationships formed between you and your agent, for business and sometimes even personal reasons, can be an effective tool in dealing with your insurer. Your agent depends on people and organizations like churches for income and repeat business. If you are dissatisfied with your insurer, then your agent realizes that you probably will take your business elsewhere. Thus, you should attempt to enlist your agent's assistance if you ever encounter difficulties with a claim. For the most part, agents are sensitive to the problems encountered in the claims process and, through their experience and contacts, may be able to assist you with your claim while staying true to the duties which they owe to the insurers which they represent. An agent's motivation is to keep you as a customer and you may find that he can be a more persuasive voice with your insurer than you can be.

Insurance companies have some interests in common with property owners, business entities, and others who consider themselves lawsuit targets because a majority of premium dollars come from these institutions. The church now fits into the target category. Insurance interests consistently lobby legislatures to modify civil laws and procedural rules to protect those entities' interests. Why? The insurance companies' public rationale is that they are seeking fairness and justice in the law and are attempting to promote a more stable business environment. However, insurance companies simply are doing what comes naturally in a free market. They are politicizing a business issue to better their own bottom line. Simply put, as in other industries, it all comes down to money. Fairness and justice may sit in the passenger seats, depending on who is defining those terms, but money is driving.

What do you get when you obtain a policy? If good neighbors, good hands, and pieces of rocks come to mind, then this industry's marketing has worked, but you need a serious jolt into the twenty-first century. All of those advertising slogans, lyrics, and graphics are designed with one objective: to persuade you to write a check every month. You will realize that the comfort which you derived from a catchy jingle is absolutely worthless when you begin to fill out claim forms to substantiate a loss.

A policy generally provides coverage for a certain time period, during which a claim either must occur or be reported to the insurer. You pay an initial premium or several premiums in installment fashion for the policy's coverage. Some policies may provide coverage only for incidents which occur during that period, sometimes referred to as "occurrence" policies.[294] Other policies may provide coverage only for claims which are made during that policy period, sometimes referred to as "claims made" policies.[295] Still other policies may require that the incident occur and the claim be made within the same policy period in order for coverage to exist.

A policy can provide for payments from the insurer when some defined incident occurs and you suffer a loss, commonly referred to as a "first party" claim, or when some defined incident occurs, someone else suffers a loss, and that person looks to you to pay for it, commonly referred to as a "third party" claim. When a claim is made, the insurer assigns an adjuster or claims manager to handle your claim. This person will provide forms for you to complete; direct you as to how to proceed with any necessary actions after the incident; communicate with the claimant and his attorney, if any; and make a decision on whether or not, who, and how much to pay.

You should read into these remarks that an adjuster has a certain amount of discretion in evaluating a claim. While property damage claims usually are more straightforward, personal injury claims, by their nature, are more complicated and subject to greater difference of opinion. I have represented many clients involved in automobile accidents and, unfortunately, also have been involved in several automobile accidents. The entire ordeal is never a fun or profitable one for those injured by another's negligence, despite any delusions which the public may hold about the injured striking it rich. I never have heard one of my clients say that she would volunteer for the process again.

Property damage claims may seem very simple at first, but even they can become complicated. Common disputes in this situation involve the materials chosen to repair or to replace damaged parts of a building and whether or not particular claims are within the scope of your policy's coverage. If your church chose a particular grade or type of material with which to construct a building and that building is damaged, then you should be careful in monitoring the replacement materials to ensure that a lower, cost-saving grade is not substituted. I am not saying that insurers should be forced to pay for the most expensive type of repair or replacement product, only that you should receive the benefit of your premiums and should be made whole after a loss. If you paid for custom copper gutters and downspouts, then you probably will have a problem when the contractor shows up with do-it-yourself materials from the local hardware store. In that same vein, what if the gazebo which church members constructed during a few weekend workdays collapses under gale force winds? Is your church covered? The adjuster may not think so, because your church did not bother to inform its agent of the addition of this "building," even though the materials may have cost $5,000.00 or more. Adding buildings or even improving existing buildings without checking your coverage is a predictable route to an insurance dispute.

Within the personal injury claims process, I have been amazed at how claims which appear to be similar from my perspective are evaluated differently by adjusters, even adjusters within the same company. Conversely, I am certain that adjusters would have the very same comments about how attorneys evaluate claims. I have listed below some of the factors which I believe may affect the value of any given personal injury claim.

- whether or not the plaintiff has prior claims
- whether or not the plaintiff has a criminal record
- whether or not the plaintiff is credible
- whether or not the plaintiff is sympathetic
- whether or not the plaintiff makes a nice appearance
- whether or not the plaintiff and insured agree on how the accident happened
- whether witnesses exist and, if so, whether they support the plaintiff's or insured's version of the accident
- whether or not the plaintiff contributed to causing the accident
- whether or not parties other than the insured contributed to causing the accident
- the shock value of the insured's conduct, *i.e.* could this have happened to anyone or was the insured's negligence in some way shocking?
- the plaintiff's and defendant's income and / or assets
- the availability of other insurance (*e.g.* personal health insurance or personal injury protection) to the plaintiff
- the coverage limits
- whether or not the plaintiff's injuries can be substantiated medically, *i.e.* injuries which are more objectively demonstrable, without merely subjective complaints, are evaluated more seriously
- whether or not the plaintiff's medical and counseling treatment appears to be reasonable, necessary, and related to the accident

- the amount of past and future medical and counseling bills incurred by the plaintiff
- any past and future physical impairment suffered by the plaintiff
- past and future loss of consortium by the plaintiff's spouse or children
- past and future earning capacity or wages lost by the plaintiff from being unable to work
- past and future physical pain and mental anguish endured by the plaintiff
- any disfigurement suffered by the plaintiff
- the plaintiff's attorney's reputation
- the insured's attorney's reputation
- the doctor's or counselor's reputation
- the county in which any suit would be filed and that county's reputation for stingy or generous jury verdicts
- the court in which any suit has been filed and that judge's reputation in favoring plaintiffs or defendants in rulings

Self-Insurance

Some nonprofit institutions feel secure and stable enough to set aside funds to pay claims before they arise. Thorough treatment of this strategy, commonly referred to as "self-insurance," is beyond this book's scope, but it remains an option for large business and non-profit corporations. These institutions usually employ professional risk managers and safety consultants, perhaps even contracting with third party administrators, to analyze the risks and claims to which they are subject. When they arrive at some consensus about how much they think they may be required to pay in claims and defense costs during a given period, then they begin to set aside funds to address these potential claims. It is, at the outset, a rather expensive proposition until a sufficient reserve is compiled to allow existing policies to lapse. However, these institutions may save money over the long haul, in part because they are not contributing to an insurer's profit margin and also because they have a more personal interest in both preventing future claims and preserving their own money.

Types of Risk

I started to write about the types of policies which every church should have. Every church has different circumstances, though. Thus, as circumstances dictate needs, trying to tell you what you need without knowing your circumstances is senseless. Further, in an attempt to compete in the marketplace, insurance companies have created flexible feature policies, multi-peril policies, and other cafeteria style policies which provide different types and combinations of coverage for different risks, only adding to the confusion. Thus, telling you that you need policy "X" will not really assist you in evaluating your circumstances. I can discuss different types of coverage, though, and how those coverages apply to hypothetical risks. It may be helpful to phrase this material in terms which the insurance industry uses so that you can speak to an agent intelligently about the scope and extent of your insurance coverage.

- Errors and Omissions - Also referred to as "Officers and Directors" or "Officers, Directors, and Trustees" insurance, this coverage indemnifies those serving the church in a leadership capacity for their negligent actions.
- Professional Liability - Similar to errors and omissions insurance, this coverage indemnifies those serving the church in a professional capacity, e.g. counselors, for their negligent actions.
- Property and Casualty - This coverage provides indemnification for losses which you suffer from certain types of damage to your real property, fixtures, and, in certain circumstances, personal property used with your real property.
- Sexual Misconduct - This coverage provides indemnification for claims made by third parties based on the sexual misconduct of someone associated with your church, usually excluding from coverage the person whose misconduct creates the claim.
- General Liability - This coverage provides indemnification for claims made by third parties against your church for personal injuries, wrongful death, and property damage.
- Medical Expenses - This coverage provides reimbursement for the medical expenses of someone injured on your premises, usually excluding employees, though.
- Flood - While many people believe that flood coverage generally is included with property and casualty, it is not. This separate policy must be purchased to protect your real and personal property against flood losses.
- Theft - We would like to think that no one would steal from the church, but outsiders and even church employees have been know to steal. This coverage provides reimbursement for stolen items.
- Employee Dishonesty - Somewhat similar in scope to a theft policy, this coverage provides reimbursement for losses which your church sustains as a result of employee dishonesty.

- Workers' Compensation - This coverage protects you from claims brought by employees who are injured while on the job. It also provides benefits through a structured, statutory scheme to the injured workers, who release their claims against you in consideration of the statutory benefits.
- Group and Individual Health and Dental - These coverages provide protection from health and dental care bills for church employees and/or their dependents.
- Disability - This coverage provides benefits when an employee becomes disabled and cannot work to support himself and/or his family. The benefits, usually determined as a percentage of salary or a fixed sum, are paid directly to the employee after a stated period after the onset of the disability.
- Life - This coverage provides benefits when an employee dies. The benefits usually are paid directly to the employee's designated beneficiary.
- Automobile - This coverage indemnifies you against claims incurred as a result of the operation of the church's vehicles. Additionally, vehicles not owned by the church and/or drivers not employed by the church may be covered if they are in the church's service when a loss occurs.
- Umbrella - This coverage applies when the limits of certain other coverages have been exhausted by a claim.

I cannot emphasize too strongly your obligation to review any policy very carefully before you purchase it. You must understand its scope of coverage, limitations, exceptions, and requirements. You should ask questions of your insurance agent, because he should be the person most familiar with the policy. You also may want to question your attorney regarding what you can expect of your insurer and what it will demand from you.

COVERAGE AMOUNTS

Many types of policies, especially liability policies, have different coverage limits. These limits set forth the maximum amount of claim dollars which an insurer will have to pay during the policy period, sometimes with separate limits per claim and in the aggregate for the entire coverage period. If a claim exceeds these limits either through a demand or a judgment, then the insurance company generally will not be obligated to pay the amount in excess of the policy limits.

An important point to remember about policy limits is that the adjuster will not write a check for those limits just because you have a claim. She still will force you to prove every dollar which you seek. It is her job to do so, as every claim dollar retained is a profit dollar. An adjuster is not paid to give away the farm and she will attempt to save her employer money at every turn. Her performance reviews depend on how well she does her job and you should not expect blank check treatment under any circumstance.

DEDUCTIBLES AND CO-PAYMENTS

When a loss occurs in a first party or third party policy, the policy may require that the insured bear some of the loss. If that is stated as a percentage of the covered loss, then it is called a co-payment. However, a deductible is different, requiring that the insured pay the first $X of any given claim. If you think that you are well insured when a property and casualty insurance policy provides that you have a $5,000.00 deductible, then please review the following example. You sustain property damage to one of your buildings. The covered loss is determined to be $20,000.00, although the replacement cost is $30,000.00. When your $5,000.00 deductible is subtracted from $20,000.00, that leaves $15,000.00 for your insurer to pay. You and your insurance company just paid $15,000.00 each to restore the *status quo*. Were you well insured?

In another example, your group health plan provides for a $1,000.00 deductible, with your insurer paying seventy-five percent of all covered claims. After a short hospital stay and minor surgery, you are faced with a $9,500.00 bill from the hospital, surgeon, radiologist, pathologist, pharmacy, emergency room physician, physical therapist, and other necessary health care providers. The insurance company deducts $1,500.00 of your claim because it denied coverage for those extra two days at the hospital because you did not feel strong enough to go home, even though your doctor recommended that you stay. Your insurer then deducts $500.00 from other providers' bills as being higher than "reasonable and necessary" charges, another standard policy provision. After these exclusions, you must pay the deductible, leaving the insurer responsible for seventy-five percent of $6,500.00, that being $4,875.00. You just paid $4,625.00, almost one-half of the bill. Were you well insured? If you think that either of these scenarios is improbable, then you need that jolt into the twenty-first century that we discussed earlier.

It is important to consider these factors when purchasing insurance. It is in your best interests to have as low a deductible as possible, but the downside is that your monthly premium will increase as your deductible decreases. Further, the percentage of your co-payment will affect your monthly premium under almost all applicable policies. If you are willing to accept a policy with a higher insured co-payment percentage, then that policy should reward your willingness to shoulder that burden with a comparably lower monthly premium.

Replacement cost coverage also may be of value for churches, especially in times of escalating real estate values and price increases for building materials. In the example above, there is a difference between the actual cash value of the loss and the replacement cost. Even ignoring the two factors stated immediately above, it invariably costs more to replace something that has been damaged than it was worth before the loss. Some of the factors which may contribute to this phenomenon include the following:

- the costs of demolition and site preparation
- the added expense of the contractor not working with economies of scale
- compliance with newer, stricter, building codes
- ever-increasing labor and material costs.

If a substantial portion of a building or an entire building is lost, then your church may have difficulty restoring that building to its original status if it only receives eighty percent of its replacement cost from the insurer. That is a tremendous burden for a congregation to bear and a tremendous risk to take in connection with a potential loss, especially given the recent wave of arson cases and other attacks on church properties.

ADDITIONAL INSUREDS

There must be a named insured on each insurance policy. Generally, the named insured will be the person or entity purchasing the policy. Occasionally, someone else should be named as an insured on that policy in order to receive its protection. In real estate, lenders are usually accorded additional insured status because they are interested in protecting the value of their collateral. Thus, if a loss to the property occurs, they want to be included in the decision-making process of how much of, if, and how their collateral is restored.

In the context of third party policies, additional insureds usually benefit from a policy when they are sued individually, along with the church, for their conduct in a claim. The most obvious example of this concept is that of the volunteer church van driver who is involved in an accident. While he may have other, individual coverage to protect him, churches usually purchase a policy which covers those driving the church's vehicles, as well as the church. Thus, as an additional insured, the driver benefits from the obligations owed to him by the church's insurer, regardless of the fact that he did not take out the policy, pay a premium, or even know of the policy's existence.

RELEASES

Releases are discussed more extensively in Chapter 5 in connection with contractual protection and in Chapter 15 in connection with youth and children's activities. A release, sometimes referred to as a hold harmless agreement, is a type of contract executed by a participant in an activity which releases the sponsor or others affiliated with an activity from liability for accidents associated with the activity. Just as insurance policies operate to transfer risk, so do releases. This transfer of risk is generally good, as it encourages churches and their members to participate in activities which they otherwise might avoid and usually apportions responsibility for behavior more appropriately to those directly involved in the activity.

However, a perhaps unintended consequence of an enforceable release is that your insurer may use it to avoid paying an otherwise covered claim. Imagine the situation in which a church volunteer causes an automobile accident on a youth trip. The release may cover transportation to and from the event and expressly release the church and its agents from their own negligence. If the release is enforceable, then you should assume that your insurer will assert that defense in court. The legal reasoning is that the insurer is obligated to pay only those claims which you are obligated to pay. If you have a defense to the claim, *i.e.* the release, then the insurer will take advantage of that defense to the greatest extent possible, reveling in its good fortune to have insured such a church.

This maneuver may leave the injured person without a remedy. While a release may be a fine piece of lawyering, it may deny recovery to someone whom a church member, acting negligently, has injured. Is this the result which you want? I am not suggesting that releases be abandoned. I am only suggesting that their use may bring about unintended consequences and that our zeal to protect the church may result in a situation which leaves us with an uneasy feeling at the end of the day.

YOUR DUTIES - DUTY TO PAY THE PREMIUM

This may seem like a self-evident duty, but many insureds allow their policies to lapse because they fail to pay the premium in a timely manner. Some policies have a grace provision, allowing late payments to be made through a certain date as a matter of course. Other policies, however, provide that the acceptance of premiums after their due date has passed is at the insurer's discretion. Some insurers require an insured to certify, prior to the insurer's decision to accept or to reject a delinquent premium or to reinstate a lapsed policy, that no claims have occurred since the date on which the premium was due. If a claim has occurred during that period, I leave you with one guess as to whether or not the insurer will accept the delinquent premium and / or reinstate the policy.

A church's decision on whether or not to pay premiums usually arises during times of financial stress. Equally forceful arguments can be made for the payment of this bill over that bill, but losing coverage, even for a short time, can have potentially disastrous effects on a church. Further, if a congregation believes that certain coverage exists and a claim occurs when that coverage has lapsed, then that congregation will be looking for the one who did not forward the check in a timely manner. Consider these possibilities when deciding whether or not to pay the premium.

Your Duties - Duty to Notify Insurer of Claim

Your duty to notify an insurer of a claim is defined in the insurance policy. Most policies contain provisions requiring you to notify your insurer "as soon as practicable," "at the earliest opportunity," *et cetera*. This duty is a condition precedent to the enforcement of the insurer's duties to defend and to indemnify you. That means that your failure to notify your insurer that an incident has occurred may void the coverage contained in the policy.[296] Further, if the coverage is voided by your breach of the contract, your premium payments probably will not be refunded, not to mention that you will be faced with the prospect of paying for your own defense and any judgment or settlement arising out of the claim.

The following are not defenses to your failure to notify your insurer of a claim:

- you meant to notify your insurer of a claim, but simply forgot about it
- you did not believe that the claimant would eventually file suit[297]
- you believed that the claims were being satisfied by another insurance policy[298]

Thus, in order to maintain effective coverage, you must notify each insurer whose policy potentially may provide coverage for an incident precipitating a covered claim "as soon as practicable." Simply notifying the only insurer whose policy you think applies to the incident could have disastrous results.

In addition to making an oral report, your church should send written notice to its insurance company and its insurance agent, regardless of whether or not its policy requires written notice. Further, the notice should be sent by certified mail, return receipt requested, or by other traceable means of delivery. Consider the following hypothetical example: a church gives oral notice of an incident to its insurance agent, who fails to forward the report to the insurer. The insurer successfully denies coverage for the claim, asserting that it should not be charged with notice when the church had an opportunity to notify it directly, as required by the policy, but chose to rely on the agent. Thus, that church faces a claim without the benefit of the policy for which it paid. These suggestions apply equally when your duty to notify your insurer that you have received notice of a suit arises.

YOUR DUTIES - DUTY TO NOTIFY INSURER OF SUIT

Even if you have notified your insurer of a claim, you still must notify it when you are served and you must forward a copy of all of the papers served on you to the insurer.[299] Again, most policies contain a specific provision spelling out your duties in this regard.

As with the duty to notify your insurer of a claim, your failure to notify your insurer that you have been served with citation and a copy of the petition or complaint (or other papers, if applicable) can have dire consequences. An insured's "failure to comply with the notice of suit provision of the insurance policy" usually will relieve the insurer of any obligations under the policy, including the duties to defend and to indemnify.[300] The reasoning behind this seemingly harsh rule is that an insurer, in order to defend you properly and to avail itself of all of your defenses, wants as much time as possible to respond to a lawsuit and to prepare a defense.[301] If the insurer shows that "the lack of notice prejudiced [its] . . . defense of the suit," then it can escape its obligations.[302] Conversely, an insurer's actual knowledge of a suit, even without the insured's notification, can be sufficient to invoke its duty to defend in limited circumstances.[303]

YOUR DUTIES - DUTY TO COOPERATE WITH INSURER

The duty to cooperate with your insurer may be difficult to accomplish at times. An example in the liability arena is when a church member is hurt at your church and the church is legitimately at fault. For legally sound reasons, your church's insurer will direct your church and its members not to discuss the matter with the plaintiff, his family, and, especially, his attorney. It is difficult to minister to someone and to avoid discussing his problems with him, though. I do not have any suggestions to resolve this dilemma, except to hope that the plaintiff understands the restrictions which you are under and that violating those restrictions could place the insurance funds which he is seeking to recover at jeopardy.

In any such situation, your insurance company will have assigned an adjuster or claims representative to handle the claim. Your insurer also will retain an attorney to represent you, but generally only after suit is filed. Your concerns regarding ministering to or speaking with an injured church member should be explained to the adjuster or attorney. Their response may not be what you expect or want, but, if you desire to speak with the injured person, you should at least address the situation with your insurer's representatives and make an attempt to explain yourself.

The duty to cooperate with insurers encompasses several distinct areas. First, you must cooperate with your insurer by making those employed or otherwise controlled by the church available for investigative and strategic discussions with the adjuster or attorney. Second, those employed or otherwise controlled by the church should avoid discussing any aspect of the incident with anyone not affiliated with the church or the insurance company. Next, the church should forward a copy of any investigative materials which it has to the insurance company to assist it in evaluating the claim. The church also must allow the insurer to inspect any premises or items involved in an incident. Finally, if the claim proceeds to litigation, the church must make itself, those employed or otherwise controlled by it, its premises, and certain of its records available to its attorney to aid the attorney in defending the church.

It is vital to remember that the insurance company is paying the attorney and any settlement or judgment. These are sometimes referred to as the insurance companies' duties to defend and to indemnify your church, respectively. Your church's insurer has a vested interest in keeping as much of its own money as possible, regardless of whether or not your church believes that the plaintiff has a worthy claim. Thus, the insurance company and its attorney, who probably receives business from the insurance company on a regular basis and whom the insurance company is paying, will be attempting at every turn to minimize or to defeat the plaintiff's claim. That is the attorney's job. The duty to cooperate contained in the insurance policy for which you paid requires you to cooperate with that very objective, with which you may or may not agree. Your failure to do so may void the coverage extended by that policy and make the church's assets viable targets for the plaintiff's recovery. Thus, if you desire for your church and, potentially, for any claimants to receive a benefit from the premium dollars which you paid to the insurer, then you should take heed of your duty to cooperate.

YOUR INSURER'S DUTIES - DUTY TO DEFEND

We have looked at what you must do to cooperate with insurers. The law also places certain duties on them as to how they must handle claims and communicate with their insureds and claimants. One of the primary duties which an insurer undertakes in a policy is the duty to defend you. "The duty to defend arises when a third party sues the insured on allegations that, if taken as true, potentially state a cause of action within the terms of the policy."[304] The corollary to this rule is that the duty to defend does not arise if a petition's factual allegations do not raise a claim within the policy's scope of coverage.[305] Thus, a certain amount of gamesmanship can occur when a plaintiff's attorney wants his client's claims to be covered by the defendant's insurance policy, especially when the defendant is unable to pay a judgment without insurance proceeds. This is sometimes referred to as the "complaint allegation rule."[306]

The duty to defend includes paying an attorney to defend you if you are sued, a benefit which may equal or exceed the settlement paid to the claimant. However, do not rush to call your favorite attorney to represent you when you are sued under an insurance policy. Your insurer maintains relationships with one or more attorneys to whom it regularly assigns cases. Known as insurance defense lawyers or insurance defense firms, these attorneys represent clients who have been sued and who are insured by the companies who, in turn, regularly refer cases to these attorneys. Further, the insurance company usually will control how you are defended, since you are requiring it to play your game with its money. "Generally, an insurance company may step into the shoes of its indemnitee, assert various defenses, appoint counsel, and manage the defense."[307] Thus, while you will be defended, do not expect to control any significant aspect of your defense.

Your Insurer's Duties - Duty to Indemnify

Perhaps the most important duty which your insurer undertakes is the duty to indemnify you for losses. As discussed before, these losses may be damage to your property or claims made against you by third parties. In either case, the insurance company's obligation is to pay the claim or loss according to the policy's terms.

The critical element in determining whether or not a duty to indemnify you exists is determining whether or not the loss or claim is covered by the policy. If it is a covered loss or claim, then the duty to indemnify arises.[308] Conversely, if the claim is not a covered loss or claim, then there is no duty to indemnify and probably no duty to defend, either.[309]

An insurer occasionally will offer a defense conditioned on its setting forth a reservation of its right not to defend or to indemnify you. This usually occurs when a petition or complaint alleges some claims which may be covered and some claims which may not be covered. The extent of the duty to indemnify is determined subsequently by the claims under which the plaintiff recovers. For example, if the plaintiff recovers under a contract theory, but not under a negligence theory, then the insurer may not indemnify you if your general liability policy does not cover contract claims. However, if the plaintiff's ground of recovery rests in his negligence claim and that is a covered claim, then you should be indemnified.

If an insurer offers a conditional defense to you, then it is wise to seek independent counsel to protect you against what may be an improper coverage determination by your insurer and to advise you about defending any claims which truly are outside the scope of coverage. However, you probably will have to pay this attorney out of your own funds. While the attorney assigned to you by the insurer may defend you against all claims, the entity paying his fees is better situated if, in the example above, the jury returns a verdict based on a contract claim. At that point, the insurer is absolved of any obligation to indemnify you, although it has provided a defense. Thus, the insurer's interests conflict directly with yours. In such a situation, it is better to have a second attorney, chosen and paid by you, not your insurer, at least reviewing the status of the case, if not participating directly in your defense.

Your Insurer's Duties - Claims Handling Duties

Less frequently discussed are the claims handling duties which your insurer owes to you. While this group of statutes and laws are not as widely applicable as they might be, do not prohibit as many unfair insurance practices as they might prohibit, and do not have the enforcement teeth which they might have, they nonetheless offer some protection to the insured or claimant who finds himself the target of unfair treatment by an insurer.

Insurers owe a duty to their insureds to comply with the Prompt Payment of Claims Act (the "PPCA").[310] The PPCA requires an insurer, within fifteen days after receiving a notice of claim, to acknowledge the claim, to begin its investigation, and to notify the insured of "all items, statements, and forms that the insurer reasonably believes . . . will be required from the claimant."[311] After receiving all of the documentation which it has required from its insured, an insurer must notify its insured of its acceptance or rejection of the claim within fifteen business days. If the insurer accepts the claim, then it must pay the claim within five days.[312] If the insurer rejects the claim, then its notice of rejection "must state the reason for the rejection."[313] Finally, if the insurer cannot accept or reject the claim, then it must notify the claimant of the reasons for its inability to make a decision on the claim, but in no case will the insurer be allowed more than forty-five additional days in which to accept or to reject the claim.[314]

There are several insurance lines which are exempt from the PPCA's coverage. Among these are workers' compensation, mortgage guaranty, and title insurance claims.[315] Another significant limitation on the PPCA is that it applies only to first party claims.[316] Thus, when you have a claim against another person or entity and are forced to deal with an opposing insurance company, the PPCA does not apply.

Insurance companies owe a duty of good faith and fair dealing to first party claimants.[317] When an insurer breaches that duty, the result is often called a "bad faith" case. An insurer creates a bad faith case "by denying a claim when the insurer's liability has become reasonably clear."[318] Insurers do not owe that same duty to third party claimants, though.[319] Moreover, damages for insureds when that duty has been breached have been hard to prove and harder to collect, given insurers' proclivity to avail themselves of the appellate process. Insurance companies also have been very successful in almost eliminating the imposition of punitive damages in these cases.[320] Thus, while you may receive social courtesy from an adjuster when you are asserting a third party claim, you should not expect them to conduct their communications and negotiations with you as if they were under a duty of good faith and fair dealing. You are an opposing claimant to whom little, if any, duty is owed and you should expect to be treated as such.

When you notify your insurer of a claim, your insurer probably will ask what happened, how it happened, who else can be blamed, and whether or not other insurance exists. However, that should not be the end of your adjuster's communications with you. Every insurer providing coverage under a liability policy should report to its insured the status of negotiations and any settlement agreements. When your insurer receives a settlement offer, it has a duty to report the material terms of that offer to you within ten days after the date on which the claimant makes the offer. Further, when your insurer settles a claim, it has a duty to report the material terms of that settlement to you within thirty days after the date of the settlement.[321] Proving that you have been damaged by your insurer's failure to notify you of a settlement may be difficult, though.[322]

This may not seem to be an important point. However, consider this scenario. The claimant's attorney and the adjuster have not been getting along well. The claimant offers to settle within your policy limits, but your adjuster refuses because he thinks that he may fare better with a jury, even with the increased attorney's fees which he will pay to try the case. A trial occurs in which a judgment over your policy limits is taken. You are now liable for the amount of the judgment in excess of your policy limits when the case could have been settled within policy limits and without your having to have paid a dime.

Do you now wish that you had been informed of the status of settlement negotiations in accordance with the statute? You may have to pay the excess judgment, but all is not lost. You also may have a claim against your insurance company for negligently failing to settle as long as a reasonably prudent insurer would have settled that same claim within policy limits. Such was the situation in the *Stowers* case and in many subsequent cases.[323] Claims such as these are commonly referred to as *Stowers* claims or as claims arising under the *Stowers* doctrine.

As stated earlier, insurance companies are motivated by the thought of spending as little money as possible to settle a case. Sometimes, an all or nothing mentality takes over a case and an adjuster will risk a large judgment, even an excess judgment, for the prospect of a favorable defense verdict, also known as pouring a plaintiff out. Your interests in settling a claim, avoiding an excess judgment, and getting on with business as usual directly conflict with your insurer's interests. Where there is conflict, there may be smoke and where there is smoke, there may be litigation. Thus, you should remain extremely interested in observing how your adjuster is handling your claim and, if you sense that something is amiss, tactfully remind him that you expect his company to fulfill each of the duties which it owes to you.

When a claim is made, an insurer's conduct also is governed by the Unfair Claim Settlement Practices Act (the "UCSPA").[324] Although it would be nice to assume that insurance companies play by the golden rule, the Texas Legislature has seen fit to make its expectations of their conduct more explicit. The following practices, among others potentially, "constitute unfair claim settlement practices."

- misrepresenting facts or policy provisions relating to coverage
- failing to communicate with claimants promptly
- failing to adopt and to implement procedures to investigate claims
- failing to attempt to settle claims promptly in which liability is reasonably clear
- forcing insureds to file suit to recover benefits
- offering insureds less than amounts actually recovered in suits
- failing to maintain adequate records of complaints[325]

If an insurer commits any of these acts, then it has violated the UCSPA, has committed a deceptive trade practice, and is subject to claims under the Texas Deceptive Trade Practices-Consumer Protection Act.[326] Again, however, the application of the UCSPA is limited to first party claims, excluding third parties from its protection.[327] Thus, it will apply only in limited circumstances.

PART THREE

PEOPLE, LAW, AND MINISTRY IN SPECIAL SITUATIONS

CHAPTER 11

Safe And Sound: Security

GENERAL CONSIDERATIONS

I have represented many clients in premises liability and security matters. I also have managed a commercial office building. That project entailed more security concerns for me as a property manager than I ever envisioned as a lawyer. Thus, I have some exposure to these issues both as a lawyer and as a property manager and, while I certainly have not concentrated on this field as much as other attorneys and security professionals, I also have some personal experience as well.

One of those experiences involved shots being fired at the school which one of my daughters was attending. As word spread over local media and the internet, we heard and read reports about bullets hitting walls and stacks of papers on desks. That shots had been fired was clear, but no one seemed to know any further details in the first few hours. The school had reacted immediately and began following its drill: lock the doors to classrooms, have the students sit on the floor behind desks, and turn the lights out. The police raced to the scene, patrolled the hallways, and took positions. The children knew that this was not a drill. They sat on the floor of darkened, locked classrooms, frozen in time at the moment when the signal for lockdown was heard. Neither I nor thousands of parents, grandparents, brothers, sisters, and other loved ones could do anything about it. I could not pick her up or even drive to the school, as officials had cordoned off the campus. All that any of us could do was to wait for news and to pray. That day thankfully ended with no injuries.

Similar days have ended tragically and have ended or changed lives. Our town is a relatively small town, with little history of violent crime, and the school district has been rated as an exemplary district year in and year out. These were prime considerations when we had moved three years earlier. A house might be wrapped once in a while, but we certainly never expected a shooting, even in the wake of the April, 1999, Columbine High School slayings. We had moved out of the big city for a better school district and a cow pasture, literally, next to our house. In the following days, I spoke to a police officer at a gas station and expressed our thanks for the job that his department did. I spoke to a school board member, expressing our support of the district's policies, and sent a note of appreciation to the principal, staff, and faculty for all that they did. We all were shocked, but in hindsight they handled the situation about as well as could be expected.

When people are injured, killed, or even just angered in these types of events, they or their survivors look for someone to blame. After the adrenaline of the moment fades, we find that those who actually did the shooting, bombing, raping, and stabbing usually are dead, bankrupt, judgment-proof, or incarcerated. Thus, we tend to look to institutions, which usually have significant assets or insurance policies, for restitution and justice.

In our legal system, it is a district attorney's job to prosecute the criminal offenders and to put them in jail. We all applaud him when he does his job well, for he has made the world a safer place, in theory, anyway. On the other hand, it is a plaintiff's lawyer's job to prosecute civil claims and to turn those claims into settlement proceeds or judgments with dollars attached to them. Depending on which side of the case we stand, we may not be applauding him at all.

Suing the shooter (who will be dead, bankrupt, judgment-proof, or incarcerated) makes little sense to a plaintiff's lawyer, who is evaluating the case financially from the moment that the plaintiff walks in the door. Remember that law is a business and that the plaintiff's lawyer probably will be footing the bill to prepare the case. He will spend his own money for a year or two, perhaps more, before he sees any return on his investment. He will pay filing fees, court reporters' bills, expert witnesses, document production costs, preparation costs for exhibits to be used as evidence, private investigators, living expenses for the plaintiff, and more. It is the only industry in which a consumer walks in the door with no money and expects an experienced service provider with a doctorate degree and overhead to finance a project and to invest weeks, months, or even years of his and his staff's time with no guarantee of a return. There is little else that the lawyer can do to restore his client and to pay himself than to target the institution.

Security claims fall squarely within the scenario that I just described. They are claims which usually are made against institutions for failing to take some action which would have prevented another party from injuring the plaintiff. While the one who pulled the trigger may be included in the suit, ninety-nine percent of everyone's energy will be focused on the institution's role and conduct in the incident, because, for reasons enumerated above, those who pull the trigger do not write settlement checks. Although I discuss these types of claims briefly in Chapter 4, we now need to look at them from a prevention standpoint.

SECURITY THEORY

If you are looking for me to write the definitive security manual for churches, then look elsewhere. I have discovered, though, mostly through trial and error, a few helpful pointers which I have distilled into a five point theory of security. I love mnemonics and would not have completed junior high without them, so I suggest that in connection with security matters, you consider being a PRUDE.

- Be Prayerful. As you pray, keep one eye open. Jesus promised that trouble will find us.
- Be Reasonable. Know that some will find your efforts lacking, while others will say that you are going overboard. Remember that your role in the "reasonable-ness" equation is to act with foresight; a jury's role is to evaluate your actions in hindsight. As between you and the jurors, you definitely did not draw the high card. Accept it and make the best of the situation.
- Be Up-to-Date. Educate yourself and avoid complacency *vis a vis* your security system. Security is a relatively new and growing field. Technological advances, some of which can help you save money over existing security components, happen fairly regularly. New ideas, based on experiences which others have had, can improve your system without costing a dime.
- Be Diligent. Despite your diligence, you occasionally will forget to check something. This usually will occur only when someone is reviewing what you were supposed to have done, but did not do, after an incident occurred. What happened, of course, easily could have been prevented if you only had done the thing that you were supposed to have done.
- Be Expectant. Expect the unexpected. Keep reminding yourself that you cannot fathom the destruction that depravity, determination, ingenuity, and easy access to weapons can wreak.

SECURITY THEORY - BE PRAYERFUL

When Jesus confesses that He will remain in the world no longer, He acknowledges that we will remain in the world for a time and prays in John 17:11, "Holy Father, protect them by the power of your name - the name you gave me - so that they may be one as we are one." He continues praying in John 17:15, not that God will remove us from the world, but that God will protect us from "the evil one." May our prayers be identical.

Dealing with security issues is a burden and a privilege which falls to someone and, if you are reading this book, then you probably are that someone. Thus, as you deal with your own emotions and misgivings about the subject and as you push for your church to implement a security system, prepare yourself for the possibilities that the church will resist security measures and that a security incident may not occur for years. You might start to feel like kicking yourself for foolishly spending money, time, and other resources on a security system. If you are fortunate enough to find yourself in that situation, then stop kicking yourself for a minute and point out to your critics, including yourself, that the difference between the occurrence and absence of an incident probably was your preparation and prayer and God's protection.

SECURITY THEORY - BE REASONABLE

You literally cannot spend enough money to guarantee any one person's or group's security. It is impossible and impractical. Having said that, your church will not always be under attack from the Judean Peoples' Front Suicide Squad. "First Fortress Church" is not the idea here. You may simply be facing a couple of ten year olds who will not stop throwing rocks at windows or breaking into the playground. Your job is to assess the foreseeable dangers confronting your church and to take reasonable security measures to deter those dangers or to minimize their consequences. You may also want to refer to Chapter 4's discussion of the "reasonable man" standard for a few more thoughts on that issue.

If you attend First Church of the Inner City, then what is reasonable at that church may be different from what is reasonable at First Church of Cowtown. Crime rates generally increase correspondingly with population densities. If you attend First Church of Everyone Has Known Everyone For Generations, then what is reasonable at that church may be different from what is reasonable for First Church of Transient Bedroom Community. Knowing who attends or is likely to attend your church can impact the level of security you need just as much as the presence of a combination crackhouse / sawed-off shotgun emporium next door to your church.

Another factor could include the accessibility of your church's facilities and personnel to outsiders during operating hours and the frequency of walk-in traffic. Homeless and transient people may try to use your church's facilities as shelter. The frequency of their visits to your church may suggest a heightened need for security measures. I would never advocate that churches and their members stop being charitable or benevolent. That is not my point. When dealing with these people, however, many reasonable people believe that you face an increased risk of erratic, unstable, and violent behavior. If you agree with that analysis, then your security risk rises. If you disagree, then by all means do that with which you are comfortable. Legally, though, if something poses a danger of which you are aware or should be aware, then you should consider implementing some type of security measure to deter that danger or to minimize its consequences.

SECURITY THEORY - BE UP-TO-DATE

Read about and discuss security concerns with other ministers and church members. Form a security committee comprised of church members, some of whom hopefully will have some expertise. Join a professional association. Bookmark security sites and visit them often. Subscribe to a trade journal. While I have listed at the end of this chapter many ideas, features, and strategies that a church could implement to maintain some degree of security, those ideas may be old hat by the time that you read them. Further, they may be inappropriate for your circumstances. They simply are ideas which I have used or have considered for my clients' needs. Some of them cost nothing; some cost a lot. Most are affordable. You may choose one or two ideas from each group or the whole hog, plus a few ideas that I have not listed or even considered. In putting your security system together, though, remember that, while you assess your "reasonableness" in foresight, jurors judge it hindsight.

SECURITY THEORY - BE DILIGENT

Develop checklists. A smoke alarm with dead batteries does absolutely no good. Should someone be checking the batteries on a regular basis to ensure that the unit is in good working order and that it at least will have a chance of functioning properly when it is needed? The obvious answer is yes, but we rarely have systems in place that allow us the luxury of a well-earned night's sleep. We may sleep well, but, if we do, then we have traded insomnia for denial. That is not much of a bargain.

I maintain checklists at work which are pages long and which we complete weekly, monthly, quarterly, and annually. I could reproduce them here, but a checklist should be tailored to your individual needs. To create your checklist, simply write down the elements of your security system and do what you need to do on a regular basis to ensure that they are working. If an item is missing or not working, then replace it or fix it and remind yourself that it would have remained missing or broken for a long time, but for your checklist.

Security Theory - Be Expectant - Expect the Unexpected from People

In my daughter's situation from earlier in this chapter, a teacher was implicated, although criminal charges ultimately were dismissed. The mere suggestion that a teacher, any kind of teacher, could hatch such a plot never would have crossed my mind. That a teacher could be responsible for a shooting at a school is shocking, but the ministry also harbors its own dangers. David Koresh, Marshall Applewhite, James Jones, and Jeffrey Lundgren are ministers who ultimately led their followers to death. They were not the first ministers to hurt people and they will not be the last. The entire Catholic priesthood recently has come under intense scrutiny for the horrendous acts committed by a few. We should not be so naive as to think that abuse of parishioners is limited to that denomination, though. Other professions are not immune, as seen in Dr. Harold Shipman's murder of hundreds of his medical patients in England before being discovered. The point is that danger lurks everywhere and we cannot trust someone based simply on a professional affiliation.

The abduction and murder of my friend's sister when I was in third grade, Wedgwood, Columbine, September 11, and other personal and global tragedies for which I do not have the answers continually drive home I Peter 2:11: we truly are "aliens and strangers in the world." All around us are men and women, described in II Peter 2:17, who are "springs without water and mists driven by a storm. Blackest darkness is reserved for them." In Jude 13 "[t]hey are wild waves of the sea, foaming up their shame; wandering stars, for whom blackest darkness has been reserved for ever." They are, in the times of Revelation 16:10–11, men who "gnawed their tongues in agony and cursed the God of heaven because of their pains and their sores, but they refused to repent of what they had done." If men like this reject God in the final judgment, then why should we be surprised one bit at their capacity and eagerness to inflict suffering on us?

Security Theory - Be Expectant - Expect the Unexpected from Places

When we attend church, many of us worship in what we refer to as a sanctuary. It is the place where we worship together; witness baptisms, marriages, and funerals; and attend business meetings and choir and drama practices and performances. We feel safe and secure in it. If life were a game of tag, then the sanctuary would be base. We can leave our troubles at the door and bring in only our faith, if we chose to do so. That has been the practice in the past, but it is beginning to change. While we may continue to worship in sanctuaries and to consider them sacred for the purposes of our faith, the immunity from breaches of the peace which they and other parts of church campuses have enjoyed in the past is vanishing.

Violence on church property is too widespread for much anecdotal evidence. One recent episode occurred in September, 1999, at Wedgwood Baptist Church in Forth Worth. A gunman entered the sanctuary during a worship service, opening fire. Before killing himself, he killed seven people and injured seven others. There was little, if anything, that any of us could have done to prevent this incident from the standpoint of security. To repeat myself, you cannot fathom the destruction that depravity, determination, ingenuity, and easy access to weapons can wreak.

Security Theory - Be Expectant - Expect the Unexpected from Things

A few years ago my family and I were driving to church on a Sunday night. As I pulled out of our driveway, I noticed that something was wrong with the mailbox. I was running late, as usual, and only had a cursory look as I drove by, already creating a suspect list from a mental roster of former Sunday School students. Upon returning, things looked more suspicious than my first impression belied. I called the police and a few hours later the hazardous materials trucks, the police department squad cars, and the fire department pumpers left. Someone had placed a bomb in our mailbox. By God's grace, it exploded when no one was around. Amazingly enough, no one even heard it explode, although the police told us that it probably had been fairly loud. While it was a crude bomb and had no trigger or timing mechanism other than chemical reaction, it had contained enough acid and shrapnel to kill, to blind, or to disfigure anyone standing in front of or opening the mailbox at the wrong time.

In 1990, Lisa Comes, daughter of then Pastor John Osteen of Lakewood Church in Houston, opened a mail package which contained a pipe bomb. Although it exploded in front of her, she miraculously survived. In 2001, we witnessed the anthrax virus being spread slowly and silently through the mail. On September 11, 2001, we witnessed religious terrorists use commercial airplanes loaded with jet fuel and passengers as weapons of mass destruction. That day sent our nation and parts of the world into economic, spiritual, and physical shock and simultaneously awakened us.

The point to all of this is that almost anything can be a weapon. Bomb recipes calling for products located under your kitchen sink, in your garage, or at your hardware store are readily available on the internet. Handguns can be stolen or borrowed from "secret" hiding places. Rifles and other firearms can be purchased at gun shows for cash with little, if any, identification required. Knives, martial arts weaponry, and swords are sold at the mall. Computer viruses destroy software and valuable data at alarming rates and computer hackers steal the same (sometimes confidential) information that viruses destroy. Any vehicle that can be directed at a target and loaded with an explosive, whether fuel or a bomb product such as that used in the April, 1995, Oklahoma City federal building bombing, can be a weapon of mass destruction or a surgical strike aimed at one person.

In conclusion of this section, remember that there will never be a completely effective deterrent for a premeditated, unanticipated act of violence. We certainly should do our best to prevent these situations by expecting the unexpected, but we shall never fully accomplish that goal. With thoughts of futility racing in your head, please consider my first point: be prayerful.

IDENTIFYING SECURITY NEEDS

Before writing a check for even one door lock, you should consider just what you are trying to protect. Give some thought to the following issues and try not to be NERVS:

- Nature of the Items to be Secured
- Ease of Replacement of the Items to be Secured
- Risk to which the Items to be Secured may be Subjected
- Value of the Items to be Secured
- *Situs* of the Items to be Secured (location, but I needed an "s" word)

Items to be secured certainly should include people, the most irreplaceable item on any security checklist. As discussed in the premises liability section, the church's mission pretty much demands that it maintain an open door policy as to any one who wants to come on the property. With rare exception, anyone on the church's property is likely to be an invitee (someone whom the owner has invited, either directly or indirectly, to be on the property). While churches should not have guard stations at the driveway, staff offices may need a little more protection. For example, your church may want to secure its exterior doors during office hours if no activities are planned. A receptionist with a view of the exterior door and / or an intercom could open the doors remotely after confirming a visitor's identity and purpose. That may be a fairly radical departure from your current situation, but some churches have adopted this procedure.

Items to be secured also include property. Churches now have sophisticated and expensive office equipment, original works of art, antiques, and valuable collections. There are ready markets for equipment and furnishings, even when these items have been stolen from a church. Among the office equipment which might be found in your church and which might be worth securing are copy machines, printing and publishing equipment, telephone systems, mail and postage equipment, computers and network equipment, sound systems, desks, chairs, file cabinets, and conference tables. Just open your telephone directory and look under "used furniture" or "used business equipment." Is there a chance that your church's property might wind up for sale a few hundred miles away? If you think that your church has nothing worth stealing, then dismiss that thought immediately.

Other property worth securing includes information. Personnel files, contribution records, payroll information, confidential communications, notes from counseling sessions, and financial account records are just a few types of the information that needs to be secured. Other records, *e.g.* baptismal records, church membership rolls, and attendance records may have no financial value and may not be confidential, but are very valuable nonetheless. When you have quantified all of these factors and have reflected on how they impact each other, you should be ready to start considering what types of security measures should be in your system.

SECURITY STRATEGIES

If you play the "first words that pop into your head" game with someone, a likely response to "security system" is "burglar alarm." However, you should think of security systems much more expansively. A security system should encompass anything that protects people or property from anticipated danger or loss and should be comprised of many different elements. Here comes the mnemonic: GATES.

- General Strategies
- Accessible Information Strategies
- Technology Strategies
- Employee, Staff, and Volunteer Strategies
- Surrounding Grounds and Buildings Strategies

None of these strategies will be successful in isolation. When utilized wisely and as part of an overall strategy, though, they can assist you in achieving your security goals. While this list is comprehensive from my experience, a security professional probably will have other ideas to add to it. Thus, you should use this chapter only as a springboard for discussion and preliminary planning and speak with a professional when the need arises.

SECURITY STRATEGIES - GENERAL STRATEGIES

- make friends, not enemies, of your neighbors and they will be more likely to watch out for your property and *vice versa*
- start or join a neighborhood watch program
- introduce your church and its leaders to the local law enforcement officials
- open your church for local law enforcement officials to present community-wide safety and security lectures
- identify property by placing hard-to-remove inventory tags in less visible places
- maintain a current property inventory list
- control building access when the doors to the public do not need to be open
- retain on-site or drive-by security services for any needed security presence, either permanently or on an as-needed basis
- report immediately any anticipated, suspected, or actual security incidents to law enforcement
- enforce accountability for those responsible for opening and closing buildings, closets, offices, desks, computers, outside facilities, *et cetera*
- avoid leaving employees unprotected and alone; fish school for very good reasons
- instruct all employees on the use of the telephone system and "911"

- interview all service contractors, *e.g.* janitorial services, with access to your church's people and property to satisfy yourself with that company's reputation, hiring safeguards, employment policies, insured status, and bonded status
- maintain current key lists
- maintain a locked key box where all keys which are not used on a daily basis or which are not taken home by employees are kept
- change locks and keys when a key is missing
- require keys to be surrendered when an employee or trusted volunteer no longer needs the key
- avoid attaching descriptive labels to keys, such as "Key to Front Door of First Church of the Open Doors"; use serial numbers or codes instead so that a lost key does not identify its owner and, thereby, invite a burglary
- maintain a current code list for serial numbers or codes describing keys so that you can avoid playing "which key fits the lock"
- do not use the "hide the key in the cute rock by the door" trick; professionals know all of the hiding places and are always a step ahead of you
- create rotating duty security patrols, which could double as traffic assistance groups, using deacons or other church members to patrol the parking lot during services, as a parking lot full of cars but devoid of parishioners presents ample opportunity for vandalism and theft
- create a plan for notifying all present of a pending security incident, with instructions for rendezvousing, accounting for those present and missing, locking down the buildings and offices, notifying emergency personnel, notifying family members, and administering any needed first aid until emergency medical personnel arrive
- limit community access to your church's facilities to those groups whom you can identify as low security risks, as someone may pose as a member of a community interest group simply to case the church

SECURITY STRATEGIES - ACCESSIBLE INFORMATION STRATEGIES

- limit access to combinations, keys, and passwords to a need-to-know basis
- maintain current virus software
- install firewalls in your computer system
- avoid using "guessable" passwords; everyone at the church knows your birthday, your street address, and your dog's name

- the best passwords are combinations of upper case letters, lower case letters, numbers, and other typographical symbols
- change passwords regularly
- memorize your passwords
- if you find yourself needing password reminders, then assign telephone keypad values to a word and use the numbers as a password; *e.g,* the password "letmein" becomes "5386346."
- if you must record your passwords, then do so at a remote location where they cannot be accessed by someone at the office
- do not write your password on a piece of paper and then tape it to the monitor
- avoid using "remember my password" features on web sites; anyone who gains access to your computer gains access to those sites if the site remembers your password and user id
- set a short "sleep" cycle for your computer; typing your password again to access your computer is a cheap price to pay for denying access to vital information while you take a quick restroom break
- maintain current property inventory lists with identifying serial numbers and photographs
- lock office doors when they are not in use
- lock all file cabinets containing confidential or sensitive information when not in use
- clean desks at lunch and the end of the day of all confidential or sensitive information
- observe all United States Postal Service guidelines for opening mail and packages[328]

SECURITY STRATEGIES - TECHNOLOGY STRATEGIES

- install a monitored alarm system consisting of a combination of the following:

  - an audible and visible on-site alarm, *i.e.* loud noise and flashing lights
  - security zones (*e.g.* Zone 1 - entire building, Zone 2 - general office, Zone 3 - ministers' offices, and Zone 4 - senior pastor's study) which allow employees access only to those zones for which they have clearance
  - magnetic contact sensors on doors and windows
  - heat and smoke detectors
  - photoelectric beams, glass break sensors, and interior motion sensors

- telephone lines which trigger alarms if they are cut
- controlled access doors using card and fob readers, magnetic contacts, concealed entry buttons, and one-way door knobs, among other types of access control

- install motion sensors connected to exterior lighting, especially around doorways and vulnerable windows
- install exterior lighting sufficient to illuminate all building sides and the parking lot
- install exterior lighting high enough to prevent tampering and to thwart little boys with rocks, good aim, and good arms
- install interior lighting to illuminate hallways at night
- install irregularly scheduled interior lighting in offices or other strategic locations which is activated at night with timers or light-sensitive photocells
- install a secure interior key box containing keys to all locks
- install closed-circuit television cameras feeding supervised or recording monitors
- install fire extinguishers (preferably multi-type, ABC extinguishers) in numerous locations sufficiently near each other to ensure availability in an emergency
- ensure that your telephone system has an intercom system so that trouble in one room or another building can be broadcast to others who can summon help
- ensure that your telephone system has speed dial numbers for local law emergency assistance and that everyone is familiar with how to use either those numbers or the 911 system, if available

SECURITY STRATEGIES - EMPLOYEE, STAFF, AND VOLUNTEER STRATEGIES

- maintain a current, comprehensive employee handbook specifically defining your church's expectations for employee conduct and outlining the consequences of violations
- conduct initial background checks
- conduct timely background checks for employees demonstrating suspicious behavior
- conduct drug testing in compliance with employment law issues
- maintain fidelity bonds for staff with access to financial assets
- require employees to wear visible identification tags while on duty

- take appropriate employment action against any employee engaging in or threatening violent behavior or otherwise behaving inappropriately toward another employee or parishioner
- take appropriate action against any volunteer engaging in threatening or violent behavior or otherwise behaving inappropriately toward another parishioner or employee
- institute appropriate safeguards and systems for teachers and nursery workers to monitor infants, toddlers, and children while in your church's care and to release those young ones only to appropriate parents or guardians

SECURITY STRATEGIES - SURROUNDING GROUNDS AND BUILDINGS STRATEGIES

- attach labels to windows and doors and plant small signs in the landscaping advising all who are interested in such matters that the property is protected by an alarm system
- erect view-obstructing fences with locked gates for areas containing anything likely to be stolen or vandalized
- have fewer, not more, access points, while maintaining building and fire code compliance
- erect fences with locked gates for areas containing HVAC, playground, and similar equipment or anything which might be considered to be an attractive nuisance
- close gates to driveways to prevent after hours vehicle access to parking lots
- build garages for church vehicles and grounds-keeping equipment
- plant thick and thorny shrubbery underneath windows to deter break-ins
- eliminate access to second story windows by pruning nearby trees to at least eight feet above ground level and by removing architectural features which allow access to roofs and nearby windows
- use graffiti-resistant paint
- install tamper-resistant burglar bars over windows
- install protective films, plastic, or glass over stained glass windows
- remodel entries with windows next to doors or windows in doors to remove the easy access presented by breaking the window and reaching through it to open the door
- avoid using landscaping stones which easily transform into window-shattering missiles

CHAPTER 12

Safe and Sound: Health

THE GOOD SAMARITAN LAW

When a medical emergency occurs at the church, the first two things that anyone should do are to consider activating the local emergency medical response team, usually by calling 911, and to locate a doctor, nurse, or emergency medical technician on the premises. Knowing the location of trained medical personnel during church activities is a good idea. Some churches post Sunday School class or other church activity schedules and their locations on bulletin boards around the church so that trained people can be found immediately when an emergency occurs. Depending on your church's size, there may or may not be a health care professional present. If anyone with medical training can be found and is willing to assist, then everyone should defer to that person's judgment and handling of the situation. However, accidents sometimes happen without a doctor in the house and liability concerns over emergency care should be addressed prior to an emergency arising.

The Texas Legislature has enacted what is referred to as the Good Samaritan Law. Similar laws exist in most states. It applies to a "person who in good faith administers emergency care, including using an automated external defibrillator, at the scene of an emergency" and states that such a person will not be "liable in civil damages for an act performed during the emergency unless the act is wilfully or wantonly negligent."[329] The defibrillator language was added in the Texas Legislature's 1999 session.

That portion of the statute applies to most of the situations in which people find themselves. However, there are several exceptions to the statute's coverage. It generally does not apply to

- health care professionals
- anyone who expects to receive payment for the care rendered
- anyone at the emergency scene who "was soliciting business or seeking to perform a service for remuneration"
- anyone whose negligent actions were a "producing cause" of the emergency[330]

Thus, the focus of the statute is on the exact situation with which the church could find itself faced: when an innocent bystander, without training, must respond to another person's medical emergency. The statute provides that when she responds, she will not be civilly liable for any negligence unless her actions are wilfully or wantonly negligent or caused the emergency. That is a fairly rigorous standard for a plaintiff to prove and should provide encouragement for us to do the right thing in the face of an emergency.

ORGAN DONATION

Churches usually rally around a family when one of its members is in need of an organ transplant. These difficult medical situations can lead a congregation to heightened sensitivity to the need for organ donations. The Texas Anatomical Gift Act provides that a person "may give all or part of the person's body" to a hospital, a specified donee, a physician, an accredited health care teaching facility, a storage facility, a person specified by a physician, an eye bank, or the Anatomical Board of the State of Texas.[331] The general purposes for which these donations may be made are for medical and dental research, education, and transplantation.[332]

There are several ways in which an anatomical gift can be made. The most popular and, perhaps, convenient way is to make the gift known on a donor's card. Prior to September 1, 1997, gifts could be made on your driver's license. However, the law changed at that point and now the law states that a person who wishes to be an organ donor may make that intention known by executing

a card designed to be carried by the donor. To be effective, the document must be signed by the donor in the presence of two witnesses. If the donor cannot sign the document, a person may sign the document for the donor at the donor's direction and in the presence of the donor and two witnesses. The witnesses to the signing of a document under this subsection must sign the document in the presence of the donor.[333]

Another method is to make such a gift through the execution of a will containing an express gift provision. The will does not need to be probated for the gift provision to be effective. There also is a provision allowing the relatives of a person who has not made a gift to do so after that person's death. This statute lists a hierarchy of those who may make such a decision and lists several criteria for the propriety of a gift under these circumstances.[334]

BLOOD DRIVES

Almost every church of which I have been a member has had blood drives. Different blood banks have different operating procedures, but most seem to offer individual and group plans. These plans provide for the donation of blood by a person or persons with corresponding credit given for that donation if a covered member needs blood during the plan period, which usually equals one year from the date of donation.

One way to think of blood drives is that they are like insurance policies. You have to pay a premium (giving blood), the coverage lasts only for a certain period, and a covered person receives a benefit if he makes a claim. Not being covered under a blood plan or lacking health care insurance can become extremely expensive in accidents or when surgery is needed. While we all would like to think that everyone in our church has adequate health insurance coverage, the fact is that there are many, perhaps many more than you would expect, that do not have any coverage at all.

Congress passed the National Blood Policy in 1974. It was designed "to encourage, foster and support measures to enhance resource sharing . . . in the distribution and utilization of blood, in order to make the most efficient use of the national supply." Seldom has Congress made more sense. Giving blood beforehand allows us to provide others, whom we may know or whom we may never know, with an inexpensive and sometimes free resource in a time of critical need.

FIRST AID TRAINING

Larger corporations have awakened to the fact that whenever groups of people gather for extended periods of time, such as in the workplace, medical problems can arise. Whether in the form of job-related accidents or unrelated health problems, businesses have responded to these situations by implementing and enforcing more and stricter safety standards and providing some level of safety training and, sometimes, medical training to its employees. Some businesses which can justify the expense have gone so far as to employ professional medical personnel on site, although this generally occurs in industries in which the probability or seriousness of job-related accidents is highest. Churches should share many of these concerns with big business. Serious accidents can and do happen every day in office, clerical, and maintenance situations. It is proper to do what we can to prepare for these contingencies before they happen and to prevent them from happening in the first place.

Organizations such as the American Red Cross,[335] the American Heart Association,[336] and the National Safety Council[337] offer first aid training programs which vary from covering only the basics to providing higher certifications. Some of the topics included in these training programs include basic and advanced first aid and emergency care, cardiopulmonary resuscitation, use of automated external defibrillators, workplace safety, and accident prevention. These training agencies will emphasize obtaining a well-equipped first aid kit, as well as an automated external defibrillator, and having people trained and willing to use these items when emergencies occur. With some churches employing significant numbers of people on every working day and with the hundreds and sometimes thousands of people who visit a church during regularly scheduled worship services, we need to consider equipping our staffs and members to deal with these problems more effectively than they have dealt with them in the past.

CHAPTER 13

Between a Rock and a Hard Place: Pastoral Issues

Privileges

Keep it on the down low. Just between you and me. Speaking confidentially. Don't tell anyone that I told you. Let's keep this confidential. When we hear these words, our first response usually is "sure." We want to be trusted. We want to be trustworthy. If we are professionals, though, we can count on our "confidentiality" being regulated. Sometimes we must break that confidence and speak when we rather would remain silent. Sometimes we must keep that confidence and remain silent when we rather would speak. When those conflicting feelings arise, we need to remember the rules of confidentiality under which we all operate, even if those rules may (and frequently do) differ from the expectations of those who entrusted us with their secrets.

There are several privileges recognized by Article V of the Texas Rules of Evidence, all of which are listed below. They address confidentiality within relationships and are "designed to further a specific societal interest by suppressing certain categories of evidence in civil and criminal trials."[338]

- certain confidential reports[339]
- attorney / client[340]
- husband / wife[341]
- clergy[342]

- voting[343]
- trade secrets[344]
- government informant[345]
- physician / patient[346]
- mental health[347]

The law is attempting to balance competing values in these situations. The first value is that the search for truth is an important ingredient in the administration of justice. That value demands that the truth be told, regardless of any prior commitments of confidentiality. The second value, sometimes in conflict with the first value, recognizes that certain behaviors and relationships (and the communications therein) strengthen society. The value of confidentiality inherent in these behaviors and relationships is recognized through the application and enforcement of privileges, listed below. These privileges are not absolute, however, and each has its own rules and exceptions. As only three of them have direct application to this book's scope, I limit discussion to the clergy, attorney / client, and mental health privileges.

PRIVILEGES - THE CLERGY PRIVILEGE

Before the advent of the 1990s, the clergy privilege was rarely discussed. However, there have been more than one dozen reported appellate cases in Texas dealing with this privilege since 1992 and we may see even more of these cases in the near future. As many staff members do not have an extremely clear idea of the scope of the privilege, it is time for us to understand the privilege before we learn some very hard lessons about it.

In the early stages of writing this book, I was discussing its progress with a young minister. I was telling him about my research on this chapter when he asked me to tell him about the clergy privilege. I was shocked at his question, but not as shocked as I have become to learn exactly how little is actually known by the very people whom it affects most. To compound the problem, a recent book on pastoral counseling advises Texas ministers that communications between parishioners and clergy members are not protected by any statutory privilege.[348]

Ignorance of the clergy privilege could lead to disastrous results. For instance, television detective shows have portrayed the struggles of a clergyman to whom a crime has been confessed. His inclination is to report the perpetrator because the act is so terrible, the victim invariably is a member of his congregation, and justice needs to be served. If the clergyman reports his knowledge, action could be taken against the perpetrator, who then might change his formerly benevolent attitude toward the clergyman. Regardless of the circumstances, though (with some exceptions noted below), privileged communications should remain privileged, for the protection of both the penitent and the priest.

The law provides that a "person has a privilege to refuse to disclose and to prevent another from disclosing a confidential communication by the person to a clergyman in his professional character as spiritual advisor."[349] The "penitent / priest privilege," as it also is known, is recognized by federal courts, too.[350] As you would expect, we simply cannot allow the plain language of the law to speak for itself. There are several unique features of the clergy privilege which are not immediately apparent.

First, the privilege belongs to the person communicating with clergy. Only he can decide whether or not the clergyman may divulge the communication to another person. If questioned regarding the communication, the clergyman must respond that the subject matter of the communication is privileged and that he cannot speak freely. While attorneys, district attorneys, policemen, journalists, and even parishioners should understand these concepts, not all of them respect the privilege and some may attempt to persuade a clergyman to divulge the communication through various arguments or outright trickery. Thus, a clergyman should not confirm the communication if someone is lucky enough to guess the truth, to say it confidently as if everyone knew it, and then to wait for the clergyman to confirm the guess.

Next, the communication must be made to a clergyman in his capacity as a spiritual advisor. For example, the clergyman's neighbor, who is unaware of the clergyman's vocation, divulges a secret to the clergyman while both are raking leaves. After a police investigation begins, the neighbor learns of the clergyman's calling and decides that his disclosure should be privileged. Although the neighbor may have sensed that the clergyman was a really nice guy, he made the communication to a yard worker, not a clergyman, in this context. Thus, the communication was not made to the clergyman in his "professional character as spiritual advisor" and should not be privileged.

Similarly, in the *Easley* case, a parishioner was charged with killing her husband by shooting him five times with a shotgun.[351] She wrote two letters to her pastor threatening to blackmail him if he did not provide an alibi for her. Her pastor took those letters to the police and they were used against her in the ensuing trial. In those letters, she threatened to make it "public knowledge that . . . [they had] been seeing each other." The court held the letters to be admissible and found that they were not written to the pastor in his capacity as a spiritual advisor. Instead, the court wrote that they were "nothing more than open threats to destroy the pastor's reputation."[352] At least two other cases, the *Kos* and *Maldonado* cases, have held that their defendants' communications with a priest were not made in the priest's capacity as a spiritual advisor to the defendants. Therefore, the priest could testify about what was said to him.[353]

Along those same lines, does the clergy privilege extend to other church employees, whether or not they are clergy members? For example, the clergyman in the first example dictates some notes to memorialize his conversation with the murderer. Has the clergyman violated the clergy privilege by revealing the communication to his secretary and asking him to transcribe the clergyman's notes? Also, does the clergyman have the right to consult with another clergy member, even in the same church, regarding a privileged communication? Again, there is no definite answer, although I would lean toward saying that these disclosures are inappropriate under the law.

However, the real world differs from the legal world. I know that some staff members discuss situations with each other and their staffs, whether or not in hypothetical terms. Such communications assist the clergy in analyzing whether or not their responses to church members are appropriate and allow the entire staff to be aware of situations within their church. There are no reported Texas cases opining on these points, though.

In contrast to *Easley*, *Kos*, and *Maldonado*, at least two significant cases have supported the exclusion of evidence in connection with the clergy privilege. In its own way, each strengthened the privilege. The *Nicholson* case is important because it enforces the clergy privilege in an extremely close case.[354] In fact, of the three judge appellate panel which decided the case, one judge filed a very well-reasoned dissent which would have allowed the chaplain involved in the case to testify. In *Nicholson* a woman discussed her husband's critical medical condition with the hospital chaplain, an employee of the hospital. The couple later sued the hospital over its alleged delay in treating the husband. The hospital sought to force the chaplain to divulge the wife's communications, alleging that the wife admitted to the chaplain that she was in part responsible for the treatment delay by attempting to have her husband transferred to another hospital, against the hospital's advice urging immediate treatment.

The court eventually upheld the chaplain's refusal to testify regarding any matter communicated to him by the wife, whether spiritual or not spiritual. The court reasoned that the law should avoid placing the clergy in the difficult position of determining "what aspects of a counseling opportunity are not privileged."[355] In so holding, the court's focus is not on whether or not the nature of the communication is spiritual or secular, but on whether the clergyman is acting in his capacity as a spiritual advisor. Thus, the court decided to protect all such communications and not to allow them to be dissected into spiritual/secular communications at a later date.

The court's other point is that the presence of people other than a minister when a privileged communication is made does not waive the privilege. In this case, a doctor and a nurse were present intermittently when the wife was speaking with the chaplain. While the court held that the hospital was "free to question any other individuals about what [the wife] . . . *said to them*" (emphasis in original), it protected what the wife said to the chaplain, regardless of whether or not the doctor and nurse heard those statements. Thus, we can glean two distinct rules from this part of the court's holding:

- anything that a communicant says directly to other people is unprotected
- anything that a communicant says directly to a clergyman in his capacity as a spiritual advisor is protected, regardless of whether or not other people hear it

Therefore, the wife's statements to the chaplain were privileged communications which the doctor and nurse cannot divulge.[356] Although this is a very fine line, it is consistent with the rule. The clergy privilege provides that a person can prevent *another*, not just a clergyman, from "disclosing a confidential communication by the person to a clergyman."[357] Thus, the rule implicitly contemplates that persons other than a clergyman may be present when a communication is made. With *Nicholson*, the rule apparently now precludes anyone who hears the communication from divulging it.

The other notable case is the *Simpson* case.[358] In *Simpson*, the church partially disassembled and set aside a faulty piece of playground equipment two days before regular worship services. A still unidentified person returned that piece of equipment to the playground before Sunday School without any repairs having been made. No one ever warned three year old Jennifer Simpson's Sunday School teachers or her parents that there was a problem with the equipment. Jennifer began playing on it, an accident happened, and she sustained life-altering, permanent injuries. She is now a quadriplegic and will need constant care for the rest of her life.

In his deposition, the church's minister admitted that he had received a communication after Jennifer's accident regarding the faulty playground equipment. He refused to divulge the content of that communication or the identity of the communicant, but stated that it concerned who put the equipment back and when they did it. The court then went on to provide a thorough discussion of the clergy privilege, relying on *Nicholson*, law review articles, and cases from other jurisdictions in deference to the fact that "virtually no caselaw" exists on this point.[359] However, the court eventually enforced the privilege, leaving the Simpsons wondering who knew what and why they would not come forward.

While this holding gave no particular comfort to the Simpsons, it is somewhat comforting to the church that the court refused to "set in motion . . . [the] piecemeal erosion" of the clergy privilege and joined the *Nicholson* court in strongly affirming "the vitality of the communications-to-clergy privilege."[360] Thus, *Simpson's* unique rule is this: without permission, a minister cannot reveal the communicant's identity in an otherwise privileged communication. When read together, *Simpson*, *Nicholson*, and their progeny reveal that "litigants can expect that the courts will broadly interpret Rule 505, protecting confidential conversations when clerics are acting in their spiritual role."[361]

Simpson may have a significant legal point to make about the clergy privilege, but it also carries a much more important message for those with ears to hear. That message is this: as Christians we must consider the care and precaution which that church should have exercised before allowing an innocent child to play on a broken, dangerous piece of equipment. Jennifer could have been your daughter or my daughter. The careless person who placed that broken piece of equipment on the playground could have been you or me. The assertion of the clergy privilege, in view of what happened to Jennifer and how we are supposed to relate to and to minister to each other, was simply legal gamesmanship. This case highlights the tension between law and ministry like few others and is well worth reading from start to finish.

PRIVILEGES - THE CLERGY PRIVILEGE - SUPPORT GROUPS

A rather narrow area of related litigation may surface in the near future. Churches have been turning to support groups in recent years for several reasons, chief among which are that such groups assist the church in ministering to more people on a more effective basis, by decreasing staff members' already considerable workload, and by equipping individual members to minister to the congregation and the world. As such, some of the communications which typically were made to staff members in years past are now being revealed and dealt with exclusively in support groups.

There usually is no licensed "minister, priest, . . . or other similar functionary of a religious organization" present when these communications are made.[362] That is the present requirement to invoke the clergy privilege. The person making such communications may have an expectation that, since the church is sponsoring these support groups, providing a meeting place, and training members who serve as group leaders, her communications are privileged. That expectation may be reasonable from a lay perspective, but it is incorrect.

I see the benefit in extending the clergy privilege to such communications. Extending the privilege would uphold its purpose, that being to encourage open communication between the penitent and the priest. As the concept of the "priesthood of the believer" is espoused by many denominations, I believe that extending the privilege is consistent with a common evangelical belief that every Christian is a minister or priest in a theological sense.

However, the law does not support that view. A good argument against an extension is that it would lead to rather quick and probably widespread abuse, as a person could claim that his communication with a fellow criminal was a communication made to a fellow spiritual believer, without regard to the nature or genuineness of their belief. For that specific reason, I do not believe that the clergy privilege will be expanded any farther than it exists today in connection with the definition of minister.

Many of these support groups require confidentiality pledges. The members of these groups trust each other's pledge of confidentiality. How then should we advise the leaders and members of support groups as to the confidentiality of their communications? The unvarnished truth is that, if an attorney or court wants to compel testimony from a group member about a communication that has been divulged, then the confidentiality pledge is not worth the paper upon which it is written and the group members probably can be compelled to testify regarding their knowledge.[363] Thus, members have three options. The first is that they can break their confidentiality pledge and answer any questions asked by anyone, whether or not under threat of contempt of court. Next, they can remain true to their pledge and risk being held in contempt of court, with an accompanying fine and/or imprisonment. Finally, they can be honest with each other in the beginning, acknowledge the limitations placed on these confidentiality pledges, and make their own decision about just how honest they want to be with a group of people who are struggling just like they are.

On a related point, how should we advise the leaders and members of support groups when they learn of a matter which they have an affirmative duty to divulge, such as child abuse or neglect, as opposed to learning of a matter which merely may impact a civil or criminal proceeding? One possible solution includes training each group leader to report any such knowledge up the chain of command until that report reaches an appointed person who will report and ensuring that all group members understand the limitations on the confidentiality pledge. That chain of command may be very short in a small church, so that the group leader reports directly to the pastor. In a large church, there may be two or three different levels through which the report needs to filter. In any case, if a communication alerts any group member to a matter which that group member has a duty to report, then there should be a procedure by which the church ensures that the matter is reported. Further, the person who made the initial admission should be informed immediately that the group leader or a staff member is legally required to disclose the communication. The church's failure to do so may bring into play civil and criminal provisions for failure to report, may result in a child's prolonged suffering (in the case of child abuse and neglect), and/or may give the person who makes the admission an undeserved expectation that it will remain confidential.

PRIVILEGES - THE ATTORNEY / CLIENT PRIVILEGE

In addition to the attorney / client privilege, ethical rules governing attorneys' conduct prohibit attorneys from revealing confidential information entrusted to them by their clients.[364] There are numerous exceptions and limitations on this rule, making meaningful discussion of it in this limited space fairly difficult. Generally speaking, though, an attorney may not reveal confidential information unless he does so under the following circumstances, all of which are addressed in the ethical rules governing attorneys:

- with the client's consent
- to prevent the client from committing or using the attorney's services to commit fraud
- to prevent the client from injuring or killing another
- to defend a claim by or to prosecute a claim against the client
- to comply with a court order or other duties owed to the court
- to inform those assisting the attorney in representing the client

An interesting aspect of the attorney / client privilege, compared with the clergy privilege, is how the two treat a relatively "limited" disclosure of confidential information to those associated with the respective attorney or minister. In a ministry context, one clergyman probably should not reveal a confidential communication to another. However, the attorney / client privilege contains language, lacking in the clergy privilege, which allows disclosures by an attorney to anyone assisting that attorney in representing a client. Thus, confidential communications may be shared by an attorney with and even forwarded by the client directly to associated attorneys, secretaries, paralegals, clerks, *et cetera*. The *Ballew* case recognizes this exception and holds that an attorney can disclose privileged information to "agents whose services are required by the attorney in order to properly prepare his client's case."[365] Those agents then are bound by the same privilege. Again, I can find no reported cases dealing with this issue in regard to the clergy privilege. However, I would not expect a court to extend the clergy privilege as far as the attorney/client privilege has been extended, based in large part upon the exception found in the attorney / client privilege rule, but missing in the penitent / priest privilege.

Privileges - The Mental Health Privilege

Yet another statutory privilege which arguably could apply to some pastoral situations is the mental health privilege. The immediate situation which comes to mind is that of the staff member who is a licensed professional counselor or licensed marriage and family therapist. However, any person who is "licensed or certified by the State of Texas in the diagnosis, evaluation or treatment of any mental or emotional disorder" is subject to the mental health privilege.[366] There are others who are defined as professionals in this context, such as psychologists, social workers, and chemical dependency counselors, but professional counselors and marriage and family therapists are the ones usually associated with churches.

The person claiming the privilege, the client or patient, is anyone who is interviewed or evaluated by or consults with a mental health professional for the purpose of being treated or evaluated by that professional.[367] Importantly, the privilege may be claimed by the patient or his representatives, a category including his parents, guardians, personal representatives, and any other person bearing his written consent.[368] The rule of privilege states that the patient or his representative may prevent the disclosure of any information communicated among the patient, his representatives, and a professional.[369]

The basic rule of confidentiality for mental health professionals is that "[c]ommunications between a patient and a professional, and records of the identity, diagnosis, evaluation, or treatment of a patient that are created or maintained by a professional, are confidential."[370] The law carves out several exceptions, though, and in these situations confidentiality must be abandoned, but only to the extent necessary to protect those in harm's way. They include situations in which the following may exist.

- child abuse and neglect[371]
- elder abuse, neglect, or exploitation[372]
- "abuse, neglect, and illegal, unprofessional, or unethical conduct" in a mental health facility[373]
- sexual exploitation[374]

There are some other exceptions, albeit infrequently encountered, which should be noted.[375]

A related comment on confidentiality, discussed in more detail in Chapter 14, is that licensed professional counselors are under an ethical obligation to disclose to their clients the exceptions to their confidentiality obligations.[376] This requirement is subject to the same criticism on which I elaborate in Chapter 14, i.e. if you disclose to a client that you have a duty to break confidentiality under certain circumstances, then you essentially foreclose any possibility of ever learning of those circumstances. It is, however, a legal and ethical requirement with which licensed professional counselors must comply. Finally, as if you needed to be reminded, the statute provides that violating confidentiality gives rise to a civil cause of action in the patient's favor, all of which leads to the discussion of an extremely important scenario.[377]

PRIVILEGES - WEARING TWO HATS

Imagine that your church's pastor is a licensed professional counselor or licensed marriage and family therapist. He engages in a counseling relationship with one of the parishioners and later determines that this parishioner is behaving in such a manner that church discipline is appropriate. In order to effect that, he informs the congregation of her conduct. While his revelation may or may not be appropriate in a ministerial context, he probably has violated the confidentiality provisions applicable to that counseling relationship by informing the congregation of the counselee's behavior and, perhaps, by instituting church discipline. The kneejerk reaction may be that his duties as pastor are far more important than his duties as a mental health professional and, therefore, should take precedence. That is a fine argument, but it is a waste of breath.

The scenario described above comes from the *Penley* case, which has not been finally resolved as of this book's publication. However, the appellate court, in reversing the trial court's findings favoring the minister, made several observations of which all staff members should take note. First (and gladly), it observed that "Texas does not recognize [a] cause of action for 'clergy malpractice.'" However, it noted that "the First Amendment [upon which *Penley's* pastor attempted to rely heavily] does not extend to insulate 'secular component[s]' of otherwise religious relationships."[378] In doing so, the *Penley* court followed the Supreme Court of Texas' opinion in *Tilton*, which noted that:

> the free exercise of religion does not go so far as to be inclusive of actions which are in violation of social duties or subversive of good order. Although freedom to believe may be said to be absolute, freedom of conduct is not and conduct even under religious guise remains subject to regulations for the protection of society.[379]

Further supporting this reasoning is the *Casa View* case, in which the Fifth Circuit Court of Appeals held that "the First Amendment's respect for religious relationships does not require a minister's counseling relationship with a parishioner to be purely secular in order for a court to review the propriety of the conduct occurring within that relationship."[380] In other words, a minister must affirmatively demonstrate that his counseling relationship with a congregant was based solely and exclusively on moral, religious, and spiritual grounds in order to escape judicial scrutiny. A minister licensed as a mental health professional rarely will be able to do that, because her license is a secular license. Further, even ministers who are not mental health professionals usually will fail to meet that burden, as any secular component of their counseling, even components merely alleged to be secular, probably will be enough to keep the case in court.

Thus, the road to the courthouse is paved as follows. Texas still recognizes the free exercise clause and does not recognize a claim for clergy malpractice. However, if the plaintiff can characterize misconduct as based in whole or even in part on secular counseling, violative of social duties, or "subversive to good order," then there will be few roadblocks to placing the case in a jury's hands. The *Penley* court reinforces this observation, stating that, if the counselee revealed confidential information to the pastor within the confines of a secular counseling relationship and he revealed that information without obtaining her consent, then the "fact finder will resolve such issues."[381]

The real issue involved in cases like this is akin to the problems inherent in serving two masters. In the pastoral role, the minister answers to a certain set of rules. In the secular counselor role, the minister answers to a different set of rules. As is evident in *Penley*, these rules sometimes conflict, leaving the minister to fall short of the standard of care and conduct in one or both areas. Before a minister finds himself having to answer to conflicting standards of care, he should find a way to resolve that conflict. Appropriate boundaries built into either or both sides of the equation sometimes can forestall any problems, although the issue may best be answered simply by referring congregants with counseling needs to outside professionals who do not owe any duties to your church, particularly those church-related duties which *Penley's* pastor felt compelled to perform. I do not doubt that many ministers and counselors have set wise boundaries which avoid the conflicts generated in *Penley* and *Casa View*. I also do not doubt that there are ministers and counselors who, having been licensed by the State of Texas as mental health professionals, are not taking their responsibilities to the law and their clients, churches, and respective state boards seriously enough.

REPORTING CHILD ABUSE

We learned the English language by remembering that, for every rule, there is an exception. So it is with the privileges set forth above. The clergy member or counselor who is charged with keeping all communications confidential, whether spiritual or secular, must report any knowledge of child abuse or neglect. There apparently is no exception to this exception in Texas, though, regardless of conflicting laws in other states. Informing the appropriate authorities of child abuse or neglect is discussed in much more detail in Chapter 14. However, I shall hit the high points here.

The law defines child abuse or neglect very expansively.[382] To paraphrase, abuse is any conduct which exposes or subjects a child to a substantial risk of mental, emotional, or physical injury or harm, including any exposure to sexual, obscene, or pornographic conduct or material.[383] Neglect is exposing a child to potential abuse or failing to provide for the child's medical, housing, nutritional, clothing, and other developmental needs.[384]

If you determine or suspect that abuse or neglect has occurred, then you are required to report the conduct in question. First, every person who knows of or suspects abuse or neglect, regardless of his relationship to the church, the child, or the perpetrator, must report the incident to the appropriate authorities immediately.[385] Second, the law requires professionals to report the incident within forty-eight hours of obtaining knowledge of or suspecting the occurrence of an incident.[386] Although the statute does not define immediately, I suspect that it means something much less than forty-eight hours.

The report is not required to be made orally, but the objective of reporting the information quickly is to diminish the possibility of further abuse or neglect. Thus, you should report such an incident in person or by telephone. Mailing in a written report, without taking other steps to ensure more prompt notice, may raise a suspicion in someone's mind that you were not too concerned about preventing further abuse or neglect. It also may create doubts as to your compliance with the statute's requirements. The report can be made to any of the following authorities:

- a local or state law enforcement agency
- Child Protective Services, a division of the Texas Department of Family and Protective Services
- the state agency charged with oversight of the facility at which the abuse or neglect occurred
- another agency designated by a court for the protection of children[387]

The person reporting should state that he believes that a child has been or may have been abused or neglected, along with the name and address of the child, the person responsible for the child, and "any other pertinent information."[388]

Reporting Sexual Misconduct

Sexual misconduct can take many forms. It may be a case of child abuse. If so, then a minister is required to report that incident under the child abuse reporting laws.[389] It may be that a minister is having an affair with someone outside of the church. In that case, there may or may not be any reporting requirement. It may take the form of unwelcome sexual advances or suggestions, perhaps simply inappropriate language, with a church employee. That may give rise to a sexual discrimination claim. However, if a minister is engaged in sexual misconduct with a church member or other person seeking counseling or mental health services, then he may have engaged in sexual exploitation, a civil cause of action discussed in more detail in Chapter 4.[390]

If you determine that the latter is the case, then you are under a duty to report that misconduct. You must do so by contacting the prosecuting attorney in the county in which the misconduct occurred and any state licensing board with oversight authority for the person who committed the misconduct within thirty (30) days after you become aware of the situation.[391]

Additionally, you must inform the alleged victim of your intention and duty to report and you should inquire if the victim wishes to remain anonymous.[392] In the report, you should identify yourself and the alleged victim, if anonymity has not been requested, and state that you suspect that an act of sexual exploitation has occurred.[393] This statute also contains an immunity clause very similar to the immunity clause applicable to the good faith reporting of child abuse or neglect.[394]

These types of claims may involve liability not only for the minister and your church, as the minister's employer, but also for your association or other denominational agency.[395] As noted by Peter Mosgofian and George Ohlschlager in *Sexual Misconduct in Counseling and Ministry*, this statute essentially "wraps the church into its jurisdiction like no other statute has done."[396] As such, you should involve an attorney on your church's behalf at the earliest possible stage in any situation remotely resembling sexual misconduct by a minister.

If your church or insurance company foresees even the remotest possibility of liability, then retaining separate counsel for that minister is advisable. I know that this increases the legal fees involved, but that is not why I make this suggestion. In any sexual misconduct case, unless it is patently frivolous and groundless, there is the very real potential and almost certainty for one attorney to have a conflict of interest in representing the church and the offending minister. The plaintiff probably will assert different causes of action against different defendants. If he alleges that the church should have exercised more care in hiring the minister, then the church may want to point out, in an appropriate case, that the minister falsified his application to conceal prior misconduct and that the church could not have discovered this fact when hiring him, even through reasonably diligent efforts. If there is one attorney, then he would have to choose which defendant's interests to serve. That is an untenable situation and one of many reasons why separate counsel is advisable.

AVOIDING SEXUAL MISCONDUCT

I was sitting at my desk, complaining about how the church needs to get its act together in all aspects of the legal arena. Kimberly was enduring this rant patiently and suggested, while I paused to catch my breath, that I actually do something about it, instead of complaining, and write a book. Only days before I had been sharing those same concerns, probably more tactfully than I had discussed them with Kimberly, with a minister who has been a friend to our families for decades. He recounted for me a story about a man who had shown a list to him. That list held the names of men whose ministries had been destroyed by sexual misconduct. The man's concern over the list's stories of loss and tragedy seemed curious at the time. He quickly tucked the list away, despite having raised the issue, uncomfortable with discussing it any further.

The man with the list was a preacher, one of the best that I have heard. He was a teacher, with a gift for illuminating and applying God's word to our lives that I seldom have seen. He was a counselor, who could empathize with the most troubled, share a word of encouragement, and help find clear paths in the forests of life. He was a pastor, whose flock quickly followed him. He was a writer, whose works you may have read. He was many things to many people.

My friend and I were discussing that list while piecing together our own intimate details of that man's life and trying to draw strength from his many strengths and lessons from his weaknesses. Little did my friend know it when the incident occurred, but the reason that the man kept the list was because it reminded him of his own guilt. He knew that his name already was on that list. It was a self-inflicted scarlet letter and that man was Kimberly's father.

Although the problems had existed for a while, we discovered them very abruptly. As usually is the case, it had not been an isolated incident. Rather, it had been a first step away from the straight and narrow, then a short detour, and finally a fall off the edge of the mountain. As I was proposing to Kimberly, her parents' marriage was disintegrating. Their divorce was final shortly thereafter. We saw Kimberly's father only sporadically during the next few years. Her family was devastated.

His story follows James 1:13–15's timeless progression: temptation leads to desire, desire leads to sin, and sin leads to death. He attempted to stay in the ministry, never approaching the effectiveness which he previously had enjoyed, and passed away, estranged from his family, almost ten years to the day after his problems were exposed. That does not seem to be an uncommon path for others with similar problems. Dr. Billy Graham writes the following account.

> It seems to me that an evangelist, and the clergy for that matter, especially faces temptation in three areas: pride, money, and morals. . . . / I have seen some tragic consequences of young evangelists who could not resist the temptations that we have mentioned. I remember one, when I first started out. He had a gift of evangelism beyond that of almost anyone else I have ever met or heard. He could sway and move great crowds. There was a great response to his ministry. But pride and ego became his stumbling block. This led to sexual immorality. Within five years he died a tragic death.[397]

I did not have to pass the bar to tell this story to you. I tell it to warn of the consequences of sin, though, consequences which can affect your church legally as well as in other ways. These examples are supported by Proverbs 5:4–5 and 14, where we are warned that adultery is as "bitter as gall, sharp as a double-edged sword" and leads to death and "the brink of utter ruin." As noted by John H. Armstrong in *Can Fallen Pastors Be Restored?" The Church's Response to Sexual Misconduct*, "sexual immorality has such serious and lasting consequences that its reproach never fully departs in this life."[398] What more warning do we need?

That question may be rhetorical, but I shall answer it, anyway. Sexual misconduct has far-reaching, yet predictable consequences. It explodes in all directions, leaving scarred, destroyed relationships and painful, uncertain paths to healing. Professionally, it may result in disciplinary action, criminal charges, civil suits, unemployment, and your last opportunity to work on a church staff. Your spouse and children feel justifiably betrayed. You tarnish your witness and publicize your own hypocrisy. Complete strangers, who judge the church and Christianity by your conduct, mistakenly latch on to yet another rationalization to reject God. You associate the church with your sin and damage its ministries and witness. God's, your own, and others' forgiveness seems more suspect as the gravity of the situation weighs upon you. Finally, you sin against your own body and God. It is hard to imagine pulling the pin on any more personally destructive grenade.[399]

While the law allows consenting adults to engage in almost any behavior imaginable, there is a higher standard to which we all need to adhere. Among other attitude adjustments, we need to conform our opinions of vulnerable people to reflect the dignity and respect belonging to someone for whom Christ died and to renew our decisions each and every hour of the day to resist the temptations flung in our faces by a society fixated on sex. This is the "inner transformation and outer control" of which Mosgofian and Ohlschlager speak.[400] This is fleeing from sexual immorality, as Paul urges us to do in I Corinthians 6:18.

You cannot watch television without the fun of sexual promiscuity being extolled. You cannot drive your car without seeing a billboard in which sex is selling something. You cannot listen to the radio or read a magazine without it infiltrating the message. Even what is seemingly innocuous by today's standards, when analyzed properly, carries improper messages. These messages ignore God's plan for sex and degrade and trivialize each of us as mere objects for each other's selfish enjoyment. With that background and the staggering legal consequences of sexual misconduct in mind, a few of the following suggestions may be helpful in avoiding some of the circumstances in which temptation or at least the appearance of impropriety can arise. To simplify these guidelines, I use a married minister as a model.

- Commit yourself to habitual growth in your Christian walk through daily prayer and study.
- Give your spouse and marriage their deserved respect and priority, a "fierce loyalty," in your life.[401]
- Ensure that any secretaries, associates, and professional peers of the opposite gender with whom you must work closely understand your commitment to and respect for your spouse and marriage.
- Avoid close or intimate friendships with members of the opposite gender.
- Observe appropriate boundaries when counseling or meeting, making and keeping professional appointments, and working on projects closely with members of the opposite gender.
- If possible, arrange your office and/or conference room so that your secretary or assistant can see you at all times, perhaps while shielding guests from that view.
- Keep your office door open as much as possible.
- If you are away from the office, then ensure that your secretary or assistant knows your location and can contact you or put your spouse or another staff member in contact with you.
- If you find yourself in an uncomfortable situation, then trust your instincts, stop what you are doing, and discuss a subsequent meeting with more suitable arrangements.
- Develop a close friendship or mentoring relationship with someone of the same gender with whom you can discuss these issues, find mutual support, and remain accountable.

- When traveling away from home without your spouse, be especially mindful of these guidelines.

There obviously is nothing foolproof about these suggestions. Man is creative enough to adhere to each one of them and, despite that, he still can find a way to miss the mark. Further, they arise from my experience as a lawyer, not as a pastor or counselor, and are inherently limited by that perspective. You will find, perhaps, much more informative discussions in further reading. These are, nonetheless, some practical steps to build appropriate boundaries into your ministry.

Exceptions to these suggestions must exist, though, exceptions which we struggle to define and to justify. There have been occasions when I have had lunch with a female colleague or have met with a female client alone. On those occasions, I informed Kimberly beforehand and I took any other appropriate measures to ensure that there was no appearance of impropriety. While admitting that I did not follow my own suggestions, I do not feel that I acted inappropriately in those instances. I certainly do not make a habit of it, though.

Some authorities have questioned whether or not such artificial or arbitrary policies constitute an overreaction *per se*. For example, Marie M. Fortune, whose work has been so important in the area of raising our collective consciousness about sexual misconduct in churches, comments that "[l]awyers and insurance companies rather than theology and scripture have too often shaped the policies and practices set forth by judicatories."[402] I agree with her analysis to a great degree. Promoting artificial form over real substance does little to promote the goal of eliminating sexual misconduct among the clergy. I do not believe, though, that it is healthy for us to be completely without a tangible moral compass on this issue.

Thus, if these guidelines work for you, then use them and any others which assist you in staying on the straight and narrow path. In urging you to consider these guidelines, though, I agree with Ms. Fortune that scripture and theology, not artificial rules, should guide our conduct. Jesus warned the Pharisees about the excesses and errors inherent in their legalistic approach in Matthew 23. He also gave us a beautiful example of breaking unnecessary boundaries in speaking to the Samaritan woman at the well in John 4. Some practical suggestions and danger signs should be heeded in this litigious world, though. If you choose to ignore these or other guidelines, then it might be a good exercise to try to identify the reasons which justify setting them aside. As Paul warned us in I Corinthians 10:12, "if you think you are standing firm, be careful that you don't fall!"

Commentators such as Arnold in *Pastoral Responses to Sexual Issues*, Fortune in *Is Nothing Sacred?* (among other works), and Karen Lebacqz and Ronald G. Barton in *Sex in the Parish* have written far more extensively and have made far more informed comments about boundaries and I unhesitatingly refer you to them for further study. However, since I mention boundaries in response to guarding yourself and others from sexual misconduct from a legal perspective, I shall briefly address some of them here.

First, your church should implement a written policy regarding sexual misconduct involving the staff. Such a policy should "encourage common sense provisions for care in maintaining appropriate boundaries of all kinds in order to preserve the integrity of the pastoral relationship."[403] Simply putting a written policy in place demonstrates a minimally desirable level of commitment and sensitivity to these boundaries and places us all on notice that the church recognizes the potential for problems. While boundaries are not failsafes, the church can minimize potential problems and protect its ministers and members to a greater degree if proper boundaries are created and maintained. Arnold separates these boundaries into five distinct categories, which I unapologetically and with attribution borrow: space, time, language, touch, and your own feelings.[404]

You should observe the boundary of personal space. Practically, this means that you should not have a sleeper sofa in your office and that every person in your office, unless you are working with couples, should have their own seating. Close spaces between people imply intimacy. Counseling and other pastoral conduct certainly involve some degree of intimacy, but it should be appropriate as to the space between minister and parishioner. While couches may be appropriate for a couple seeking counseling, you should have your own chair and should have some space between you and those whom you are counseling. This does not mean that a moat should be dug and filled around your desk, only that maintaining inappropriately close distances with a parishioner may leave her with a feeling that she is more special to you than you would wish for her to believe. You can fulfill your responsibilities without ignoring the boundary of space.

Next, observe the boundary of structured time. Allotting an appropriate amount of time to deal with any person and / or her problems is a good boundary to have in place. Spending too much time with a parishioner may leave the parishioner with that "special" feeling. This boundary can be enforced by not allowing an employee, counselee, or other parishioner unrestricted periods in which to discuss matters and unrestricted access to your office. In other words, schedule regular beginning and ending times and stick to those times. If issues are not resolved within the designated time period, then schedule another meeting.

Alternatively, if your schedule is too busy to accommodate another demand, then delegate responsibility for meeting with a person to another staff member or refer that person to a professional outside of your church. Alternatively, inform that person beforehand of the limited time which you can devote to a particular problem or issue. If that person demands or needs more time than you have available, then you should anticipate a problem. Clergy members should not overextend themselves, yet parishioners' demands on their time are often a primary cause of that overextension.

Observe the boundary of appropriate and timely language. Some words convey an inappropriately close relationship in a situation. The words which you use, especially in the counseling context, should convey not only comfort, empathy, and appropriate options, but also should serve to inform the person being counseled of the limits which should be imposed on your relationship. Further, to the extent that you can, avoid premature decisions, and, especially, comments concerning who is right and who is wrong in a given situation. In many cases, you will be dealing with conflicts among church or family members. When the first person to speak with you tells you his side of a story, omitting all of the nasty facts which do not reflect well on him, and you side with him, you become a judge having heard only one side of the case. Proverbs 18:17 states it succinctly: "[t]he first to present his case seems right, till another comes forward and questions him."

Observe the boundary of touch. Hugs and pats on the hand or shoulder are normally appropriate. However, they sometimes can be misinterpreted. A vulnerable parishioner may interpret any touch to have conveyed an unexpected, yet welcomed, closeness. In contrast, an overly sensitive parishioner may interpret a purely innocent gesture which you meant to convey only comfort or friendship as an offensive or suggestive touch. If a parishioner tells you that your touch makes her uncomfortable, then stop. Similarly, if you sense that a parishioner is uncomfortable, even in the absence of her telling you so, then you either should stop or ask her if she is uncomfortable with the situation. If you remain aloof without ever offering a comforting hug, then you may not be accused of inappropriate behavior. You also may not be accused of being an effective minister. Years of experience are often most helpful in developing your own sense of what is and is not appropriate in certain situations or with certain people, but even experienced ministers have been accused of improper conduct when their motives were entirely innocent. Failing to offer a comforting touch to a parishioner in need, though, will not strengthen your ministry.

Finally, observe the boundary of your own feelings. If any aspect of your relationship with a congregation member makes you uncomfortable, then take appropriate steps to remedy those feelings. If you believe that you can correct the problem by modifying your behavior or discussing the problem with the person whom you are counseling, then you may want to try that first. If that means ending a counseling relationship, though, then do it. It is likely that any problem significant enough to keep you feeling uncomfortable in a relationship, especially after you have tried to remedy the problem, is significant enough to warrant ending that portion of the relationship. Be respectful of the other person's feelings and needs for further counseling by referring them to another counselor, without accusing them of being at fault for the relationship's termination, but end that portion of the relationship. This does not mean that the person cannot continue attending your church, singing in the choir, serving on committees, or participating in any other aspect of church life. It does mean, though, that you should observe your own feelings, even if they cannot be articulated sufficiently for you to express them cogently, and slam on the brakes before an accident happens.[405]

Clint Eastwood's famous character, Dirty Harry, once muttered something about a man's need to know his limitations. His advice is particularly appropriate in the counseling and ministry situations in which clergy members constantly find themselves enmeshed. The educational, training, and experience levels of staff members run the gamut, from those with high school diplomas to those with one or more doctoral degrees. Yet parishioners rarely distinguish between what a minister may be trained, qualified, and experienced to do and what they expect him to do. When you fail to set limits or to establish appropriate boundaries, you ignore your own limitations and invite trouble into your house, even if only out of a motivation to serve. Ignoring your limitations should set off bells and whistles, because it usually is a sign that you are failing to do what a reasonably prudent man would do in similar circumstances. If the word "negligence" springs to mind, then you remember that discussion in Chapter 4. If you fail to remember it, then a plaintiff's lawyer will be happy to offer a refresher course to you.

CHAPTER 14

Child Abuse and Neglect

WHAT IS CHILD ABUSE? WHAT IS CHILD NEGLECT?

We all have a legal duty to report child abuse or neglect whenever we know or suspect that child abuse or neglect has occurred. The question is, do we know it when we see it? To summarize, *abuse* is any conduct which exposes or subjects a child to a substantial risk of mental, emotional, or physical injury or harm, including any exposure to sexual, obscene, or pornographic conduct or material.[406] Internet access takes on a whole new meaning in light of this definition. *Neglect* is exposing a child to potential abuse or failing to provide for the child's medical, housing, nutritional, clothing, or other developmental needs.[407] Keep in mind that these are simply working definitions. The statute contains lengthy, carefully worded definitions which may not correspond exactly to these abridged versions.

One question which arises frequently is whether or not spanking is abuse. I know what my father's answer was. The current answer, though, is that it depends. The law provides that a physical injury, such as a bruise from a spanking, is abuse, but not if it results from "an accident or reasonable discipline by a parent . . . that does not expose the child to a substantial risk of harm."[408] The statute does not define "substantial risk of harm," creating yet another grey area for all to interpret differently. Thus, the degree of corporeal punishment administered is probably what determines whether or not the child is exposed to a substantial risk of harm. As the severity of the punishment increases, so increases the child's exposure to a substantial risk of harm. Keep in mind that the statute discusses only those actions taken "by a parent." If you are not a child's parent, then do not spank that child. I do not think, though, that the Texas Legislature intended to outlaw spanking by parents, as time-honored a tradition as that is.

WHO SHOULD REPORT?

If you believe that abuse or neglect has occurred, then you must report the conduct in question. The law requires professionals, regardless of the nature and scope of any privilege involved, to report an incident within forty-eight hours of learning of or suspecting abuse or neglect.[409] That same statute requires every person to report an incident, regardless of his relationship to the church, the child, or the perpetrator, immediately.[410] Although the statute does not define immediately, I suspect that it means something much less than forty-eight hours. While no court has opined on exactly what "immediately" means, one opinion rejected a challenge to the "immediately" standard on constitutional grounds.[411] Thus, immediately, whatever that means, remains the standard and you should err on the side of being "more immediate" than "less immediate," if indeed such distinctions can be made.

At first glance, the statute seems to catch ministers under the first requirement and church members under the second requirement. As to ministers, a potential problem arises, in that the statute's definition of professional does not include clergy members. The law states that

> "professional" means an individual who is licensed or certified by the state or who is an employee of a facility licensed, certified, or operated by the state and who, in the normal course of official duties or duties for which a license or certification is required, has direct contact with children.[412]

While some clergy members may be licensed or certified by the state (*e.g.* a licensed professional counselor), most are not. Further, although many evangelical denominations engage in ordaining ministers, there also may be ministers who either object to ordination or simply have not been ordained yet. Thus, many ministers would lack the statute's licensure or certification requirement.

This analysis assumes that ordination is comparable to being licensed or certified by the state. It is not an equivalent process, though. Ordination is a traditional process in which individual churches and denominations, not the state, recognize the training, qualifications, and experience of a person who has responded to God's call to the ministry. I am unaware of any denomination which even reports the names of those ordained to the state. Thus, I do not believe that most ministers meet the statute's definition of professional.

It could be argued that churches are licensed or certified by the state *via* incorporation and that, as ministers act as a church's agent, ministers meet the definition of professional. That argument really stretches logic, though, and there are no licensing or certification agencies with oversight responsibility for churches. Further, the state certainly does not operate churches. While the Secretary of State may issue corporate charters, Texas courts have gone to great lengths to stay out of church affairs, holding that "questions of church discipline and government are left to the church, limited only by the courts' supervision of property and civil rights."[413] Thus, this argument should fail, also.

I do not mean to say that a minister is not a professional by way of this analysis. I am simply pointing out that the Texas Legislature probably intended to include the clergy in the definition of professional, but failed to do so. The problem is somewhat academic, though, because the statute states in a different subsection that the "requirement to report" applies to "a member of the clergy," regardless of whether or not the clergy member learned of the abuse or neglect during an otherwise privileged conversation.[414] To resolve the ambiguity, I suggest that clergy members make a report under the stricter "immediately" standard, just in case someone argues that the requirement that a clergy member report is more properly made under the general, non-professional standard.

If any questions remain, the Attorney General of Texas has issued a formal opinion stating that clergy members are required to report instances of actual or suspected abuse or neglect, even if a church member discloses the abuse to the clergy member in a privileged conversation.[415] While an attorney general's opinions do not constitute law, they generally are regarded as persuasive authorities by most courts.

Where does all of this analysis lead? Very simply, it leads to fulfilling your legal duty in a manner which protects you, the child involved, and your church. Consider the scenario in which you could have reported an incident of child abuse immediately, but waited forty-eight (48) hours because you thought that you had the legal right to do so. At hour forty-five (45), another, more serious incident occurs in which the parent beats the child. If you had reported the initial incident immediately, Child Protective Services ("CPS") probably would have intervened and the subsequent incident and injuries would have been averted. Would you like the child's attorney cross-examining you in a courtroom regarding what good you thought would come from waiting? If I represented that child, I certainly would argue that the "immediate" standard applied to you and that your failure to report contributed to causing my client's subsequent injuries.

Another aspect of the reporting requirement is that professionals may not delegate the task of reporting to someone else.[416] Thus, if you inform other professionals within your church of the situation and you are a credible person upon whose word they may rely, then you may have imposed upon them a duty to make a separate report. There is no specific statutory language or case law addressing this situation. However, the statute imposes a duty to report upon every person who learns of the abuse. If the duty is non-delegable by a professional, then this seems to be a reasonable, although perhaps unintended, interpretation of the statute. Further, does the delegation ban on professionals and the absence of such a ban on non-professionals implicitly authorize a non-professional to delegate the duty to report?[417] Any answer would be mere speculation, as there is no specific statutory language or case law addressing the question. In the absence of clear instruction, no one should delegate his duty to report.

If a volunteer or other paid worker learns of or suspects abuse or neglect, then he should immediately report his knowledge to the staff member with oversight responsibility for the affected child or the staff member otherwise designated to deal with these situations. That minister then will be confronted with a decision. He must review the facts and determine whether or not he knows or suspects that an incident of abuse or neglect has occurred. If he determines that he has a duty to report, then he should make the report as outlined below and inform the initial reporter that he has made the report.

However, if the minister determines that he does not have a duty to report because he does not know or suspect that an incident of abuse or neglect has occurred, then he should tell the initial reporter of his decision. If the minister is mistaken in that belief, then, perhaps weeks or months later, the initial reporter will not be allowed to rely on that minister's poor decision if it is determined that the minister should have made a report. Informing the initial reporter that a report will not be made allows the reporter the opportunity to follow his own conscience and to make his own decision regarding whether or not to report. In the final analysis, the law requires that of each of us and we should not allow a church member to go forward blindly, having trusted a staff member to perform an arguably delegable duty and remaining oblivious to the fact that a report was not made.

I may be analyzing this statute too finely. However, my desires are to educate those reading these materials regarding their duty to report abuse and neglect and, in so doing, to assist those children in need of the statute's protections. The statute should have been more carefully worded. However, we must work with what is on the books. Until the Texas Legislature recognizes the problems, I believe that clergy members should undertake the requirements of reporting as non-professionals and professionals, *i.e.* to report immediately and not to delegate. In this manner no one will have cause to complain that you should have done more.

Making the Report

The concept of reporting the information quickly is designed to decrease the possibility of further abuse or neglect. Thus, you should report such an incident in person or by telephone. If you make the report by telephone, then I advise you to tape record the conversation and to alert the person to whom you speak that you are recording the conversation. At a minimum, you should write down the name of the person to whom you spoke, the telephone number which you called, the agency to which you made the report, the date and time of the call, and the contents of your conversation. Always remember that you are obligated to report your knowledge and you may be called on to prove that you complied with the statute at a later date when the details are not so fresh.

If you record your conversation, then instruct the person to whom you are making the report that you are recording the conversation at the beginning of the conversation. Some CPS offices record "intake" calls, also, although there are anecdotal reports of those tapes being lost when they are needed most. Identify yourself and, if possible, start recording before you dial the number. Ask the person to whom you are speaking to identify himself and the agency for which he works. Before relaying your knowledge, state that you are making a report to ensure that everyone who subsequently hears the recording understands your motivation for making the report and your intention to rely on statutory immunity.[418] Further, if you can record the conversation with an inline recording device, the resulting tape quality is much better than if you simply hold a recorder close to the handset or speakerphone.

As an aside, I can find no statute requiring you to identify yourself, although proving that you made a report anonymously may be quite difficult when there are no intake records with your name on them. Further, while we usually think of these reports as being confidential, they can be brought into the public record under certain circumstances.[419] There are safeguards built into these statutes which prohibit disclosure when it is not essential or when someone's life or safety would be jeopardized by the disclosure, but the point to remember is that, no matter who tells you differently, the report is never absolutely confidential.

While it may seem natural in today's legal climate to make the report in writing, I cannot find any requirement that it must be made in writing. Indeed, it seems absolutely counterintuitive to the purpose of the statute to require a written report. Although the United States Postal Service is fairly reliable, children's lives are at stake here. If we are really concerned about stopping abuse and neglect, then we should care enough to pick up the telephone when we learn of an instance of abuse or neglect. I have discussed this issue with officials at CPS and they, also, are unaware of any requirement to file a written report.

The law provides that the report can be made to any one of these four different groups:

- a local or state law enforcement agency
- Child Protective Services, a division of the Texas Department of Family and Protective Services
- the state agency charged with oversight of the facility at which the abuse or neglect occurred
- another agency designated by a court for the protection of children[420]

There are no statutory guidelines which dictate to whom a report should be made among these four agencies. However, experience suggests that, if the incident does not involve a person responsible for the child's care, then the report should be made to a local or state law enforcement agency. The phrase "person responsible for the child's care" includes parents, guardians, conservators, foster parents, family members, household members, and school and daycare personnel and volunteers.[421] If the incident involves a person responsible for the child's care, then you should report it to CPS at (800) 252–5400, the agency's toll-free hotline, or to your local CPS office. It is a rare occasion when you will need to report an incident to a state agency overseeing a facility at which an incident occurs and an even rarer occasion for a report to be made under the fourth category.

The person reporting should state that he believes that a child has been or may have been abused or neglected and should relate the name and address of the child and the person responsible for the child, along with "any other pertinent information."[422] The employee who receives the report also may inquire about the some or all of the following:

- the identity of the perpetrator
- the existence of prior incidents
- the location of the incidents
- the specific allegations regarding the incidents
- the identity of any witnesses to the incidents
- the identity of the child's parents, guardians, conservators, foster parents, relatives, and others with whom the child has regular contact
- the child's schedule and current location.

Even if you record the conversation, take written notes regarding every facet of the situation and keep those notes in your records.

A person required to report is under no obligation either to furnish any information which he does not have or to investigate the situation.[423] In fact, I advise my clients against making further inquiries, as those inquiries may serve to exacerbate a situation. Once the report is made, you should allow those trained in dealing with these situations to do their jobs. Although we hear of exceptions, case workers have children's best interests at heart and will do everything possible under the law to protect the children whom they serve. After observing my wife and others who have worked as sexual abuse case workers for CPS for many years, I can tell you that, although their hands may be tied in some very difficult situations, they are dedicated people who do the best that they can with the resources and options available to them.

INFORMING THE COMMUNICANT

If the person who informed you of the abuse or neglect does so in what otherwise would be a privileged communication, then you may feel uneasy when you tell him that you have a duty to report the abuse or neglect. However, you should do so or at least stop him from telling you more than necessary to avoid any subsequent claim that you enticed him to tell you more than he wanted to tell you. In many cases, criminal penalties are possible for the person who abuses or neglects a child. If you sit silently and allow someone to confess his life story, divesting himself of every detail, then you will be required to report all "pertinent information."[424] After he has told you everything and realizes that you could have stopped him and informed him that you had a duty to report the information which he first relayed to you, he probably will wish that he had not said so much and may attempt to sue you and the church for not stopping him sooner. He probably will not prevail on that claim, but it always is better to avoid, rather than to engage, an unnecessary battle.

The gray of this black and white situation rests in exactly when to tell the person sitting across from you that you must report what he is telling you to the government. Telling him before he leaves your office could lead to a situation in which there is time to orchestrate and to implement a coverup. Children in these situations are afraid and confused, at best. Telling a five year old that "talking to the policeman or the social worker about what Daddy did will make Daddy go to jail" is an extremely effective way to ensure that five year old's silence. It also will result in that five year old continuing to live in an abusive situation. Thus, if you believe that this is a possibility, then you have a judgment call to make regarding when you tell the communicant of your duty to report. While stopping him from telling you more is always a good idea, you may want to hesitate before proceeding to tell him that you must report the abuse until after you have had a chance to make the report and to discuss your concerns with the proper authorities. This is an extremely fine line and one which is best walked only after years of experience and, perhaps, prior consultation with other professionals. Even at that point, so many different subjective factors will weigh upon this decision that reaching a consensus on exactly when to notify the communicant of your duty to report may be impossible.

One of the statute's goals is to prevent further abuse or neglect. You probably will have enough information to turn the matter over to the authorities upon learning the identity of the child and the person responsible for that child's care. You should stop there. There is no reason for you to play investigator and there are plenty of reasons for you not to do so.[425] First, you probably are not trained to do so.[426] Second, you have little, if any, authority to do anything about the situation which will benefit the child. Next, you are interfering with the state's interest in protecting children and investigating and prosecuting violations of its criminal laws. Finally, you are exposing yourself and your church to liability if you do anything else. Place yourself and your actions within the immunity provided by the statute. In so doing, you obey the law and protect a child, yourself, and your church. You also are taking the only action which, at least temporarily, will stop further abuse. That usually is the first step that an offender needs for someone to take for him.

Some professionals advise that you provide prior, written disclosure of your duty to report to those with whom you speak regarding spiritual matters. You might choose to disclose this duty on an appointment log on which clients sign in, a client intake sheet signed by the client, or similar form. Doing so provides you with solid evidence to prove that you advised the person of your duty to reveal a confidential communication prior to it being made.

There is another side to that issue, though. The law does not require that you inform anyone of this exception to the clergy privilege rule. Doing so would require each person with whom you potentially may have a privileged communication to sign a disclosure form with a specific warning similar to the following:

> Our conversations normally are privileged. That means that I am prohibited from divulging to anyone what you say or any advice which I may give to you. However, I must warn you that an exception to this privilege exists. If you reveal any information to me that leads me to suspect that a child has been abused or neglected or is being abused or neglected, then I must report that information to the proper authorities immediately after you reveal that information to me.

Someone reporting suspected or known abuse or neglect to a clergy member certainly could be discussing a spiritual matter. However, taking this advice to its logical conclusion could have a tremendously chilling effect on a minister's relationship with his congregation. More importantly, taking this advice would almost certainly rule out ever hearing of abuse or neglect. That should not be the objective. Jesus cautioned us in Luke 17:1–2 to avoid placing stumbling blocks in children's paths. Our failure to remove the stumbling blocks of abuse and neglect is tantamount to cementing those blocks in place and to compounding the prior damage done by ensuring that it continues. It is a rejection of Jesus' explicit warning. If you do not want to help a child, then you should not place yourself in the position of potentially learning that a child needs your help.

If someone communicates to you that he has abused or neglected a child, then that person needs help. As such, your church should not close its doors. It should be willing to minister to these troubled people as best it can, despite what they may have done. While throwing the perpetrator and the affected child in a room for them to sort it out, to shake hands, and to emerge victorious over deviant conduct which has lasted for years is certainly not the answer, there is always an appropriate theological response for a community of faith to offer to a sinner, a victim, and their families short of abandoning them in their own wilderness. As Lee W. Carlson said, "the church of Jesus Christ has a critical responsibility in alleviating this life-crippling scar upon humanity. Ministers and priests have a key role to play in any such healing ministry."[427] The church should accept that role, disquieting as it may be.

I have encountered several abuse and neglect situations in my practice. They are never easy to deal with and I must admit that I have not handled them perfectly each time. It is not easy to tell a client or a church member that you have to report an incident. These people come to us with a misguided sense of absolute secrecy which we must disregard. Relationships ultimately may be damaged or destroyed. However, the statute's and our overriding concern should be for the welfare of the child. As such, we must follow the law and express our concern for the one who cannot express concern for herself. I personally disagree with those who disclose their duty to report prior to a consultation. I sympathize with the reasoning which they use to support their disclosure, but I still disagree with it. I believe that such action crosses the fine line of letting legal concerns override ministry concerns. We should trust God to provide ways for us to cope with the law and to perform our ministries without letting the law minimize those ministries. A child, whose life could be changed or saved, may later thank you for doing so.

CRIMINAL PENALTIES, CIVIL LIABILITY, AND IMMUNITY

The law creates two different scenarios in which criminal penalties can be assessed. First, a knowing failure to report a known or suspected case of abuse or neglect is a Class

B misdemeanor.[428] Second, knowingly or intentionally making a groundless report under this statute is also a Class B misdemeanor.[429] Obviously, avoid each scenario. The tendency of some churches and staff members to tackle these problems from within has led to disastrous results for the children, churches, and staff members. If you think that the government will not prosecute a person for violating these statutes because they belong to a church, then you simply need to revise your thinking. It has happened before and it will happen again.

The law provides that any person who is sued for making a report in good faith or assisting in any manner in an investigation or judicial proceeding relating to actual or suspected abuse or neglect "is immune from civil or criminal liability that might otherwise be incurred or imposed," excepting only the perpetrator for obvious reasons.[430] The first thought that goes through any professional's mind when he is required to divulge a privileged communication is that he will be sued, especially in an area as emotionally charged as child abuse or neglect. However, this statute has been very effective in limiting claims against those professionals, such as:

- Physicians[431]
- Teachers[432]
- Mental Health Professionals[433]
- Social Workers[434]
- Clergy[435]

The statute also provides for the recovery of attorney's fees and other reasonable, related expenses if one who reports abuse or neglect is sued and the court finds that the claim is "frivolous, unreasonable, or without foundation because the defendant is immune from liability."[436]

However, woe to him who is required to make a report, but does not make that report. If that child or his parents ever find out that you should have made a report, but did not make a report, and that your duty to make that report arose out of your duties as a member of the clergy at a church, then you and your church can expect to be sued. Not only will you and your church be sued, but the plaintiffs probably will sue you under a negligence *per se* theory, meaning that you violated a law which was designed to spell out the obligation which you owed to the child. That creates another barrier to defending yourself and the church. Further, juries love children and love to reward children who have suffered. If the only defendants left standing at the end of the day are you and your church (the perpetrators in abuse and neglect case are usually bankrupt and either in jail or otherwise unavailable) and the jury believes that your action could have prevented something from happening, then you might want to wire home for extra cash.[437]

Finally, if your church operates a child-care facility, then it should post a sign in a conspicuous place notifying all employees and customers of their duty to report child abuse or neglect and the penalties for failing to report child abuse or neglect. The term "child-care facility" is a term of art which should be understood by reference not to any common meaning, but by reference to its statutory definition. The law provides that a child-care facility is one which "provides care, training, education, custody, treatment, or supervision for a child who is not related . . . to the owner or operator of the facility, for all or part of the 24-hour day."[438] Simply holding Sunday School or providing child care while a parent attends a worship service does not necessarily mean that your church is required to obtain a child-care facility license, though.[439] While the subject of child-care facilities is outside of the intended scope of this book, you need to be aware that operating a child-care facility at your church without posting that sign constitutes a Class C misdemeanor.

EDUCATING CHURCH STAFF AND VOLUNTEERS

Many staff members and parishioners are unaware of how widespread abuse and neglect cases are and of the necessity for reporting incidents when they see or suspect them. Thus, compliance problems may be more frequent than we would suspect. First, we sometimes do not recognize or want to recognize abuse and neglect. While conventional wisdom or simple prejudice may point to society's lower economic classes accounting for a majority of abuse and neglect cases, that generally is not the case. Studies have shown that abuse and neglect cases run the gamut of socioeconomic classes. Thus, simply because your church may be in a middle class or affluent neighborhood or may be composed of people belonging to those classes, do not assume that it will be immune from these problems. The church that assumes that it only happens at other churches will be the one with a problem.

Second, educating people is vital to the integrity of any reporting program. Without an understanding of the prevalence of abuse and neglect and the absolute need to report, there will be little, if any, real effort toward compliance. Thus, take advantage of existing educational videotapes and other resources promoted by groups such as Christian Ministry Resources and Center for the Prevention of Sexual and Domestic Violence. Arrange educational meetings on the subject for staff members and those working with children and youth and make attendance at those meetings mandatory for continuing service with children and youth. Take advantage of CPS' policy of providing public service speakers on the subject free of charge to community groups. There is no more effective voice of concern for children than a case worker who has to deal with abuse and neglect issues on a daily basis. Local law enforcement departments also may make officers available to speak with church groups regarding their perspective on this subject. Finally, if common sense and appeals for the protection of children fail, then copy some of the appellate opinions in which a church has been sued over abuse and neglect.[440] You also might look into any of the numerous Roman Catholic clergy cases proceeding through various United States courts at the moment. Distribute those opinions to those unwilling to be educated. If that fails, then tell them to look for another area of service if they are unwilling to change in order to adapt to changing times.

In addition to these steps, the staff member responsible for this project or the senior pastor should draft and distribute a short statement regarding the church's policies and procedures and the necessity of educating the church and screening workers. Having all workers countersign such a statement to indicate their agreement and placing these documents in a file may assist in reinforcing the seriousness of our corporate resolve to deal with this problem and in demonstrating that the church has done something tangible to obtain a member's agreement to its policies and procedures.

Any of these steps may upset some church members. You even may lose some members. We should be a little more tolerant of the inconveniences caused by the law, but some people will choose to take offense at being asked about their background. When that happens, there are three potential reasons for a person to resist completing a screening questionnaire in the face of having been educated about growing liability concerns. He is trying to hide something, thinks that he is the exception to the rule, or genuinely does not understand the importance of these issues. If a person refuses to comply with the screening process, then it is appropriate to redirect his desire to serve to another area of the church's ministries.

SETTING UP A SCREENING SYSTEM

Your church should implement a screening procedure for all staff members, volunteers, and other paid workers working with children and youth. In today's society, many jurors believe that it is negligent to allow a person to have access to children and youth without knowing and verifying their background. The state requires similar screening methods for day care workers, whose contact with children is identical to the opportunities afforded to church workers, but for the amount of time involved. If a volunteer provides information which raises a question regarding his potential fitness for working with children and youth, then you have a duty to ask followup questions, perhaps through checking references, criminal records, employment records, prior church records, and, most importantly, a personal interview with that person. Your screening brochure should ask personal questions. Let us deal with that point immediately. If it does not, then it does not ask the right questions. Be forthright about this issue with those affected by it and you will have fewer arguments about it over the long run. The questionnaire should include the following information, which can be divided roughly into three parts.

General Personal Information

- applicant's full name, current employment and home addresses, and current employment and home telephone numbers
- birth date, social security number, and Texas driver's license number with expiration date
- prior employment and home addresses for a reasonable period
- marital status, spouse's name, children's names and ages
- emergency contact information (name, relationship, and telephone number)
- statement of faith and description of salvation experience
- prior church memberships with telephone numbers and addresses
- description of prior experience in working with children and youth in and away from church settings
- description of education, training, gifts, talents, *et cetera* applicable to working with children and youth
- indication of area, age group, or other classification of children and youth with which applicant is interested in working
- description of applicant's other church-related activities
- description of applicant's medical training, if any

Confidential Personal Information

- list of at least three unrelated references with telephone number and address
- at least one staff reference from the church previously attended by the applicant
- question regarding convictions for drug use
- question regarding hospitalization or other medical or psychological treatment for use/abuse of drugs (including alcohol)
- question regarding arrests for criminal offenses (excluding minor traffic violations)
- question regarding accusations, arrests, and/or convictions for sex crimes
- question regarding accusations, arrests, and/or convictions for child abuse or neglect

- question regarding life experiences that could adversely or beneficially impact applicant's ability to work with children or youth
- question regarding whether or not applicant has been a victim of abuse or neglect (placing an asterisk next to this question with an explanation that a written answer is not required and, in the alternative, an applicant may desire to discuss his answer with a member of the staff may be a good idea)
- space to explain any affirmative answers

Agreements and Releases

- statement regarding veracity and completeness of information disclosed on questionnaire
- statement of acceptance and obedience to church policies regarding abuse and neglect of children and youth
- statement releasing employers, churches, and references who can provide information which they otherwise might be unwilling to provide from liability for disclosing information
- statement authorizing criminal records check, employment history check, and any other background checks deemed appropriate by your church
- statement regarding confidential nature of information disclosed
- signature and date of signature

Your church should designate one or more staff members, but not lay members, to be responsible for reviewing the questionnaires. I suggest excluding the laity from this duty because any confidentiality pledge contained in a questionnaire arguably could be breached automatically if the questionnaire is reviewed by one other than a licensed "minister, priest, . . . or other similar functionary of a religious organization."[441] If a question arises regarding an applicant's fitness, then it should be dealt with discreetly by that minister, who should be empowered and directed by the church to make absolutely final decisions regarding a person's fitness for serving in this capacity. Alternatively, the minister charged with the initial review of the applications could forward applications which raised questions to another staff member or members as an internal appeal or review procedure. Even if challenged by an adversely affected applicant, this type of decision should be outside the scope of the current limits of judicial review of church conduct. As noted elsewhere, judicial inquiries into whether or not a church follows its own policies and procedures violate the First Amendment of the United States Constitution.[442]

Many churches have a mandatory church membership period (six months to one year) prior to an applicant even being considered for work with children and youth. One of the purposes of this requirement, quite simply, is to place an obstacle in the path of the pedophile who joins a church looking for his next victim. This is not an absolute deterrent, though. People with psychological disorders react in unpredictable ways and may decide to stay in a church during this quasi-probationary period if there is not a more attractive alternative available to them. Most churches would disqualify any person with a criminal conviction for abuse or neglect from serving in that capacity at that church. I agree with that position, but a criminal record should not result in a person being denied any area of service. To do so is to deny the power of any redemptive work in that person's life. It is appropriate, though, to monitor that person's behavior and to place limits on his areas of service. For example and, of course, depending on the circumstances, a church might want to limit such a person's access to children and youth, even to the point of prohibiting him from working with minors, sitting with or near them in services, or being in their Sunday School or church training rooms or areas.

Aside from these instances, any person's background must be dealt with on an individual basis. One guideline which I can suggest is that a church should increase the diligence which it uses to verify an applicant's questionnaire if an applicant's references or the facts disclosed raise any questions regarding that applicant's fitness. This may rise to the level of running various types of background checks on every applicant, regardless of whether or not an application raises questions. Further, if an applicant regarding whom questions exist is allowed to work with children or youth, then consider heightening the supervision level over that applicant, imposing restrictions on him, and holding frequent reviews of his performance until those questions have been satisfied. You also may want to develop more familiarity with characteristics common to pedophiles and child molesters through reading more specialized books and other materials. Educating ourselves about these topics will better enable us to recognize warning signs that we may have dismissed more easily in earlier times. Such actions are, in general, what reasonably prudent men should do in similar circumstances.

Are Child Abuse and Neglect Really That Big of a Problem?

This may be the ultimate rhetorical question. It would be a better world if we did not have to deal with this scourge, but we must and, if you spend any time at all in dealing with the public, then you will encounter situations in which you will have a duty to report child abuse or neglect. CPS reports 203 homicides involving child abuse and neglect cases in Texas in 2002, a shameful record. That is a staggering number which bears repeating: 203 children were killed through abuse and neglect in our state in 2002.[443]

The numbers break down during this period as follows: 4 children were killed every week in 2002 in Texas as a result of child abuse and neglect.

CPS received 183,057 reports of child abuse and neglect in 2002. After preliminary investigations, CPS confirmed 47,409 victims of child abuse from those reports.[444] Those numbers break down as follows: CPS received a daily average of 501 reports of child abuse or neglect and confirmed a daily average of 130 victims, roughly twenty-five percent (25%) of the reports received. The real numbers must be higher than the confirmed numbers. This is happening right now in your county, your town, and maybe even your church.

CHAPTER 15

They Did What?!: Youth

GENERAL CONSIDERATIONS

The church ministers to youth in ways which differ from every other age group. No other segment of the church goes harder and faster at life or needs more supervision. Junior high school and high school students need to question, to explore, and to test their spiritual, intellectual, emotional, and physical boundaries. Children, *i.e.* future youth group members, are simply watching the older youth, making note of what seems to work and not to work and biding their time until they feel up to the challenges. Thus, children and youth present special challenges to the church in how it traditionally has ministered to them and how it legally positions itself to do so.

Having said all of this, I am not a sociologist. I am an attorney who is keenly aware of the risks involved each time that my wife and I take our class canoeing for a break from the Sunday School routine. Further, although Jesus directs me not to worry five times in Matthew 6:25–34, I tend to worry. I worry that the one taking his own car to an activity, against a sponsor's wishes, will have a wreck. I worry about the varsity football players playing flag football with the seventh graders. I worry about my response to any emergency situation and am all too familiar with the phrase "accidents happen." We never plan on an accident happening and that is exactly when we needlessly complicate situations.

If I could give anyone remotely interested in youth activities one piece of practical advice, it is this: be prepared for any contingency. That is one of the best strategies that I have found to deal with worry. If you are taking the youth group to a water park, then ensure that an adequate number of lifeguards will be present. If you anticipate that any physical activity will take place, then have a first aid kit ready and have someone present who is trained and willing to use it appropriately. It is easy enough to dial 911, but a bee sting, absent an allergic reaction, or a minor cut or scrape should not require the local emergency medical corps to race to the scene. Your church also should have enough sponsors and transportation available to respond to an emergency. In other words, if ninety-nine of your sheep are obedient and one is lost, then have enough shepherds to maintain the watch while another shepherd searches for the lost sheep. Ninety-nine untended sheep do not sit still for long.

I remember a cartoon showing the home of a lawyer with signs in the front yard. They disclaimed liability for slipping on the grass, tripping on the steps, spraining a finger while ringing the doorbell, *et cetera*. Although it may be tempting to take that approach with a youth group, it cannot be done. Pushing the limits is part of growing up. When limits are pushed, accidents happen. So it was with me and so it is with my children. Denying youth appropriate opportunities to push those limits only will result in those limits being pushed outside of our knowledge as parents and as youth workers. Thus, perhaps it is better to be in the middle of a football game with the kids, exposing ourselves to potential injury, than to sit on the bench exhorting everyone to be careful. Perhaps it is better to offer medical assistance to the one who cuts his foot at the beach than to tell him that the beach is dangerous. Perhaps it is better to have something happening which attracts youth to our churches and our Lord than to be on the committee which restricts youth activities because there is too much risk. I rather would risk and be prepared for the accidents of life than sit safely in my house and deny those accidents a chance of ever happening.

RELEASES AND AUTHORIZATIONS

After reading the last paragraph, it should not surprise you to learn that Kimberly and I scuba dive and that we take our fun seriously. We study very hard, gain experience on every dive, and push our limits, diving to the increasing levels that our training and experience take us and worrying our relatives in the process. The risks inherent in diving are extreme and require that we execute releases for just about every facet of any dive that we make. Those releases are important in that they set the rules for the activity. The person asking to be released will not allow you to proceed until you assure him that you understand the risks involved, are qualified to address those risks, and do not hold him responsible if an accident occurs, regardless of who causes the accident.

A release, sometimes referred to as a hold harmless agreement, is a

contractual arrangement whereby one party assumes the liability inherent in a situation, thereby relieving the other party of responsibility . . . [or an] agreement or contract in which one party agrees to hold the other without responsibility for damage or other liability arising out of the transaction involved.[445]

In the case of most youth, their parents must sign a release on their behalf, as anyone under the age of eighteen in Texas does not have the legal capacity to enter into a binding contract.[446] Some attorneys advise that, in addition to the parents' signatures, the minor's signature should be obtained, also. While there is no legal effect to the minor's signature, it does reinforce the notion that he has been made aware that your church is seeking a release and that he has made promises in that document, even if they are not legally binding.

Authorizations are more like permission slips. Many churches, however, fail to distinguish between the two. I have seen some church forms, entitled "Authorization" or "Permission Slip," which are an attempt to release the church from potential liability. For reasons set forth under the "express negligence doctrine," a fairly detailed legal doctrine addressing the enforceability of certain types of releases, the release language in those documents may be unenforceable. I also have seen forms entitled "Release" which were nothing more than permission slips. If those churches thought that they had been released from any potential liability by using a document simply entitled "Release," then they would have been very surprised if an accident had occurred and an attorney had reviewed those documents. Churches need to be familiar with each document's characteristics and need to determine which situations call for which documents.

RELEASES AND AUTHORIZATIONS - ENFORCEMENT PROBLEMS

Releases discourage us and make us think about the possibility of accidents happening long before an activity even occurs. That is perhaps their best quality, though, *i.e.* they help us to prepare for life's contingencies by making us think about the consequences of our actions. However, they are difficult to draft and even more difficult to shove into parents' hands, along with a demand that they be executed. They breed suspicion and make the people signing them look cautiously at the people demanding that they be signed. That reaction may or may not be justified, but it can be a reaction, nonetheless. Requiring the execution of a release, in effect, may deter a child from attending an activity.

Another disadvantage rests in the issue of just who is being released. Releases are almost always utilized when someone is engaging in a hazardous activity. Companies offering bungee cord jumps, high-speed miniature race car tracks, sky diving, rock climbing, paint gun wars, and similar amusements have very viable reasons for requiring releases. A church should realize, though, that releases obtained by commercial operators generally will not assist that church in avoiding a claim if an accident happens during one of these activities. These releases usually protect only the operator, which may place a church in the unenviable position of being the more attractive defendant, a significant drawback. Since these activities (and others which could become hazardous under adverse or abnormal conditions) are generally considered to be more hazardous than other, more traditional events, the law may require that a church exercise a higher degree of supervision or care than normally expected in order to meet the reasonably prudent man standard.[447] I am not advocating that these activities be abandoned, only that you understand the extent to which a church's conduct may be scrutinized if an accident occurs. Thus, you may want to examine more closely your youth group's involvement in these activities, the strength of your church's release forms, or both.

A significant limitation on releases, despite any amount of planning which you may have devoted to their use, is that courts and juries sometimes have been willing to disregard them. Plaintiffs have argued that they are unenforceable or voidable based on a variety of arguments, *e.g.* that a particular release was:

- unenforceable because no consideration existed for its execution, essentially arguing that since the plaintiff received nothing in exchange for granting the release, it is unfair to give the defendant the benefit of that release[448]
- unenforceable because it was executed by mistake[449]
- unenforceable because of a disparity in bargaining power[450]
- void because it was obtained under duress[451]
- void because it was ambiguous[452]

A related observation is that courts and juries may be willing to disregard or to enforce releases primarily based on the amount of sympathy generated either by the plaintiff or defendant.

Another problem rests in enforcing releases on the most basic level. Take the scenario in which a group of ten teenagers is ready for a trip and only nine of them have releases. Naturally, the one without a release cannot find his parents. It is possible, perhaps probable, that the sponsor will allow the one without a release to participate. I have witnessed this exact situation several times and, more often than not, the sheep without the proper documentation is let out to play with the other sheep.

One last problem with releases rests in what to do with them after an event. Take the situation in which a church hosts a fairly large event in which it is impossible for a youth minister to keep track of all of the participants. Also, assume that an accident, which may have seemed fairly inconsequential at the time, happens and that the volunteer in charge fails to tell the youth minister about it, either through oversight or embarrassment. The youth minister may have determined that it was appropriate for the church to have secured releases for this event. After having gone through the trouble to do that, it would be a shame for the youth minister to throw the releases away simply because he never heard of an incident. One month later, after the releases have been discarded, a letter from a lawyer arrives making a claim against the church for that small problem, which now has grown into a major problem, since the claimant's parents do not remember executing a release.

It may require the purchase of another lateral file, but a church should retain all releases until the statute of limitations has lapsed. Thus, the releases should be maintained at least until each child involved in the activity passes his twenty-second birthday, that being the age of majority plus four (4) years for the longest potentially applicable statute of limitation. This may seem like a lot of work, but it is a simple matter of creating and labeling a file, putting all of the releases in that file, and retaining it in the church's permanent records for the appropriate amount of time.

RELEASES AND AUTHORIZATIONS - ROLE OF THE NOTARY PUBLIC

From a church's perspective, there are two goals for requiring that a notary public sign a release or authorization. First and foremost, a notary public's signature and seal should allow a minister or volunteer to rely on the signature on the page actually being a parent's signature. Forgery can be a problem, not just for the one doing the forging, but also for the minister or volunteer. Remember, any parent whose signature has been forged is going to be upset. That parent can just as easily be upset with her child as she can be with a minister or volunteer, especially if she believes that he should have recognized that the signature was a forgery.

A notary public's signature is a pretty strong deterrent to this type of misconduct. Further, requiring this is not pharisaical legalism. It simply acknowledges that young people are tempted to misbehave at times, just like adults who forge signatures. In the latter case, the motivating factor usually is greed. In the former case, a young person usually has focused his eyes on the prize, *e.g.* a fun trip to an amusement park, a little too much and has allowed honesty to take a back seat to fun. It happens.

What about the upset parent from the first paragraph? Is it fair that she holds you responsible for verifying that the signature on the release is actually hers? No, but when was the last time that you actually looked at a release to ensure that the signature on the bottom line looked anything like an adult's signature, much less compared it to known handwriting examples? We are guilty far too often of just telling the kids to put the releases on the corner of our desks. The kids see that we do not even look at the releases; we just count them to make sure that the number of releases matches the number of kids. By not treating the document with the seriousness which it deserves, we are sending a message to the youth that a release is really something that we do simply to placate the lawyers. If it is alright for you as a minister to disregard the release as inconsequential or an inconvenience, then why should it not be alright for a youth to forge a signature? You should not expect rationalization to be logical. It simply serves to justify our conduct when it otherwise cannot be justified. Thus, if you want to use a release, then put some effort into it and do not give anyone an excuse to base their conduct on how you treat releases. If you do not want to put the effort into it, then forget the release and save a tree.

Next, what happens when, two days after the youth group's Scripture memorization / skateboard party, someone's mother calls you to inform you of a broken leg? First, you find the signed release and congratulate yourself on your administrative skills. Next, call your attorney when the mother denies having signed the release. Your failure to require a notarial acknowledgement has allowed the mother to claim that the signature is a forgery and, therefore, not binding. Further, since the seventeen year old son who may have forged or may not have forged his mother's signature is a minor and does not have the capacity to enter into a contract, there is little, if any, wiggle room to argue that he released your church through the forgery. You have gone to a lot of trouble to hold on to a potentially worthless piece of paper.

Requiring a notary public will dissuade all but the most hardened cases from raising these issues. It is a shame that we have to go to these lengths to protect the church, but the fact that it is a shame has nothing to do with whether or not we should do it. Thus, if your church decides that it should be using releases and authorizations, then I recommend having those documents properly acknowledged by a notary public. Doing so is the reasonably prudent thing to do.

Once you have decided to require this step, please try to make it as convenient as possible for the parents, who unfailingly will grumble about it. If you have a youth group volunteer who is a notary public, then have him present as parents drop off their kids for an activity at the church. Consider making the youth minister a notary public. Consider making other employees, ministers, and staff members notaries public. I rarely have seen too many notaries public helping with the process, but I have seen a quite a line waiting on Kimberly, the only notary public present, to sign her name twenty times.

The process of becoming a notary public is quite simple. It can be done with a few telephone calls through private companies who specialize in streamlining the process. Once a person has become a notary public, he is "a public servant with statewide jurisdiction who is authorized to take acknowledgments . . . [and to] administer oaths." Notaries public take an oath to perform their duties and they are required to post a bond with the Secretary of State. Their duties are to demonstrate to the signatory that the document being signed is important, to receive evidence from the signatory as to the authenticity of her "identity, signature, and reasons for signing the document," and to memorialize the signing of that document in a separate journal by keeping notes about just who signed what, when, and where. A notary public's seal and signature are not conclusive proof of the authenticity of a signature, but they go a long way (distinguished from conclusive proof as being *prima facie* proof) in establishing that you can rely on a signature as the real deal when you are faced with a forgery claim. The State of Texas places a great deal of trust in and responsibility on notaries public, so it should come as no surprise that there are civil and criminal penalties for notarial misconduct, along with the possibility of license revocation. Thus, notaries public should take their duties seriously.[453]

RELEASES AND AUTHORIZATIONS - STRATEGY AND OPTIONS

Churches typically decide which document to use based on a variety of factors, including the nature, duration, and location of the specific activity. Most churches do not require any authorization or release for on-site activities, regardless of the nature of the activity. To require a release or an authorization for the youth to play basketball in the church parking lot is extremely cumbersome. A signed authorization from a parent may be required for an off-site activity, though, indicating simply that the parent is aware that her child will be attending a church-sponsored activity away from the church and that the church will be providing transportation to and from, along with supervision at, the activity. If the activity is far away from the church, perhaps even involving an overnight stay, a church might require that the authorization be notarized. It is an unhappy mother who learns that her boy has forged her signature to an authorization and that the son is several hundred miles away, instead of sleeping over at a friend's house, as the story initially began. The degree of risk involved also affects the choice of document, as certain activities generate far more risk than others. Importantly, though, an authorization does not release anyone from liability. It merely formalizes a parent's consent for her child to participate in an activity.

If a church cannot afford the types of insurance required by the Charitable Immunity & Liability Act, as discussed more fully in Chapter 5, then it may be prudent to insist on releases. However, that scenario begs another question. If a church cannot afford such insurance, then it may need to ponder whether or not its members should be participating in activities which expose it to the exact type of risk for which insurance coverage exists. Conversely, if a church can afford the minimum insurance, then I believe that it is appropriate for that church to question the wisdom of using releases as a kneejerk reaction in every situation. If a church purchases insurance to manage risk and pays the premiums, then why does that church want to remove potential coverage for accidents by providing itself with the defense of a release? Again, the answer turns on so many individual factors that each church may answer this question in a slightly different way based on its own circumstances.

Needless to say, we should eliminate those risks which are unnecessary and reduce those risks which are manageable, being ever vigilant not to damage any ministry while doing so. After that, there are essentially three responses to potential liability:

- avoid participating in or sponsoring any activity
- obtain releases prior to participating in or sponsoring any activity and/or
- maintain insurance covering your participation in or sponsorship of an activity

The first scenario is unacceptable. Withdrawing from the world is not part of any viable ministry. The second plan is unreliable, problematic, and may alienate some church members. Although releases may be appropriate in some circumstances, they should not become a kneejerk reaction for every youth activity. Finally, as much as I dislike paying the premiums, maintaining insurance provides a degree of protection from claims. Thus, in many cases, it is a more appropriate safeguard against potential claims than the alternatives.

RESPONDING TO ACCIDENTS

Even if a church decides to pay an injured person's medical bills and even if that person accepts the church's offer to do so, you should not assume that these payments have ended the matter. Offering to pay someone's medical bills is simply that, an offer. Unless tied to a settlement offer and unless accompanied by the proper execution of an enforceable release, your payments have not necessarily purchased peace, although they may have been an admirable gesture. An injured person easily can make a claim for other types of compensable damages usually associated with personal injuries. These types of damages include past and future

- mental anguish
- physical pain
- lost earning capacity
- lost wages
- physical impairment
- loss of consortium
- disfigurement
- medical and counseling expenses

Without an agreement, simply paying the medical bills does not guarantee an end to the matter.

That does not mean that a church never should offer to pay someone's medical bills. It simply means that the issue is a little more complicated than it may appear. The law is a bit of a two-edged sword on this point, in that it attempts to protect such gestures of goodwill from being used against defendants, but is only partially effective in doing so. The law prohibits introducing evidence of making or offering to make such payments "to prove liability for the injury."[454] A plaintiff's lawyer might attempt the following argument: "this church must have been negligent because it felt guilty enough to pay for my client's medical bills." That may be an improper argument, but that does not mean that the plaintiff's lawyer will forego trying to make it.

A significant limitation is that the medical payments rule only applies when a party tries to introduce evidence for the purpose of proving liability. Thus, the plaintiff's lawyer might attempt to let the jury know that your church paid certain bills for a purpose other than proving liability, perhaps for calculating the amount of bills that remain unpaid, simply leaving the impression that the church felt responsible without having said it directly. Your church's attorney may try to counter this by asking the trial judge to prohibit the plaintiff's lawyer from ever mentioning any payments or may try to mitigate any damage done by the plaintiff's lawyer by arguing that, among other motivations, the church, although not feeling responsible, simply was trying to be a good neighbor by assisting with the medical bills. I am not trying to discourage any church from doing what it feels is the right thing in any situation, only to ensure that all churches are aware of the possible consequences of their actions.

Another aspect of responding to an accident is expressing sympathy to the injured person, a concept which should not be limited in any way to youth. Sometimes the most important thing that a church can do is to communicate its concern for an injured person and regret over, if not responsibility for, the incident that caused the injury. Such expressions are appropriate and even endemic to our faith. Yet, far too often, we allow concerns over law suits or, worse, apathy to dissuade us from expressing our concerns. Finding a way to express those sentiments without violating our duty to cooperate with the church's insurance company will be difficult in many cases, as discussed more fully in Chapter 10. Yet, we should not have to go so far as to confess liability in a contested claim when we confess concern.

MEDICAL CARE CONSENT FORMS

The law states that a parent has, among other rights, the right to "direct the moral and religious training of the child."[455] The statute does not require written authorization for any activities related to these purposes. Thus, with a parent's oral permission, a church can take a child out of town on a retreat or other activity without written permission from that child's parents or other guardians. The question should not focus on the minimum legal requirements, though. The question should revolve around determining the measures which a church should take to prepare for the contingencies of having a child away from his parents.

One of the more common situations arising in these circumstances involves a child who needs medical care. Obviously, her parents should be contacted immediately, as the parents are primarily responsible for the child's medical care.[456] However, what happens when she needs medical attention before the parents can be contacted? Absent life-threatening emergencies, health care professionals may be reluctant to render medical care to minors, whose right to consent is extremely limited.[457] Without a parent's permission, the law usually does not allow a health care professional to presume that the sponsor has that authority. To resolve this dilemma, the law allows parents to authorize an adult sponsor to consent to medical treatment for the child.

Such a written consent form should include the following information, some of which is statutorily mandated and some of which has a more practical bent:

- the child's and the parent's or other consenting adult's name, address, telephone number, and relationship
- a description of the activity being attended, including dates
- applicable health insurance information
- listing of allergic reactions, significant medical problems, and current medications

- the name, address, and telephone number of the church or group
- a clause granting the parent's authorization for a sponsor from the church or group to consent to reasonable and necessary medical treatment for the child
- the parent's or other consenting adult's signature
- a notarial acknowledgement[458]

A designated sponsor, whose identity and location are known to all sponsors and youth, should retain possession of an authorization for each child for the duration of a trip.

TRANSPORTATION

One of the more worrisome aspects of youth activities is transportation. Youth generally take at least as many trips together as any age group in a church and need for an adult to drive them to their destination. The process usually involves a youth minister or sponsor taking his own vehicle or a church van. Few, if any, precautions usually are observed in deciding who can drive in these situations. Youth group volunteers are difficult enough to recruit. Thus, the argument goes, we should not scare them off by asking about their driving records and offending them. However, consider the following scenario.

Don Speedalot, a recent college graduate, joins the church and begins working with the youth group. Everyone is thrilled that he has stepped up to this task. He takes the youth group on a trip in the church van and Don causes an accident in which several of the youth are injured. The plaintiffs' attorney discovers that Don had a driving record which included several accidents, moving violation citations, and a conviction for driving while intoxicated. The damages exceed all available insurance policy limits. The church is sued on a negligent entrustment theory (as discussed more fully in Chapter 4) because, if the church had bothered simply to inquire of Don's driving record, then it would have discovered that Don should not have been driving himself, much less anyone else. The church, however, never bothered to ask the right questions. It simply handed the keys to Don, even though it had ample opportunities to ask the right questions.

Negligence involves the failure to act as a reasonably prudent person under similar circumstances. If a church fails to inquire of a poor driver's record before it entrusts him with others' lives, then that church may have been negligent and may be liable for any consequential damages arising from that driver's negligence. It is simply time to put away our old thinking that volunteers are too valuable to risk offending. The stakes are too high in today's society to roll the dice with these issues and we all need to adjust our thinking to allow the church to function more effectively by screening volunteers and staff members before allowing them to serve. Doing so protects the church from potential claims and protects its members and society at large from accidents waiting to happen. Thus, screening potential drivers and limiting vehicle access to those on an approved list should become a routine part of every church's procedures, as discussed in more detail in Chapter 14.

Teenagers love to drive and there always seems to be at least one who insists on driving himself and a few friends to a youth activity. This is extremely problematic. The first time that I was primarily responsible for a youth trip to an amusement park, I was confronted with a situation in which some teenagers told me that they would be taking their own car and that they had cleared this with all of their parents. Those teenagers missed two check-ins during the next twelve hours, only making the final check-in at 10:00 P.M. We had informed their parents, were tracking our lost sheep, and knew approximately where they were. Some of the parents were shocked, though, when they learned that they supposedly had given their permission for this to happen and were rightly disappointed in me.

I allowed this problem to develop by not having rules in place to deal with it. I regret that and assure you that, absent special circumstances and parental consent communicated directly to me by that parent, no youth group member now drives a car on a trip for which I am responsible. The problem is not one of trust. The problem is not one of playing favorites with who can drive and who cannot. The problem is twofold: knowing that teenage drivers have less experience and a higher traffic accident rate than adults and maintaining insurance coverage when something goes wrong. Although we are not speaking exclusively of the sixteen to eighteen year old male in this context, insurance studies and rates certainly demonstrate that those in that profile are involved in more than their fair share of accidents. I contributed to those statistics twice when I was eighteen and I can look any of our young men straight in the eye and tell them that I know exactly how they drive when they protest my not allowing them to do so.

If an accident occurs on a church-sponsored trip, then that church may be sued for any resulting injuries, regardless of whether or not its vehicle is involved. Most policies insuring those who drive a church's vehicles require that the drivers be a minimum age level, usually ranging from twenty-one to twenty-five. Thus, an additional coverage problem could exist in the earlier example with Don, depending on his age, but the church never bothered to ask even that minimal question. We can argue about whether or not these arbitrary ages are too low or too high, but it does not change the fact that the church's insurance coverage may not apply to accidents involving an underage driver operating the church's vehicle in connection with a church-sponsored activity. If he is driving his own vehicle, then his insurance coverage should apply. However, that will not necessarily eliminate the church's exposure, as a plaintiff's lawyer probably will include the church in any claim under a negligent supervision or other theory, particularly if the negligent driver is part of a caravan of cars, as is common on youth trips, and / or only has a liability policy with minimum limits. That raises the question of whether or not the church's automobile liability coverage applies to such a situation. Lack of coverage places the church and its assets at risk. That is a high price to pay for placating someone's desire to drive.

CURFEWS

Just as parents should be concerned about how early or late their child arrives home, churches should be concerned about this issue when they host late night youth functions. Consider this example. The youth group holds a fellowship after each Friday night's varsity football game. The game is over by 10:00 and all of the youth are at the church by 10:30. The fellowship lasts for two hours and everyone goes home. Some of the youth are old enough to drive themselves, so they do. They are stopped for violating a municipal curfew ordinance at 12:30 A.M., thirty minutes after a midnight deadline. Late night youth activities are a wonderful part of being in a youth group and provide a safe alternative to other options, but they should not give us cause to violate the law.

More and more cities are enacting these ordinances. The time limits (even during school hours in some cases), applicable ages, potential defenses, and other specifics contained in these laws vary from city to city, though. To complicate the issue, some urban areas have fairly gerrymandered political boundaries, meaning that a child may have to drive through more than one municipality and may have to obey more than one ordinance in order to travel safely from church to home. That means familiarizing yourself with all of the applicable ordinances and limiting your group's activities to the earliest curfew in place.

We cannot stop any young person with a driver's license from ignoring an enforceable curfew ordinance if the determination exists. What we can do is to ensure that all youth functions end soon enough for every teenager to be home in time to avoid violating curfew. If all of the youth leave the church in time to drive home, then no one has cause to complain. If they are not released until after the curfew is in effect, then there may be some angry parents speaking with the staff on Sunday morning. If a church hosts any youth activity at which this could be a concern, then it simply should release all of the youth in a timely manner or, if it is too late to do that, then it should have enough adult sponsors to drive those youth home without violating the ordinance. Given that choice, most of the adult sponsors will begin to see the wisdom in an early end to the night's festivities. In conclusion, encouraging even one youth to violate the law by driving himself home after curfew undermines the example which we should be setting for them and their respect for us. That, in turn, undermines our ministry. No degree of personal convenience justifies that result.

LETTING GO

The following statements are all true. If you doubt that statement, as many parents have done when I have told them what the law is on a particular subject, then confirm your worst fears by referring to the actual statutes and cases cited in support of these statements. They are nothing more than a eclectic grouping of laws affecting children and, consequently, parents. You may find these oddly reassuring or frightening, but, in one way or another, they echo the Scriptural admonition that there will come a time in the life of each child when that child is less of a child and more of an adult, whether in the eyes of the law or their parents, a time when we begin to face the issue of letting go.

- A child or minor is "a person under 18 years of age who is not and has not been married or who has not had the disabilities of minority removed for general purposes."[459]
- The age of majority is 18.[460]
- Among other rights, a parent has the right to "direct the moral and religious training of the child."[461]
- Among other duties, a parent has the duties "to support the child, including providing the child with clothing, food, shelter, medical and dental care, and education" and "of care, control, protection, and reasonable discipline."[462]
- Without a parent's or judge's consent, a person 18 and over can marry.[463]
- With a parent's consent, a person 14 and older can marry.[464]
- With a judge's consent, a person under 14 can marry.[465]
- A person must be 21 or older to consume alcoholic beverages in Texas.[466]
- Parents are responsible for damages caused by the "the negligent conduct of the child if the conduct is reasonably attributable to the negligent failure of the parent or other person to exercise" the parent's "duty of control and reasonable discipline."[467]
- Parents are responsible for damages caused by the willful and "malicious conduct of a child who is at least" 10 but under 18.[468]
- A minor who is at least 16, after meeting certain criteria, may earn a driver's license.[469]

- A minor who is at least 15, after meeting certain criteria, may earn a driver's license on a hardship basis.[470]
- A minor needs to appear in person to apply for a passport. Parents must accompany minors under 14 and may be required to accompany older minors.[471]
- A person who is a soldier in the United States armed forces, legally married, or 18 and older may execute a will.[472]
- A person 15 and older may witness the execution of a will.[473]
- A physician can perform an abortion on a minor if the physician gives 48 hours notice of the intended abortion to the minor's parents.[474]
- Generally, a person younger than 18 must appear in court as a party through her parent, known as a "next friend."[475]
- A person 18 and older may vote.[476]
- Males between the ages of 18 and 25 must register with the Selective Service.[477]
- A person with testamentary capacity, regardless of age, may donate his organs without the consent of a parent.[478]
- A person younger than 18 without testamentary capacity may donate his organs without his parents' consent, but the "gift is not effective without the approval or consent of the person's parents or legal guardian if the person is younger than 18 years of age at the time of death."[479]
- A bruise from a spanking by a parent may be child abuse.[480]
- A person 16 or older, if living separately from his parents, can ask a court to remove the disabilities of being a minor if the minor is "self-supporting and managing the minor's own financial affairs."[481]
- Under certain circumstances, a person may be put to death for capital offenses committed after that person turns 17.[482]
- A minor can open a bank account without his parent being a signatory on the account.[483]
- A person at least 18 can enter into contracts.[484]
- Generally, a court may order one or both parents involved in a divorce to pay child support for the benefit of a person who has not yet turned 18 or graduated from high school.[485]

Bibliography

Adams, Jay E. *Handbook of Church Discipline*. Grand Rapids, Michigan: Zondervan Publishing House, 1986.

Aldave, B. ed. *Texas Corporations Law and Practice*, vol. 1. Albany, New York: Matthew Bender, 1984.

Anderson, Neil T. and Mylander, Charles. *Blessed Are the Peacemakers*. Ventura, California: Regal Books, 2002.

Armstrong, John H. *Can Fallen Pastors Be Restored?: The Church's Response to Sexual Misconduct*. Chicago, Illinois: Moody Press 1995.

Arnold, William V. *Pastoral Responses to Sexual Issues*. Louisville, Kentucky: Westminster/John Knox Press, 1993.

Berkley, James D., ed. *Leadership Handbook of Management and Administration*. Grand Rapids, Michigan: Baker Books, 1998.

Bush, Robert A. Baruch and Folger, Joseph P. *The Promise of Mediation: Responding to Conflict Through Empowerment and Recognition*. San Francisco, California: Jossey-Bass, Inc. Publishers, 1994.

Bush, Robert A. Baruch and Folger, Joseph P., eds. *Designing Mediation: Approaches to Training and Practice within a Transformative Framework*. New York, New York: Institute for the Study of Conflict Transformation, Inc., 2001.

Buzzard, Lynn R. and Eck, Laurence. *Tell It to the Church*. Elgin, Illinois: David C. Cook Publishing Co., 1982.

Carlson, Lee W. *Child Sexual Abuse: A Handbook for Clergy and Church Members*. Valley Forge, Pennsylvania: Judson Press, 1988.

Coffee, Blake. *One Body: Experiencing Unity in the Church*. Dallas, Texas: Baptist Leadership Center, Inc., 1999.

Crabtree, Jack. *Better Safe than Sued*. Loveland, Colorado: Group Publishing, Inc., 1998.

Cronenwett, Mark D., and Stansberry, Lindsay L. "Article V Privileges." *The Advocate*, Vol. 27, Summer 2004. Austin, Texas: State Bar of Texas.

Dunn, Ronald. *Surviving Friendly Fire*. Nashville, Tennessee: Thomas Nelson, Inc., 2001.

Fortune, Marie M. *Is Nothing Sacred?* San Francisco, California: Harper & Row, 1989.

Fortune, Marie M. and Voelkel-Haugen, Rebecca. *Sexual Abuse Prevention*, Cleveland, Ohio: United Church Press, 1996.

Fortune, Marie M. *Working Together*, Vol. 17, No. 2. Seattle, Washington.

Graham, Billy. *A Biblical Standard for Evangelists*. Minneapolis, Minnesota: Worldwide Publications, 1984.

Hagglund, Clarance and Wiemer, Britton. *Stay Out of Court & Stay in Ministry*. Lima, Ohio: CSS Publishing Company, Inc., 1998.

Hart, Archibald D., Gulbranson, Gary L., and Smith, Jim. *Mastering Pastoral Counseling*. Portland, Oregon: Multnomah Press, 1992.

Hays, Richard B. *The Moral Vision of the New Testament*. New York, New York: HarperCollins Publishers, 1996.

House, H. Wayne, ed. *Christian Ministries and the Law: What Church and Para-Church Leaders Should Know*, 2nd ed. Grand Rapids, Michigan: Kregel Publications, 1999.

Jackowski, Karol. *The Silence We Keep*. New York, New York: Harmony Books, 2004.

Laurie, Greg. *The Great Compromise*. Waco, Texas: Word Publishing, 1994.

Lebacqz, Karen and Barton, Ronald G. *Sex in the Parish*. Louisville, Kentucky: Westminster/John Knox Press, 1991.

Mazur, Cynthia S. and Bullis, Ronald K. *Legal Guide for Day-to-Day Church Matters*. Cleveland, Ohio: United Church Press, 1994.

Miller, Renee. "The Ten Commandments of Firing." *Texas Business Today*. Texas Workforce Commission, 2nd Quarter, 1997.

Mosgofian, Peter and Ohlschlager, George. *Sexual Misconduct in Counseling and Ministry*, Waco, Texas: Word Publishing, 1995.

Peretti, Frank E. *Piercing the Darkness*. Westchester, Illinois: Crossway Books, 1989.

Sande, Ken. *The Peacemaker: A Biblical Guide to Resolving Personal Conflict*, rev. ed. Grand Rapids, Michigan: Baker Books, 1997.

Shaughnessy, Mary Angela. *Ministry and the Law*. Mahwah, New Jersey: Paulist Press, 1998.

Southern Baptist Convention. *The Baptist Faith and Message*, Article VI, 1963.

Taylor, Thomas F. *7 Deadly Lawsuits*. Nashville, Tennessee: Abingdon Press, 1996.

The Holy Bible, New International Version (American Edition), © 1973, 1978, 1984 by the International Bible Society, used by permission of Zondervan Publishing House.

Waddell, Glenn G., and Keegan, Judith M. "Christian Conciliation: An Alternative to 'Ordinary' ADR." 29 *Cumberland Law Review* 583, 1999.

Wenham, David. *The Parables of Jesus.* Downers Grove, Illinois: InterVarsity Press, 1989.

Notes

Introduction

1. Karol Jackowski, *The Silence We Keep* (New York, New York: Harmony Books 2004) 180.

Chapter 1 - The Church, the Law, and Attorneys

2. *Boyles v. Kerr*, 855 S.W. 2d 593 (Tex. 1993).
3. *McCamish, Martin, Brown & Loeffler v. F.E. Appling Interests*, 991 S.W.2d 787 (Tex. 1999).
4. For a fictional, yet realistic, account of the struggles that a Christian attorney can face in representing the church and related causes, read Frank Peretti, *Piercing the Darkness* (Westchester, Illinois: Crossway Books 1989) 67–74.
5. Tex. Disc. R. Pro. Cond. 1.04(b).
6. Tex. Bus. & Com. Code Ann. § 1.201(28) and (30).
7. Tex. Disc. R. Pro. Cond. 1.12(a).
8. Tex. R. Pro. Cond. 1.12(a)-(c), (e).
9. Barbara Aldave, *Texas Corporations Law and Practice*, vol. 1 (Albany, New York: Matthew Bender 1984) 3.04[2].
10. Tex. Disc. R. Pro. Cond. Preamble.
11. *The Baptist Faith and Message*, Article VI, 1963.

12.   William V. Arnold, *Pastoral Responses to Sexual Issues* (Louisville, Kentucky: Westminster/John Knox Press 1993) 52.

Chapter 2 - Conflict in the Courthouse

13.   *The Constitution of Texas*, Article I, § 13.
14.   *<www.twc.state.tx.us>*.
15.   *<www.irs.gov>*.
16.   Robert A. Baruch Bush and Joseph P. Folger, *The Promise of Mediation* (San Francisco, California: Jossey-Bass, Inc. 1994) 63.
17.   Bush and Folger 69. 18. Tex. R. Civ. Pro. 11 and Tex. Civ. Prac. & Rem. Code Ann. § 154.071(a).
19.   Tex. Civ. Prac. & Rem. Code Ann. § 154.073.
20.   Tex. Civ. Prac. & Rem. Code Ann. § 154.027.
21.   Tex. Civ. Prac. & Rem. Code Ann. § 171.104.
22.   Tex. Civ. Prac. & Rem. Code Ann. § 171.001 et seq.

Chapter 3 - Conflict in the Church

23.   Neil T. Anderson and Charles Mylander, *Blessed Are the Peace Makers* (Ventura, California: Regal Books 2002) 60.
24.   David Wenham, *The Parables of Jesus* (Downers Grove, Illinois: InterVarsity Press 1989) 153–54.
25.   Anderson and Mylander 90.
26.   Phil Keaggy, "Salvation Army Band," *True Believer,* CD, Sparrow, 1995.
27.   Bryan Duncan, "Mr. Bailey's Daughter," *Anonymous Confessions of a Lunatic Friend*, CD, Fanatic Music / Word Music, 1990.
28.   Ronald Dunn, *Surviving Friendly Fire* (Nashville, Tennessee: Thomas Nelson, Inc. 2001) 178–79.
29.   Jay E. Adams, *Handbook of Church Discipline* (Grand Rapids, Michigan: Zondervan Publishing House 1986) 28.
30.   Lynn Buzzard and Laurence Eck, *Tell It to the Church* (Elgin, Illinois: David C. Cook Publishing Co. 1982) 29.
31.   Hays 97.
32.   Richard B. Hays, *The Moral Vision of the New Testament* (New York, New York: HarperCollins Publishers 1996) 102. *See also* Leviticus 19:17–18.
33.   Adams 47.
34.   Anderson and Mylander 201.

35. Buzzard and Eck 33–34.

36. Adams 70.

37. See Matthew 18:16, Acts 11:30, II Timothy 4:2, Titus 1:13, and Titus 2:15.

38. Adams 80.

39. Adams 80.

40. Hays 102.

41. Adams 83.

42. Hays 102.

43. Hays 102. *See also* Buzzard and Eck 34.

44. Blake Coffee, *One Body: Experiencing Unity in the Church* (Dallas, Texas: Texas Baptist Leadership Center, Inc. 1999) 63.

45. Bush and Folger 81 and 233.

46. Bush and Folger 84–85.

47. Buzzard and Eck 39.

48. Buzzard and Eck 34–38.

49. Anderson and Mylander 203.

50. Anderson and Mylander 203–12.

51. Ken Sande, *The Peacemaker: A Biblical Guide to Resolving Personal Conflict,* rev. ed. (Grand Rapids, Michigan: Baker Books 1997).

52. Glenn G. Waddell and Judith M. Keegan, "Christian Conciliation: An Alternative to 'Ordinary' ADR," 29 *Cumberland Law Review* 583 (1999).

53. <www.hispeace.org/html/church_respond_distinct.htm>.

54. <www.christianunityministries.org> and <www.lmpeacecenter.org>.

Chapter 4 - They've Sued Us for What?!: Common Claims

55. *Greater Houston Transp. Co. v. Phillips,* 801 S.W.2d 523, 525 (Tex. 1990) and *Praesel v. Johnson,* 967 S.W.2d 391, 394 (Tex. 1998).

56. *Doe v. Boys Clubs of Greater Dallas, Inc.,* 907 S.W.2d 472, 477 (Tex. 1995).

57. *Rosas v. Buddies Food Store,* 518 S.W.2d 534 (Tex. 1975).

58. *Adam Dante Corp. v. Sharpe,* 483 S.W.2d 452 (Tex. 1972).

59. *Keetch v. The Kroger Co.,* 845 S.W.2d 262 (Tex. 1992).

60. *Barker v. City of Galveston,* 907 S.W.2d 879, 884 (Tex. App.—Houston [1st Dist.] 1995, no writ).

61. *State of Texas v. Tennison,* 509 S.W.2d 560 (Tex. 1974).

62. *Lipton v. Wilhite,* 902 S.W.2d 598 (Tex. App.—Houston [1st Dist.] 1995, writ denied).

63. *Corbin v. Safeway Stores, Inc.,* 648 S.W.2d 292 (Tex. 1992).

64. *Texas Utilities Electric Co. v. Timmons*, 947 S.W.2d 191, 193 (Tex. 1997).

65. *Restatement (Second) of Torts* § 821D and *Timmons* 193–94.

66. *Timmons* 197, and *Massie v. Copeland*, 149 Tex. 319, 330, 233 S.W.2d 449, 455 (Tex. 1950).

67. *Timmons* 195–96.

68. *Stimpson v. Bartex Pipe Line Co.*, 120 Tex. 232, 36 S.W.2d 473 (Tex. 1931).

69. *Restatement (Second) of Torts* § 821D.

70. *Restatement (Second) of Torts* § 822.

71. *Ballenger v. City of Grand Saline*, 276 S.W.2d 874, 875 (Tex. Civ. App.—Waco 1955).

72. *Gillespie v. Grimes*, 577 S.W.2d 538, 540 (Tex. App.—Tyler 1979).

73. *Walkoviak v. Hilton Hotels Corp.*, 580 S.W.2d 623 (Tex. App.—Houston [14th District] 1979, writ ref'd n.r.e.).

74. *Garner v. McGinty*, 771 S.W.2d 242, 246 (Tex. App.-Austin 1989, no writ) and *Kendrick v. Allright Parking*, 846 S.W.2d 453 (Tex. App.—San Antonio 1993, writ denied).

75. *Castillo v. Gared, Inc*, 1 S.W.3d 781, 786 (Tex. App.—Hous. [1st Dist.] 1999, pet. denied) (citing *Mackey v. U.P. Enterprises, Inc.*, 935 S.W.2d 446, 459 (Tex. App.—Tyler 1996, no writ).

76. *Dieter v. Baker Service Tools, a Division of Baker International, Inc*, 739 S.W.2d 405, 408 (Tex. App.—Corpus Christi 1999).

77. *Galveston, H. & S. A. Ry. Co. v. Currie*, 100 Tex. 136, 96 S.W. 1073, 1074, 10 L.R.A., N.S., 367; *Tierra Drilling Corp. v. Detmar*, 666 S.W.2d 661, 663 (Tex. App.—Corpus Christi 1984).

78. *Dieter. See also Verinakis v. Medical Profiles, Inc.*, 987 S.W.2d 90, (Tex. App.— Houston [14th Dist.] 1998, pet. denied); *Houser v. Smith*, 968 S.W.2d 542, 544 (Tex. App.—Austin 1998, no pet.); *Robertson v. Church of God, Intern.*, 978 S.W.2d 120, 124 (Tex. App.—Tyler 1997, pet. denied); *Scott Fetzer Co. d/b/a The Kirby Co. v. Read*, 945 S.W.2d 854 (Tex. App.—Austin 1997). *Golden Spread Council of Boy Scouts v. Akins*, 926 S.W.2d 287 (Tex. 1996); *Porter v. Nemir*, 900 S.W.2d 376 (Tex. App.—Austin 1995, no writ); and *Doe v. Boys Club of Dallas, Inc.*, 868 S.W.2d 942 (Tex. App.—Amarillo 1994, aff'd 907 S.W.2d 472); *Deerings W. Nursing Ctr. v. Scott*, Tex. App.—El Paso 1990, writ denied); and *Restatement (Second) of Torts* § 315.

79. Tex. Fam Code Ann. § 261.109.

80. Tex. Fam. Code Ann. § 261.107.

81. *Moughon v. Wolf*, 576 S.W.2d 603 (Tex. 1978).

82. *Penley v. Westbrook*, No. 2-02-260-CV (Tex. App.—Fort Worth 2004, no writ); *Sanders v. Casa View Baptist Church,* 134 F.2d 331 (5th Cir. 1998).

83. Archibald D. Hart, Gary L. Gulbranson, and Jim Smith, *Mastering Pastoral Counseling* (Portland, Oregon: Multnomah Press 1992) 26.

84. *Dawes v. J.C. Penney & Co.*, 236 S.W.2d 624 (Tex. Civ. App.—Waco 1951, writ ref'd n.r.e).

85. Arnold 52.

86. *Schneider v. Esperanza Transmission Co.*, 744 S.W.2d 595, 596 (Tex. 1988) and *Avalos v. Brown Automotive Center, Inc.*, 63 S.W.3d 42 (Tex. App.—San Antonio 2001).

87. Tex. Trans. Code Ann. §§ 550.001 et seq.

88. *Brookshire Grocery Co. v. Richey*, 899 S.W. 2d 331, 333 (Tex. App.—Tyler 1995, no writ).

89. Tex. Civ. Prac. & Rem. Code Ann. § 41.001(7).

90. *Transportation* Ins. Co. v. Moriel, 879 S.W. 2d 10 (Tex. 1994).

91. *Marshall v. Mahaffey*, 974 S.W.2d 942, 949 (Tex. App.—Beaumont, 1998).

92. Tex. Civ. Prac. & Rem Code Ann. § 81.001(2)(A)-(H).

93. Tex. Civ. Prac. & Rem Code Ann. § 81.001(1) and (4).

94. Tex. Civ. Prac. & Rem Code Ann. § 81.001(4).

95. Tex. Civ. Prac. & Rem Code Ann. § 81.001(5).

96. Tex. Civ. Prac. & Rem Code Ann. § 81.001(6).

97. *See Hawkins v. Trinity Baptist Church*, 30 S.W.2d 446 (Tex. App.—Tyler 2000, no writ) for a particularly disturbing account.

98. Tex. Civ. Prac. & Rem. Code Ann. § 81.001(7).

99. *Hawkins.*

100. Tex. Civ. Prac. & Rem Code Ann. § 81.002.

101. Tex. Civ. Prac. & Rem Code Ann. § 81.004.

102. Tex. Civ. Prac. & Rem Code Ann. § 81.003.

103. Tex. Civ. Prac. & Rem Code Ann. § 81.005(a)(1)-(3).

104. Tex. Civ. Prac. & Rem Code Ann. § 81.005(b).

105. Tex. Civ. Prac. & Rem Code Ann. § 81.006(a).

106. Tex. Civ. Prac. & Rem. Code Ann. § 81.006(b).

107. Tex. Civ. Prac. & Rem. Code Ann. § 81.006(c).

108. Tex. Civ. Prac. & Rem. Code Ann. § 81.007.

Chapter 5 - What Do We Do Now?!: Defenses

109. *The Constitution* of Texas, 1876, Article I, § 13.
110. *The Constitution* of Texas, 1876, Article I, § 13, Interpretive Commentary.
111. Tex. R. Civ. Pro. 13.
112. Tex. Disc. R. Pro. Con. 3.01.
113. Tex. Civ. Prac. & Rem. Code Ann. §§ 9.011 and 10.001.
114. Tex. Rev. Civ. Stat. Ann. art. 1396-2.07.
115. Tex. R. Civ. Pro. 7 and *Kunstoplast of America, Inc. v. Formosa Plastics Corp., USA*, 937 S.W.2d 455 (Tex. 1997).
116. Tex. Bus. & Com. Code Ann. § 3.402(c).
117. *Griffin v. Ellinger*, 538 S.W.2d 97 (Tex. 1976).
118. Tex. Rev. Civ. Stat. Ann. art. 1302-7.07.
119. Tex. Bus. & Com. Code Ann. § 1.201(39).
120. Tex. Gov. Code Ann. § 312.011(14).
121. Tex. Rev. Civ. Stat. Ann. art. 1396-9.03A.
122. Tex. Civ. Prac. & Rem. Code Ann. § 16.070.
123. Tex. Civ. Prac. & Rem. Code Ann. § 16.001(a).
124. *Burns v. Thomas*, 786 S.W.2d 266 (Tex. 1990).
125. Tex. Civ. Prac. & Rem. Code Ann. § 75.001(2).
126. Tex. Civ. Prac. & Rem. Code Ann. § 75.001(3).
127. Tex. Civ. Prac. & Rem. Code Ann. § 75.002(c).
128. *Torres v. City of Bellmead*, 40 S.W.3d 662, 665 (Tex. App.—Waco 2001).
129. Tex. Civ. Prac. & Rem. Code Ann. § 75.002(d).
130. Tex. Civ. Prac. & Rem. Code Ann. § 75.003(b).
131. Tex. Civ. Prac. & Rem. Code Ann. § 75.003(c)(1)-(3).
132. Tex. Civ. Prac. & Rem. Code Ann. § 75.004(a).
133. Tex. Civ. Prac. & Rem. Code Ann. § 75.002(d).
134. Tex. Civ. Prac. & Rem. Code Ann. § 75.004(b).
135. *Lipton.*
136. Tex. Civ. Prac. & Rem. Code Ann. § 84.003(1)(B)(i)-(vi).
137. Tex. Civ. Prac. & Rem. Code Ann. § 84.003(2).
138. Tex. Civ. Prac. & Rem. Code Ann. § 84.003(3).
139. Tex. Civ. Prac. & Rem. Code Ann. § 84.003(4).
140. Tex. Civ. Prac. & Rem. Code Ann. § 84.004(a) and (b).
141. Tex. Civ. Prac. & Rem. Code Ann. § 84.004(c).
142. Tex. Civ. Prac. & Rem. Code Ann. § 84.004(d).
143. Tex. Civ. Prac. & Rem. Code Ann. § 75.004(a).

144. Tex. Civ. Prac. & Rem. Code Ann. § 84.007(g).

145. Tex. Civ. Prac. & Rem. Code Ann. §§ 84.005 and 84.006.

146. Tex. Civ. Prac. & Rem. Code Ann. § 84.007(a)-(f).

147. Tex. Civ. Prac. & Rem. Code Ann. § 41.003(b).

148. Tex. Civ. Prac. & Rem. Code Ann. § 41.009.

149. Tex. Civ. Prac. & Rem. Code Ann. § 41.007.

150. Tex. Civ. Prac. & Rem. Code Ann. § 41.008.

151. Tex. Civ. Prac. & Rem. Code Ann. § 41.006.

152. Tex. Civ. Prac. & Rem. Code Ann. § 41.011.

153. Tex. Civ. Prac. & Rem. Code Ann. § 41.005.

154. Tex. Civ. Prac. & Rem. Code Ann. § 95.001 et seq.

155. Tex. Civ. Prac. & Rem. Code Ann. § 95.003.

156. Tex. Civ. Prac. & Rem. Code Ann. § 95.003(1) and (2).

157. Tex. Civ. Prac. & Rem. Code Ann. § 33.001.

158. Tex. Civ. Prac. & Rem. Code Ann. §§ 33.012(a) and 33.013(a).

159. Tex. Rev. Civ. Stat. Ann. art. 1396-2.22A.H, I, J, and O.

160. Tex. Rev. Civ. Stat. Ann. art. 1396-2.22A.B.

161. Tex. Rev. Civ. Stat. Ann. art. 1396-2.22A.C.

162. Tex. Rev. Civ. Stat. Ann. art. 1396-2.22A.F.

163. Tex. Rev. Civ. Stat. Ann. art. 1396-2.22A.H.

164. Tex. Rev. Civ. Stat. Ann. art. 1396-2.22A.M and Q.

165. Tex. Rev. Civ. Stat. Ann. art. 1396-2.22A.R.

166. *The Serbian Eastern Orthodox Diocese v. Milivojevich*, 426 U.S. 696, 713, 96 S. Ct. 2372, 2382, 49 L. Ed.2d 151, 165 (U.S. 1976).

167. *Patterson v. Southwestern Baptist Theological Seminary*, 858 S.W.2d 602, 606 (Tex. App.—Fort Worth 1993, no writ).

168. *Williams v. Gleason*, 26 S.W.3d 54 (Tex. App.—Houston [14th Dist.] 2000, pet. denied, cert. denied 121 S. Ct. 2242 (2001)); *Libhart v. Copeland*, 949 S.W.2d 740 (Tex. App.—Waco 1997, no pet.); *Tran v. Fiorenza*, 934 S.W.2d 740 (Tex. App.—Houston [1st Dist.] 1996, no writ); and *Diocese of Galveston-Houston v. Stone*, 892 S.W.2d 169 (Tex. App.—Houston [14th Dist.] 1994, orig. proceeding).

169. *Green v. United Pentecostal Church International*, 899 S.W.2d 28, 30 (Tex. App.—Austin 1995, writ denied). See also In re: *Pleasant Glade Assembly of God*, 991 S.W.2d 85 (Tex. App.—Fort Worth 1998); *Ex Parte McLain*, 762 S.W.2d 238 (Tex. App.—Beaumont 1988, no writ); *Waters v. Hargest*, 593 S.W.2d 364 (Tex. Civ. App.—Texarkana 1979, no writ); and *Hughes v. Keeling*, 198 S.W.2d 779 (Tex. Civ. App.—Beaumont 1946, no writ).

170. *Hawkins v. Friendship Missionary Baptist Church*, 69 S.W.3d 756 (Tex. App.—Houston [14th Dist.] 2002).

171. *Dean v. Alford*, 994 S.W.2d 392 (Tex. App.—Fort Worth 1999, no writ).

172. *Lacy v. Bassett*, No. 14-02-01077-CV (Tex. App.—Houston [14th Dist.] 2004).

173. *First Baptist Church of Paris v. Fort*, 93 Tex. 215, 54 S.W. 892 (1900); Hawkins; *Green v. Westgate Apostolic Church*, 808 S.W.2d 547 (Tex. App.—Austin 1991, writ denied); and *Presbytery of the Covenant v. First Presbyterian Church of Paris, Inc.*, 552 S.W.2d 865 (Tex. Civ. App.—Texarkana 1977, no writ).

174. Tex. Rev. Civ. Stat. Ann. art. 1396-1.02.A(3) and 1396-2.24.

Chapter 6 - First Church, Inc.: Corporate

175. Tex. Rev. Civ. Stat. Ann. art. 1396-2.02.

176. Tex. Rev. Civ. Stat. Ann. art. 1396-2.14.C.

177. Tex. Rev. Civ. Stat. Ann. art. 1396-1.02.A(3) and 1396-2.24.

178. Tex. Rev. Civ. Stat. Ann. art. 1396-2.26.

179. Tex. Rev. Civ. Stat. Ann. art. 1396-1.03.A.

180. Tex. Rev. Civ. Stat. Ann. art. 1396-3.01.

181. Tex. Rev. Civ. Stat. Ann. art. 1396-2.04.A.

182. 1 Tex. Admin. Code § 79.37.

183. Tex. Rev. Civ. Stat. Ann. art. 1396-2.04 and 1 Tex. Admin. Code § 79.40.

184. 1 Tex. Admin. Code § 79.43.

185. 1 Tex. Admin. Code § 79.46.

186. Tex. Rev. Civ. Stat. Ann. art. 1396-2.15.A.

187. Tex. Rev. Civ. Stat. Ann. art. 1396-2.14.D.

188. Tex. Rev. Civ. Stat. Ann. art. 1396-2.14.C.

189. Tex. Rev. Civ. Stat. Ann art. 1396-2.05.

190. Tex. Rev. Civ. Stat. Ann. art. 1396-2.02.A(1).

191. Tex. Rev. Civ. Stat. Ann. art. 1396-9.01.

192. Tex. Rev. Civ. Stat. Ann. art. 1396-9.02.

193. Tex. Tax Code Ann. § 171.255(a) et seq.

194. Tex. Tax Code Ann. § 171.252.

195. Tex. Tax Code Ann. § 171.252.

196. Tex. Rev. Civ. Stat. Ann. art. 1396-2.07.

197. Tex. Civ. Prac. & Rem. Code Ann. §§ 84.004(a) and 84.007(b) and Tex. Rev. Civ. Stat. Ann. art. 1396-2.22.

198. Tex. Rev. Civ. Stat. Ann. art. 1396-102(A)(7) and Tex. Rev. Civ. Stat. Ann. art. 1396-2.22.
199. *International Bankers Life Ins. Co. v. Holloway*, 368 S.W.2d 567, 577 (Tex. 1963).
200. Aldave § 21.01[2] and *Gearheart Indus., Inc. v. Smith Int'l Inc.*, 141 F. 2d 707 (5th Cir. 1984).
201. *Meyers v. Moody*, 693 F.2d 1196 (5th Cir. 1982).
202. *FDIC v. Wheat*, 970 F.2d 124, 130–31 n.13 (5th Cir. 1992).
203. *FDIC v. Brown*, 812 F. Supp. 722, 723 (S.D. Tex. 1992).
204. *Brown.*
205. Tex. Rev. Civ. Stat. Ann. art. 1396-2.28.
206. Paragraphs 4 and 5 of the commentary to Tex. Rev. Civ. Stat. Ann. art. 1396-2.28.
207. Tex. Rev. Civ. Stat. Ann. art. 1396-2.25.A.
208. Tex. Rev. Civ. Stat. Ann. art. 1396-2.25.B.
209. Tex. Rev. Civ. Stat. Ann. art. 1396-2.12.
210. Tex. Rev. Civ. Stat. Ann. art. 1396-2.12.
211. Tex. Rev. Civ. Stat. Ann. art. 1396-6.02 and 6.05.
212. Tex. Rev. Civ. Stat. Ann. art. 1396-6.02 and 26 U.S.C. § 501(c)(3).
213. Tex. Rev. Civ. Stat. Ann. art. 1396-6.01.
214. Tex. Rev. Civ. Stat. art. 1396-70.01 § 1 et seq.
215. Tex. Rev. Civ. Stat. art. 1396-70.01 § 7(a).
216. Tex. Rev. Civ. Stat. art. 1396-70.01 § 12.
217. Tex. Rev. Civ. Stat. art. 1396-70.01 § 8.
218. Tex. Rev. Civ. Stat. art. 1396-70.01 § 5.
219. Tex. Rev. Civ. Stat. art. 1396-70.01 § 6.
220. Tex. Rev. Civ. Stat. art. 1396-70.01 § 7(e).
221. Tex. Rev. Civ. Stat. art. 1396-70.01 § 10(a).
222. Tex. Rev. Civ. Stat. art. 1396-70.01 § 10(b).

Chapter 7 - Rendering Unto Caesar: Taxes

223. <www.irs.gov/pub/irs pdf/p557.pdf>.
224. Tex. Tax Code Ann. §§ 111.001 et seq. and 321.001 et seq.
225. Tex. Tax Code Ann. § 26.05 et seq.
226. Tex. Tax Code Ann. § 151.310(a)(1).
227. Tex. Tax Code Ann. § 151.310(a)(2).
228. 34 Tex. Admin. Code § 3.322.
229. Tex. Tax Code Ann. § 151.314(c)(3).

230. Tex. Tax Code Ann. § 151.314(d)(2).
231. Tex. Tax Code Ann. § 151.314(e).
232. Tex. Tax Code Ann. § 151.304.
233. Tex. Admin. Code § 3.316(1).
234. Tex. Tax Code Ann. § 171.001.
235. Tex. Tax Code Ann. §§ 171.002 and 171.101 et seq.
236. Tex. Tax Code Ann. §§ 171.058 and 171.061.
237. Tex. Tax Code Ann. § 171.063.
238. 34 Tex. Admin. Code § 3.541(c)(3).
239. 34 Tex. Admin. Code § 3.541(c)(5).
240. 34 Tex. Admin. Code § 3.541(a)(2).
241. Tex. Tax Code Ann. § 171.051(a)-(b).
242. The Constitution of Texas, 1876, Article VIII, § 2.
243. Tex. Tax Code Ann. § 11.20(a).
244. Tex. Tax Code Ann. § 11.20(c).
245. Tex. Tax Code Ann. § 11.20(c)(1).
246. Tex. Tax Code Ann. § 11.20(c)(2) and (3).
247. *City of Dallas v. Cochran*, 166 S.W. 32 (Tex. Civ. App.—Texarkana 1914, writ ref'd).
248. *City of San Antonio v. Young Men's Christian Association*, 285 S.W. 844 (Tex. Civ. App.—San Antonio 1926, writ ref'd).
249. *Radio Bible Hour v. Hurst-Euless Independent School District*, 341 S.W.2d 467, 469 (Tex. Civ. App.—Fort Worth 1960, writ ref'd).
250. *Kerrville Independent School District v. Southwest Texas Encampment Association*, 673 S.W.2d 256, 258 (Tex. App.—San Antonio 1984, writ ref'd n.r.e.).
251. Tex. Tax Code Ann. § 11.20(d).
252. *University Christian Church v. City of Austin*, 768 S.W.2d 718 (Tex. 1986).
253. *University Christian Church v. City of Austin*, 789 S.W.2d 361 (Tex. App.—Austin 1990).
254. *First Baptist Church of San Antonio v. Bexar County Appraisal Review Board*, 833 S.W.2d 108 (Tex. 1992), on remand 846 S.W.2d 554 (Tex. App.—San Antonio, 1993), cert denied 510 U.S. 1178, 114 S. Ct. 1221, 127 L. Ed.2d 567 (1994).
255. *Bexar County Appraisal Review Board v. First Baptist Church*, 800 S.W.2d 892, 895 (Tex. App.—San Antonio 1990, writ granted).
256. *Bexar County Appraisal Review Board v. First Baptist Church*, 846 S.W.2d 554, 559 (Tex. App—San Antonio 1993).
257. Tex. Tax Code Ann. § 11.43.
258. Tex. Tax Code Ann. § 11.433(a).

Chapter 8 - Hiring, Firing, and Other Forms of Quicksand: Employment

259. *Sabine Pilot Service, Inc. v. Hauck*, 687 S.W.2d 733 (Tex. 1985).
260. Tex. Lab. Code Ann. § 431.006.
261. Tex. Elec. Code Ann. § 161.007.
262. Tex. Lab. Code Ann. § 276.004.
263. Tex. Civ. Prac. & Rem. Code Ann. § 122.001.
264. Tex. Lab. Code Ann. § 52.051.
265. Tex. Lab. Code Ann. §§ 101.052, 101.053, and 617.004 and Tex. Bus. & Com. Code Ann. § 15.05.
266. Tex. Lab. Code. Ann. § 451.001.
267. Tex. Lab. Code Ann. § 21.001 et seq. and the Civil Rights Act of 1964.
268. Tex. Lab. Code Ann. § 21.002.
269. *See Scott Fetzer Co. d/b/a The Kirby Co. v. Read*, 945 S.W.2d 854 (Tex. App.—Austin 1997).
270. *See* Tex. Civ. Prac. & Rem. Code Ann. § 81.003(b).
271. *See Golden Spread Council of Boy Scouts v. Akins*, 926 S.W.2d 287 (Tex. 1996); *Fetzer; Porter v. Nemir,* 900 S.W.2d 376 (Tex. App.—Austin 1995, no writ); and *Doe v. Boys Club of Dallas, Inc.,* 868 S.W.2d 942 (Tex. App.—Amarillo 1994, aff'd 907 S.W.2d 472); and *Deerings W. Nursing Ctr. v. Scott,* Tex. App.—El Paso 1990, writ denied).
272. I Timothy 5:22. *The Living Bible* (Wheaton, Illinois: Tyndale House Publishers 1971).
273. I Timothy 5:24. *The Living Bible.*
274. I Timothy 5:22. *The New American Standard Bible* (La Habra, California: The Lockman Foundation 1973).
275. *See Cox v. Nasche*, 70 F.3d 1030 (9th Cir. 1995).
276. Tex. Lab. Code Ann. § 52.031(a).
277. Tex. Lab. Code Ann. § 52.031(c).
278. Tex. Lab. Code Ann. § 52.031(d).
279. *Pioneer Concrete of Texas, Inc. v. Allen,* 858 S.W.2d 47, 50–51 (Tex. App.—Houston [14th Dist.] 1993, writ denied and *Free v. American Home Assurance Co.,* 902 S.W.2d 51, 55–56 (Tex. App.—Houston [1st Dist] 1995, no writ).
280. *See Saucedo v. Rheem Manufacturing Co.,* 974 S.W.2d 117 (Tex. App.—San Antonio 1998, writ denied).
281. Tex. Lab. Code Ann. § 61.018(3).
282. *Paniagua v. City of Galveston,* 995 F.2d 1310 (5th Cir. 1993).

283. Renee Miller, "The Ten Commandments of Firing" in *Texas Business Today* (Texas Workforce Commission 2nd Quarter 1997) 5.

Chapter 9 - Sticks and Stones, Bricks and Loans: Real Property

284. Tex. Rev. Civ. Stat. Ann. art. 6573a.
285. Tex. Rev. Civ. Stat. Ann. art. 6573a, § 15C.
286. Tex. Prop. Code Ann. § 5.008(a).
287. Tex. Prop. Code Ann. § 5.008(f).
288. Tex. Prop. Code Ann. § 92.108.
289. Tex. Prop. Code Ann. § 92.108.
290. Tex. Prop. Code Ann. § 92.103.
291. Tex. Prop. Code Ann. § 92.109.
292. *Waggoner v. Floral Heights Baptist Church,* 116 Tex. 187, 288 S.W. 129 (Tex. Com. App. 1926, opinion adopted).
293. *Waggoner* 131.

Chapter 10 - Do You Feel Lucky?: Insurance

294. *Yancey v. Floyd West & Co.,* 755 S.W.2d 914 (Tex. App.—Fort Worth 1988, writ denied).
295. *Hirsch v. Texas Lawyers Ins. Exchange,* 808 S.W.2d 561 (Tex. App.—El Paso 1991, writ denied).
296. *Broussard v. Lumbermen's Mutual Casualty Co.,* 582 S.W.2d 261 (Tex. App.— Beaumont 1979, no writ).
297. *Norman v. St. Paul Fire and Marine Ins. Co.,* 431 S.W.2d 391 (Tex. App.—Beaumont 1968, no writ).
298. *Broussard.*
299. *Kimble v. Aetna Casualty & Surety Co.,* 767 S.W.2d 846 (Tex. App.—Amarillo 1989, writ denied).
300. *Harwell v. State Farm Mutual Automobile Ins. Co.,* 896 S.W.2d 170, 173 (Tex. 1995).
301. *Weaver v. Hartford Accident & Indemnity Co.,* 570 S.W.2d 367 (Tex. 1978).
302. *Harwell* 175.
303. *Ohio Casualty Group v. Risinger,* 960 S.W.2d 708 (Tex. App.—Tyler 1997).
304. *Houston Petroleum Co. v. Highlands Ins. Co.,* 830 S.W.2d 153, 155 (Tex. App.— Houston [1st Dist.] 1990, writ denied).

305. *National Union Fire Ins. Co. v. Merchant's Fast Motor Lines, Inc.*, 939 S.W.2d 139 (Tex. 1997) and *Holmes v. Employers Casualty Co.*, 699 S.W.2d 339 (Tex. App.—Houston [1st Dist.] 1985, writ ref'd n.r.e.).

306. *Boyles v. Kerr*, 855 S.W.2d 593 (Tex. 1993).

307. *Baze v. Marine Office of America, Inc.*, 828 S.W.2d 152, 157 (Tex. App.—Corpus Christi 1992, no writ); *Dear v. Scottsdale Ins. Co.*, 947 S.W.2d 908, (Tex. App.—Dallas 1997, no writ); and *Fielder Road Baptist Church v. GuideOne Elite Ins. Co.*, 2-02-231-CV (Tex. App.—Fort Worth 2004).

308. *Trinity Universal Ins. Co. v. Cowan*, 945 S.W.2d 819 (Tex. 1997) and *Highlands Ins. Co. v. City of Galveston*, 721 S.W.2d 469 (Tex. App.—Houston [14th Dist.] 1986, writ ref'd n.r.e.).

309. *Holmes.*

310. Tex. Ins. Code art. 21.55.

311. Tex. Ins. Code art. 21.55, § 2(a)(1)-(3).

312. Tex. Ins. Code art. 21.55, § 4.

313. Tex. Ins. Code art. 21.55, § 3(c).

314. Tex. Ins. Code art. 21.55, § 3(d), (e).

315. Tex. Ins. Code art. 21.55, § 5(a).

316. Tex. Ins. Code art. 21.55, § 1(3).

317. *Arnold v. National County Mutual Fire Ins. Co.*, 725 S.W.2d 165 (Tex. 1987) and *Transportation Ins. Co. v. Moriel*, 879 S.W.2d 10 (Tex. 1994).

318. *State Farm Fire & Casualty Co. v. Simmons*, 963 S.W.2d 42, 44 (Tex. 1998).

319. *Transport Ins. Co. v. Faircloth*, 898 S.W.2d 269 (Tex. 1995).

320. *Transportation* Ins. Co. v. Moriel, 879 S.W.2d 10 (Tex. 1994).

321. Tex. Ins. Code art. 21.56(b), (c).

322. *Trinity Universal Ins. Co. v. Bleeker*, 944 S.W.2d 672 (Tex. App.—Corpus Christi 1997, no writ).

323. *G.A. Stowers Furniture Co. v. American Indemnity Co.*, 15 S.W.2d 544 (Tex. Comm'n App. 1929, holding approved); *American Physicians Ins. Exchange v. Garcia*, 876 S.W.2d 842 (Tex. 1994); and *Birmingham Fire Ins. Co. of Pennsylvania v. American National Fire Ins. Co.*, 947 S.W.2d 592 (Tex. App.—Texarkana 1997, no writ).

324. Tex. Ins. Code art. 21.21–2.

325. Tex. Ins. Code art. 21.21–2, § 2(a)(1)-(6).

326. Tex. Civ. Prac. & Rem. Code Ann. § 17.41 et seq.

327. *Rumley v. Allstate Ins. Co.*, 924 S.W.2d 448 (Tex. App.—Beaumont 1996, no writ).

Chapter 11 - Safe and Sound: Security

328. <www.usps.com>.

Chapter 12 - Safe and Sound: Health

329. Tex. Civ. Prac. & Rem. Code Ann. § 74.001(a).
330. Tex. Civ. Prac. & Rem. Code Ann. § 74.001(b), (c), and (d).
331. Tex. Health & Safety Code Ann. §§ 692.001, 692.005, and 692.006.
332. Tex. Health & Safety Code Ann. § 692.005.
333. Tex. Trans. Code Ann. § 521.401(b) and Tex. Health and Safety Code § 692.003(d).
334. Tex. Health & Safety Code Ann. § 692.004.
335. <www.redcross.org>.
336. <www.americanheart.org>.
337. <www.nsc.org>.

Chapter 13 - Between a Rock and a Hard Place: Pastoral Issues

338. Mark D. Cronenwett and Lindsay L. Stansberry, "Article V Privileges," *The Advocate*, Vol. 27 (Austin, Texas: State Bar of Texas, Summer 2004) 21.
339. Tex. R. Evid. 502.
340. Tex. R. Evid. 503.
341. Tex. R. Evid. 504.
342. Tex. R. Evid. 505.
343. Tex. R. Evid. 506.
344. Tex. R. Evid. 507.
345. Tex. R. Evid. 508.
346. Tex. R. Evid. 509.
347. Tex. R. Evid. 510.
348. Hart, Gulbranson, and Smith 36.
349. Tex. R. Evid. 505.
350. *Eckman v. Board of Education*, 106 F.R.D. 70, 72 (Missouri 1985).
351. *Easley v. State*, 837 S.W.2d 854 (Tex. Crim. App. 1992).
352. *Easley* 856.
353. *See also Kos v. State*, 15 S.W.3d 633 (Tex. App.—Dallas 2000) and *Maldonado v. State*, 59 S.W.3d 251 (Tex. App.—Corpus Christi 2001).
354. *Nicholson v. Wittig*, 832 S.W.2d 677 (Tex. App.—Houston [1st Dist.] 1992, no writ).

355. *Nicholson* 687.
356. *Nicholson* 687.
357. Tex. R. Evid. 505(a)(2).
358. *Simpson v. Tennant*, 871 S.W.2d 301 (Tex. App.—Houston [14th Dist.] 1994, no writ).
359. *Simpson* 311.
360. *Simpson* 311.
361. Cronenwett and Stansberry 23.
362. Tex R. Evid. 505(a)(1).
363. Tex. R. Civ. Pro. 176 and 201.1 and Tex. Code Crim. Pro. art. 24.01 et seq.
364. Tex. Disc. R. Pro. Con. 1.05.
365. *Ballew v. State*, 640 S.W.2d 237, 239–40 (Tex. Crim. App. 1980).
366. Tex. R. Evid. 510(a)(1) and Tex. Health & Safety Code Ann. § 611.001(2)(B).
367. Tex. R. Evid. 510(a)(2) and Tex. Health & Safety Code Ann. § 611.001(2)(A).
368. Tex. R. Evid. 510(a)(3) and Tex. Health & Safety Code Ann. § 611.003(a).
369. Tex. R. Evid. 510(b)(1) and (c)(1) and (2) and Tex. Health & Safety Code Ann. § 611.002.
370. Tex. Health & Safety Code Ann. § 611.002(a).
371. Tex. Fam. Code Ann. § 261.101(b).
372. Tex. Hum. Res. Code Ann. § 48.051.
373. Tex. Health & Safety Code Ann. § 161.132.
374. Tex. Civ. Prac. & Rem. Code Ann. § 81.006.
375. Tex. Health & Safety Code Ann. §§ 611.004 and 611.0045.
376. 22 Tex. Admin. Code § 681.41.
377. Tex. Health & Safety Code Ann. §§ 611.005(b).
378. *Penley v. Westbrook*, No. 2-02-260-CV (Tex. App.—Fort Worth 2004, no writ), citing *Hawkins v. Trinity Baptist Church*, 30 S.W.2d 446, 452 (Tex. App.—Tyler 2000, no pet.) and *Sanders v. Casa View Baptist Church*, 134 F.2d 331, 337–38 (5th Cir. 1998).
379. *Tilton v. Marshall*, 925 S.W.2d 672,677 (Tex. 1996), quoting Tex. Const. Art I, § 6 Interpretive Commentary.
380. *Sanders* 336.
381. *Penley.*
382. Tex. Fam. Code Ann. § 261.001.
383. Tex. Fam. Code Ann. § 261.001(1)(A)-(H).
384. Tex. Fam. Code Ann. § 261.001(4)(A)-(C).
385. Tex. Fam. Code Ann. § 261.101(a).
386. Tex. Fam. Code Ann. § 261.101(b).

387. Tex. Fam. Code Ann. § 261.103.

388. Tex. Fam. Code Ann. §§ 261.102 and 261.104.

389. Tex. Fam. Code Ann. § 261.101.

390. Tex. Civ. Prac. & Rem. Code Ann. § 81.001 *et seq.*

391. Tex. Civ. Prac. & Rem. Code Ann. § 81.006(a).

392. Tex. Civ. Prac. & Rem. Code Ann. § 81.006(b).

393. Tex. Civ. Prac. & Rem. Code Ann. § 81.006(c).

394. Tex. Civ. Prac. & Rem. Code Ann. § 81.007.

395. Tex. Civ. Prac. & Rem. Code Ann. § 81.003(d) and (e).

396. Peter Mosgofian and George Ohlschlager, *Sexual Misconduct in Counseling and Ministry* (Waco, Texas: Word Publishing 1995) 222.

397. Billy Graham, *A Biblical Standard for Evangelists* (Minneapolis, Minnesota: Worldwide Publications 1984) 74, 78–79.

398. John H. Armstrong, *Can Fallen Pastors Be Restored?: The Church's Response to Sexual Misconduct* (Chicago, Illinois: Moody Press 1995) 48.

399. Greg Laurie, *The Great Compromise* (Waco, Texas: Word Publishing 1994) 120–23 and Mosgofian and Ohlschlager 8–9.

400. Mosgofian and Ohlschlager 261.

401. Armstrong 190.

402. Marie M. Fortune, *Working Together,* vol. 17, no. 2 (Seattle, Washington) 2.

403. Fortune, *Working Together,* 2.

404. Arnold 48–52.

405. Arnold 48–52.

Chapter 14 - Child Abuse and Neglect

406. Tex. Fam. Code Ann. § 261.001(1)(A)-(H).

407. Tex. Fam. Code Ann. § 261.001(4)(A)-(C).

408. Tex. Fam. Code Ann. § 261.001(1)(C).

409. Tex. Fam. Code Ann. § 261.101(b).

410. Tex. Fam. Code Ann. § 261.101(a).

411. *Rodriguez v. State*, 47 S.W.3d 86, 88–89 (Tex. App.—Houston [14th Dist.] 2001).

412. Tex. Fam. Code Ann. § 261.101(b).

413. *Green v. United Pentecostal Church International*, 899 S.W.2d 28, 30 (Tex. App.—Austin 1995, writ denied).

414. Tex. Fam. Code Ann. § 261.101(c).

415. Texas Attorney General Opinion No. JM-342, 1985.

416. Tex. Fam. Code Ann. § 261.101(b).

417. Tex. Fam. Code Ann. § 261.101(a) and Tex. Fam. Code Ann. § 261.101(b).

418. Tex. Fam. Code Ann. § 261.101 and Tex. Fam. Code Ann. § 261.108.

419. Tex. Fam. Code Ann. §§ 261.101(d) and 261.201(a).

420. Tex. Fam. Code Ann. § 261.103.

421. Tex. Fam. Code Ann. § 261.001(5)(A)-(E).

422. Tex. Fam. Code Ann. §§ 261.102 and 261.104.

423. Tex. Fam. Code Ann. § 261.104.

424. Tex. Fam. Code Ann. § 261.104.

425. Marie M. Fortune and Rebecca Voelkel-Haugen, *Sexual Abuse Prevention* (Cleveland, Ohio: United Church Press 1996) 28.

426. Lee W. Carlson, *Child Sexual Abuse: A Handbook for Clergy and Church Members* (Valley Forge, Pennsylvania: Judson Press 1988) 28, 31–32.

427. Carlson 12.

428. Tex. Fam. Code Ann. § 261.109 and *Rodriguez v. State,* 47 S.W.3d 86 (Tex. App.—Houston [14th Dist.] 2001).

429. Tex. Fam. Code Ann. § 261.107.

430. Tex. Fam. Code Ann. § 261.106.

431. *Bird v. W.C.W.,* 868 S.W.2d 767 (Tex. 1994); *Dominguez v. Kelly,* 786 S.W.2d 749 (Tex. App.—El Paso, 1990 writ denied); and *Walker v. Pollock,* 981 S.W.2d 226 (Tex. App.—Houston [1st Dist.] 1998).

432. *Doe v. Rains Independent School District,* 865 F. Supp. 375, rev'd 66 F.3d 1402 (5th Cir. 1994).

433. *Bird v. W.C.W.,* 868 S.W.2d 767 (Tex. 1994); *Blum v. Julian,* 977 S.W.2d 819 (Tex. App.-Fort Worth 1998); *Morales v. Murphey,* 908 S.W.2d 504 (Tex. App.—San Antonio 1995, writ denied); *Viviano v. Moore,* 899 S.W.2d 326 (Tex. App.—Houston [14th Dist.] 1995, rehearing overruled, writ denied); and *Vineyard v. Kraft,* 828 S.W.2d 248 (Tex. App.—Houston [14th Dist.] 1994, writ denied).

434. *Albright v. Texas Department of Human Services,* 859 S.W.2d 575 (Tex. App.—Houston [1st Dist.] 1993, no writ).

435. *Bordman v. State,* 565 S.W.3d 63 (Tex. App.—Houston [14th Dist.] 2001).

436. Tex. Fam. Code Ann. § 261.108.

437. *See* Scott v. Butcher, 906 S.W.2d 14 (Tex. 1995).

438. Tex. Hum. Res. Code Ann. § 42.002(3).

439. Tex. Hum. Res. Code Ann. § 42.041(b)(3).

440. *See Society of Roman Catholic Church v. Interstate Fire & Casualty Co.,* 26 F.3d 1359 (5th Cir. 1994); *Kendrick v. East Delavan Baptist Church,* 886 F. Supp. 1465 (E.D. Wis. 1995); *Preferred Risk Mutual Ins. Co. v. Watson,* 937 S.W.2d 148 (Tex. App.—Fort Worth 1997, writ denied).

441. Tex. R. Evid. 505(a)(1).

442. *The Serbian Eastern Orthodox Diocese v. Milivojevich*, 426 U.S. 696, 96 S. Ct. 2372, 49 L. Ed.2d 151, (Supreme Court 1976); *Patterson v. Southwestern Baptist Theological Seminary*, 858 S.W.2d 602, 606 (Tex. App.—Fort Worth 1993, no writ); and *Green v. United Pentecostal Church International*, 899 S.W.2d 28, 30 (Tex. App.—Austin 1995, writ denied).

443. <www.tdprs.state.tx.us>.

444. <www.tdprs.state.tx.us>.

Chapter 15 - They Did What?!: Youth

445. *Black's Law Dictionary*, 5th ed. (Minneapolis, Minnesota: West Publishing 1979) 658.

446. *Kargar v. Sorrentino*, 788 S.W.2d 189 (Tex. App.—Houston [14th Dist.] 1990, no writ), and Tex. Civ. Prac. & Rem. Code Ann. § 129.001.

447. *Dawes v. J.C. Penney & Co.*, 236 S.W.2d 624 (Tex. App.—Waco 1951, writ ref'd n.r.e.).

448. *Victoria Bank & Trust Co. v. Brady*, 779 S.W.2d 893 (Tex. App.—Corpus Christi 1989, writ granted), aff'd in part and rev'd in part, 811 S.W.2d 931.

449. *Williams v. Glash*, 789 S.W.2d 261 (Tex. 1990).

450. *Smith v. Golden Triangle Raceway*, 708 S.W.2d 575 (Tex. App.—Beaumont 1986, no writ).

451. *Dear Creek, Ltd. v. North American Mortgage Co.*, 792 S.W.2d 198 (Tex. App.—Dallas 1990, no writ).

452. *Newman v. Tropical Visions, Inc.*, 891 S.W.2d 713 (Tex. App.—San Antonio 1994, writ denied).

453. <www.sos.state.tx.us/statdoc/edinfo.shtml#Introduction>.

454. Tex. R. Evid. 409.455. Tex. Fam. Code Ann. § 151.003(a)(1).

456. Tex. Fam. Code Ann. §§ 32.001(a)(3) and 151.003(a)(6).

457. Tex. Fam. Code Ann. § 32.003.

458. Tex. Fam. Code Ann. § 32.002.

459. Tex. Fam. Code Ann. §101.003.

460. Tex. Civ. Prac. & Rem. Code Ann. § 129.001.

461. Tex. Fam. Code Ann. § 151.003(a)(1).

462. Tex. Fam Code Ann. § 151.003(2) and (3).

463. Tex. Fam. Code Ann. § 2.101.

464. Tex. Fam. Code Ann. § 2.102.

465. Tex. Fam. Code Ann. § 2.103.

466. Tex. Alc. Bev. Code Ann. § 106.04.
467. Tex. Fam. Code Ann. § 41.001.
468. Tex. Fam. Code Ann. § 41.001.
469. Tex. Trans. Code Ann. § 521.204.
470. Tex. Trans. Code Ann. § 521.223.
471. <http://travel.state.gov/passport/get_first_apply.html>.
472. Tex. Prob. Code Ann. § 57.
473. Tex. Prob. Code Ann. § 59.
474. Tex. Fam. Code Ann. § 33.002.
475. Tex. R. Civ. Pro. 44.
476. Tex. Elec. Code Ann. § 11.002(1) and U.S. Const. Amend. XXVI.
477. 50 U.S.C. §§ 453 and 454.
478. Tex. Health & Safety Code Ann. § 692.003(a).
479. Tex. Health & Safety Code Ann. § 692.003(a).
480. Tex. Fam. Code Ann. § 261.001(1)(C).
481. Tex. Fam. Code Ann. § 31.001.
482. Tex. Pen. Code Ann. § 8.07(d).
483. Tex. Fin. Code Ann. § 34.305.
484. Tex. Civ. Prac. & Rem. Code Ann. § 129.001 and *Kargar*.
485. Tex. Fam. Code Ann. § 154.001.

Index

To order additional copies of

SHEEP AMONG
Wolves

Have your credit card ready and call:

1-877-421-READ (7323)

or please visit our web site at
www.pleasantword.com

Also available at:
www.amazon.com
and
www.barnesandnoble.com

HIEBERT LIBRARY

3 6877 00218 9065

LaVergne, TN USA
06 October 2010
199700LV00004B/2/A